THE Most Unlikely Salesperson

The story of how sales obstacles were overcome and major sales awards won in five industries

Kurt Newman

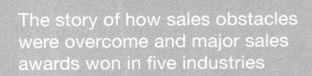

THE
Most
Unlikely
Salesperson

by Kurt Newman

The story of how sales obstacles were
overcome and major sales awards won
in five industries

Published by

◗ Sales Consultants

© Sales Consultants 2023

This work is copyright. All rights reserved, apart from any use, including for the purposes of study, research, criticism, or review, as permitted under the Copyright Act 1968. No part may be reproduced by any process without written permission from the author. Reproduction processes may include but are not limited to storage in a retrieval system, transmission in any form or by any means, whether electronic, mechanical, photocopying or recording.

For permission requests, enquiries, and bulk order purchase options:
Email info@salesconsultants.com.au
Email subject field: TMUSP
Website: www.salesconsultants.com.au

Publisher: Sales Consultants
Author: Kurt Newman

Editing, graphic design and artwork by
Linda Parker-Wood, Parker-Wood Communications Pty Ltd

National Library of Australia Cataloguing in-Publication data:

First edition published by Sales Consultants 2023

ISBN: 978-0-6458364-0-0

Paperback Edition

Disclaimer: This book is based on authentic sales situations and designed to provide accurate and authoritative information regarding the subject matter covered. In respect and for privacy, the names and identifying details of individuals portrayed in this book have been changed, except for those contacted and have granted permissions. Company and organisation names have been replaced by industry, excepted for those who have granted permissions. This book is sold with the understanding the author and publisher are not engaged to provide any type of sales, strategy, attitudinal, psychological, or any other professional advice. The advice and strategies contained herein may not be suitable for your situation. No warranties or guarantees are expressed or implied.

Limit of Liability/Disclaimer of Warranty: While the author and publisher have used their best efforts in preparing this book, they make no representations or warranties with respect to the accuracy or completeness of the contents of this book and specifically disclaim any implied warranties merchantability or fitness for a particular purpose. No warranty may be created or extended by sales representatives or written sales materials. The advice and strategies contained herein may not be suitable for your situation. You should consult a professional where appropriate. Neither the author nor the publisher shall be liable for any loss of profit or any other commercial damages, including but not limited to special, incidental, consequential, or other damages.

The author and publisher have made every effort to ensure that all attributions have been correctly noted. Should something have accidentally been overlooked, the author and publisher offer their apologies and will ensure that any error or omission notified is rectified for future editions. Contact the author and the publisher at the above email address in this regard.

Printed by FC Productions Pty Ltd Sydney, Australia

What the experts say about the breadth of knowledge and experience Kurt Newman brings to the business world

 I have had the pleasure of working with Kurt frequently over the last 20 years. I have observed his approach to mentoring, coaching and business improver in many companies in several industries.

There are three attributes that drive Kurt in his approach to business and are foundational to his character:
– Professionalism
– Discipline
– Application of Knowledge.

Kurt set up an internal sales academy for a large player in retail office supplies. He drafted learning materials based on cutting edge sales concepts. He then invested heavily in building the capability of the company sales force. Kurt spent time in the field with the sales team to show them how to apply what they had learned during the academy classes to complex selling. He then worked with outstanding sales staff to build them into trainers and mentors to the Australia-wide sales team. The results on the bottom line were significant, and the results in the professional skills of the academy trainees were transformational.

When Kurt asks a sales trainee to work hard, he leads by example, working harder than he demands of his trainees. This makes him an inspiring role model.

Nothing Kurt does is random. Every sales activity is planned. Every training session, field interaction has a measurable goal or target outcome.

Kurt is a voracious researcher of best practices in sales and the psychology of selling. This knowledge does not sit idly on the shelf, Kurt applies the knowledge in his training and in mentoring sales people. For example, Kurt has developed a Sales Competency Levels framework. This unique approach is based on extensive research. Kurt knows before he joins a salesperson in the field their level of competency, and he adjusts his approach accordingly.

Kurt's approach is unique, personal and practical. Clients respect him, and are usually clients for life."

Paul Beaumont
Process Improvement Management Consultant

He sold the vision and the rest is history.

I had the pleasure of crossing paths with Kurt when he was the Chair of Southern Highlands Chamber of Commerce. Not one to shy away from a challenge, Kurt was an instrumental figure driving change in how business bodies, government and other stakeholders collaborated to support the Southern Highland businesses and community.

Always keen to help, listen and share his thoughts, Kurt was fun to work and brainstorm with. He was also willing to help, even outside of his region.

Duncan Burck
Former LCC Relationship Manager
Currently Managing Director, MCB Business Partners

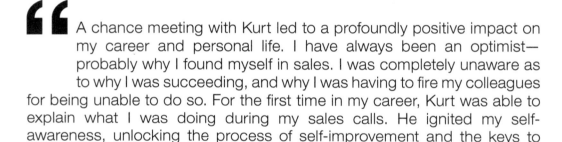 A chance meeting with Kurt led to a profoundly positive impact on my career and personal life. I have always been an optimist—probably why I found myself in sales. I was completely unaware as to why I was succeeding, and why I was having to fire my colleagues for being unable to do so. For the first time in my career, Kurt was able to explain what I was doing during my sales calls. He ignited my self-awareness, unlocking the process of self-improvement and the keys to leading sales teams to success.

Together, we built training programs and formed the Office Academy. The Office Academy challenged the status quo. In doing so, lifted performance beyond what anyone at the time thought was possible. Salespeople trained 20 years ago still remind me today of the profound impact that The Office Academy had on their lives and careers. It would not have happened if it was not for Kurt.

Kurt's passion for sales and salespeople is a delight to see in action—he genuinely cares for salespeople and the sales profession. He has dedicated his life to creating and teaching understanding of our industry to benefit us all.

I have and still hold executive leadership roles as a direct result of the professional prowess gained working with Kurt. My life has changed as a result."

Phil Saddleton
Former National Sales and Marketing Manager
Currently Managing Director, Source It Retail

I brought Kurt's expertise into a number of organisations. I have always found him to be inquisitive and empathetic. His vast experience across many different industries translates very quickly to understanding the client's business and the challenges they have.

Whether your team has rock stars, diamonds in the rough, or dead wood, you can be sure that Kurt will—tactfully—point out the strengths and opportunities and next steps. The approach Kurt recommends will persevere with those who need more help and have the furthest to travel—no one gets left behind."

Nick Fisher
Former Operations Manager
Currently Maritime CEO

 I sold correspondence courses in photography, art drawing and creative writing for an international company. No training was given, no retainer, commission only, no expenses paid and being in North Queensland huge distances had to be covered.

Several years later, I moved to Perth. I applied for and was accepted as a sales representative with the Industrial Chemical Company. I was still green-sales wise, but my attitude had changed due to family responsibilities.

I was introduced to Kurt as my sales manager. Several in-house training sessions were undertaken both for product knowledge and the company's unique sales techniques. These made the initial cold call approach much easier.

I then went out with Kurt for a week doing predominantly cold calls and a small number of existing client calls. Kurt did most of the first day and then it was my turn. My initial feeling was somewhere between petrified and intimidated. Each completed call was dissected in the car before the next call. The learning process was intensive and relentless, but I had to do it.

After a couple of months, I began to enjoy it. I had my own sales territory and an extensive list of existing clients who welcomed me back on return visits. I spent a couple of hours on a weekend rough draft planning sales calls for the coming week. Then half an hour each evening fine tuning the next day's calls. This was becoming a way of life and all due to Kurt, my mentor.

I have never come across a sales manager like him. To me he was a combination of a surgeon and a psychologist as he analysed every step of a sales call and I owe my success totally to him.

The nuts and bolts psychology of selling is in Kurt's blood, he lives and breathes it."

Graeme Mogridge
Former Sales Manager
Currently retired Insurance Broker

" At our first meeting Kurt made a very positive impression on me. We developed a good working relationship based on trust and worked together on problems and issues in the business.
One major achievement was a sales training program that was practical and outcomes focussed. The training program was coupled with a team building weekend—a calculated gamble that paid dividends within a short time. The training program aimed to develop individuals and team learning within teams and across departments.

Kurt never shied away from addressing hard issues with people in a firm and compassionate manner.

Throughout Kurt provided excellent diagnostic tools for identifying sales training gaps and improving sales through coaching and training.

Kurt was always available to impart ongoing coaching to sales staff."

David Tarento
Former State Manager and Project Manager
Currently Management Consultant

I was introduced to the Southern Highlands Chamber of Commerce by John Irwin, a long-time friend. We attended several meetings and then decided to join to associate with other business leaders in the Southern Highlands Community.

At one of the early meetings, Kurt gave a presentation on how to prepare for a phone call or a client meeting. This hit home for me as he detailed several minor, but highly relevant pre-meeting procedures I still use today.

As a financial strategist, I did not see myself as someone selling products. I provide a service/solution to my clients who have individual needs. By adopting some of Kurt's methods, client meetings flow smoother and efficiently. The result is financial products and structures that assist clients with present and future business/personal requirements.

After working with Kurt on the Chamber Board as the Membership Director for several years, I gained skills in client meetings and the importance of researching my clients, not just for suitable products. I was impressed by his management style dealing with volunteer directors on the board, all mostly working for the betterment of the Chamber and the business community. Kurt was truly clear in delegating tasks and setting goals. He made me feel appreciated and respected in my role.

I have watched him over the years achieve his goals, typical Newman tenacity."

Peter Blain,
Former Membership Director Southern Highlands Chamber of Commerce
Currently Owner Effective Finance

If you picked up this book undoubtedly you want to be a highly successful professional salesperson or entrepreneur and deliver hard results for your clients and your life.

As you read this book, Kurt will take you on a personal journey describing critical sales skills and practical business development strategies that are simple, natural and easy to employ.

You will be excited to find that Kurt brings alive the powerful principles of Ralph Waldo Emerson's Law of Compensation. Bob Proctor, one of my own mentors, enthusiastically encouraged salespeople and entrepreneurs to embrace this important law of success.

Bob repeatedly said, *"The Law of Compensation states that the amount of money or good you receive in life is going to be in direct ratio with these three things: the need for what you do; your ability to do it, and the difficulty there will be in replacing you. You can only do this by going the extra mile and getting better at what you do".*

Kurt Newman is the very personification of this law. In fact, how to get better at what you do in all aspects of sales and sales management is the essence. Kurt's exceptionally practical and engaging unpack of outstanding long-term sales and business success secrets.

As you read, you will witness first-hand Kurt in full flight in a diverse range of selling and in-field sales training and coaching, business development and account management settings across 15 industries. You will observe

Kurt emotionally and intelligently going the extra-mile, managing a broad range of business challenges, contexts and environments over several decades, overcoming difficulties and growing professionally to achieve outstanding results, accolades and a rich meaningful life while consistently delivering value for his clients.

You will learn how to apply Kurt's hard-won understanding and insights gained from marketing both tangible and intangible products and services, in just almost every sales environment imaginable. From presenting to couples in friendly kitchens and dining rooms, grimy industrial workshops, to shiny commercial and retail offices and showrooms, and all the way to the carpeted executive suites of corporate and community boardrooms.

Most importantly Kurt intimately demonstrates many up-close personal examples of the critical character attributes, qualities, skills and processes required to succeed in sales, business and life.

Of exceptional value is that he details his unique and highly successful, 'sales consultants 6 levels of sales competence coaching model' methodology and tools for developing highly effective sales professionals for business and organisation managers and leaders.

Kurt is a widely respected community, industry and business development professional. Apart from his exemplary sales success record he has been recognised as an outstanding sales leader and won major Sales Awards in five industries. His number one passion is being a sales coaching expert dedicated to elevating the reputation and recognition of sales as a being a true profession, and to assist you achieve your goals.

This book is Kurt's legacy, something that he knows will powerfully and meaningfully serve you and those you serve. There is a good reason to scan through the book's Introduction page even if you are not directly involved in sales. Most likely you'll be sold on why and how Kurt can assist you to experience a quantum leap in your performance and realise the inexhaustible and profound rewards of the Law of Compensation in every area of your life…"

Peter Harrison
Master Coach and Trainer, EmergentQx Coaching Pty Ltd

Contents

Chapter 1 Background and First Career Overview 1

Chapter 2 Discovering Sales 3

Chapter 3 Sales Role: Industrial Chemicals 7

Chapter 4 Sales Role: Publishing and Advertising Industry 43

Chapter 5 Sales Role: Long Service Leave Funding 53

Chapter 6 Sales Role: Electrical Switchgear 60

Chapter 7 Sales Role: The Scholarship Trust 77

Chapter 8 Sales Role: Computerized Motion Signs 86

Chapter 9 Sales Role: Training & Development Consultant 92

Chapter 10 The Australian Training Company 111

Chapter 11 Office Products and the Office Academy 147

Chapter 12 Warringah Chamber of Commerce 157

Chapter 13 Sales Role: Luxury Cars 166

Chapter 14 Sales Consultants 190

Chapter 15 Southern Highlands Chamber of Commerce
and Industry Ltd 215

Afterword 227

viii

Acknowledgements

Personal note of gratitude

When I started writing this book a flood of emotions and feelings took me back to the time I was a shy and nervous young salesperson. I recall the determination, commitment and an overwhelming desire to be in sales, but logically I could not reason why. Perhaps a calling at a subconscious level?

Unskilled and, on reflection, ignorant of what lay ahead or involved in sales, I am grateful for the management of the Industrial Chemical Company mentioned in Chapter 3. They gave me the first break to develop the skills to sell at a professional level. They saw something in me I did not see in myself.

Today I find similar traits in salespeople starting out who need to be given the opportunity and the skills to succeed.

Working with salespeople as a trainer, coach and mentor has been and still is a privilege. I have seen salespeople reinvent their careers with new vitality, go on to win major sales awards, own successful businesses and become Chief Executive Officers of large companies.

I want to thank everyone mentioned in the book who made the storytelling and this adventure possible. The characters and personalities I have met along the way who have provided resonating memories, thank you.

My gratitude to my wife June for her support, insights and the experiences we shared on projects.

Linda Parker-Wood for her friendship, hard work and articulate skills that have led to the final publication of this book.

Importantly, I want to thank you for purchasing the book.

With kind regards

Kurt

x

Introduction

The motivation to write this book was to provide insights and to guide or inspire you to achieve the sales success you desire. Perhaps you are not in sales, but the title caught your attention and at one level or another, sales interests you?

The book takes you on a journey—a practical journey—within a range of sales situations across a number of industries, including one-on-one sales to complex sales involving many people with different agendas. Each chapter describes the customer, client or prospective client, and the conversation, the obstacles—whether self-defeating thoughts and feelings about the sales call itself—and the applied sales skills, sales strategies and behaviour that achieved major sales records and awards across five industries.

Every sales call or sales meeting are actual events providing context as well as content—so learning is easy and enjoyable. The experiences are wide ranging from beginning in sales, the apprehension, failures and success, to sales coaching salespeople in a cross section of industries, sales management. The salespeople involved were contacted and sent a draft chapter to validate the content and permission was given to use their names. Salespeople who could not be located, replacement names have been used. I feel privileged to have worked with these and hundreds of salespeople. The lessons I learned about myself, relationships, sales and loyalty will always be with me.

In the majority of chapters, organization names have been replaced by the respective industry. Industries chosen were selected to provide the greatest learning value in terms of sales skills and practice. You may decide to read the chapters of greatest interest or start at the beginning and go for there—it is up to you. I believe everyone in sales or those interested in pursuing a career in sales will gain great value from the book.

I was born in Austria and came to Australia with my parents as a young two-year old. We lived in a rented unit situated above retail shops on the south coast of NSW. I didn't sleep much because my bedroom faced the main intersection that was so brightly lit at night—it was almost daylight.

The local school was in Port Kembla, only a suburb away. To be frank, I was an average mid-tier student and found school boring. As a high school student, everyone was interviewed by the school's career advisor.

The advisor suggested I take a trade apprenticeship with the largest employer in the region, the Australian Iron and Steel which later became BHP. I soon learned every male in the class was given the same advice.

For some time, I felt a burning desire to leave the south coast. When an opportunity came to join the Royal Australian Navy, I jumped at it. I signed up for 12 years, which at the time was the minimum period of service. The naval career lasted less than two years because I developed a medical condition in one of my kidneys and was honourably discharged on medical grounds.

The months that followed were challenging, applying for jobs, and adjusting to the new reality. After many attempts, I was not making any headway and had to do something different. A storeman position was advertised. Although I had no experience, I decided not to phone to make an appointment, instead to be at the premises before the business opened its doors. When the manager Mr McKenzie arrived, he was surprised to see an applicant waiting for him. He said he might as well interview me. A short 30 minutes later I had the job. A breakthrough at last, and one I am thankful to Mr McKenzie for the opportunity and new start.

The industries covered in the book are industrial chemicals, publishing and advertising, long service leave funding, electrical switchgear, insurance, technology, manufacturing, training & development, wholesale, shipping, not-for-profit, office products, luxury cars and management consulting. Companies and organizations mentioned are The Warringah Chamber of Commerce and Industry Ltd, The Australian Training Company, Sales Consultants, and The Southern Highlands Chamber of Commerce and Industry Ltd. The Business Chambers provide an insight into how sales and sales strategy were used to, in one instance grow membership three-fold, and the other win a 'Chamber of the Year Award'.

I believe the relationship between a salesperson and client needs to be built on shared values, commitment, exceptional service, and mutual respect. This foundation when measured in financial terms, results in business volume and solid revenues.

With kind regards,

Kurt[1]

---

1 Note: This book is intentionally written using third person. This is to provide greater focus on the story, sales skills and sales strategy, not the adventures of the person.

xiv

Chapter 1
Background and First Career Overview

During his junior years Kurt was very thin and suffered from constant tonsillitis flare ups that resulted in losing many weeks at school. His tonsils were finally removed at age ten. Immediately following, he had a new lease of energy and knuckled down to catch up on what he had missed.

Kurt had a quiet and shy demeanour, but this did not stop him from seeing how he could get away with breaking rules, particularly as a teenager. His antics were based on fun—if he thought he could get away with it, it was on. He could not understand why some rules were invented, therefore saw these to be impediments. Several examples are given in this chapter.

At 14 Kurt joined the Australian Sea Cadet Corps in Wollongong as the precursor to join the Royal Australian Navy. The unit was 'TS Albatross'. The 'TS' Stood for Training Ship. It was near the Wollongong inner-harbour, and the ship's company met every Friday evening. The Navy supported sea cadet units with uniforms, equipment, weekends at naval establishments and ships for ongoing learning and experience.

Kurt Newman as a junior recruit

Kurt resigned from the sea cadets when he was old enough to join the Navy as a junior recruit. The training involved 12 months at HMAS Leeuwin, a naval base in Western Australia. It was an exciting time learning about the navy as well as continuing high school subjects, sport and getting to know fellow recruits of the 23rd Intake. Though discipline was strict, Kurt regularly broke rules and got away with it. An example is when he had a tailor do multiple alterations to his uniform including having his bell-bottom trousers

The Most Unlikely Salesperson

taken in from the knees to the crutch creating a greater flair at the bottom half. He was never pulled up or questioned about the changes.

Kurt totally committed himself to naval life and after six months was promoted to a leading junior recruit. He was the first selected and the only one who lasted in that role for the following six months. Putting in the extra effort paid off—in his class he achieved 8th in academic subjects and topped the seamanship subjects.

Kurt was posted to destroyer HMAS Duchess, and soon got used to ducking far enough to avoid hitting his head on the top edge of bulkhead-door. Living conditions were tight but comfortable. He was one of the youngest junior sailors on board and had limited responsibilities—opening opportunities to have fun.

Being a military environment discipline is vital. Some rules, according to Kurt, were hurdles to overcome and these became an addictive adrenaline rush prior to, during and after the event. One such rule was sailors 17 years and older were given a green identification card that meant they did not have to report back on board until the following morning. Sailors under 17, only two including Kurt, were issued a pink card meaning a return to the ship by midnight. His mates were all 17, so when the fun started at a club or bar Kurt had to leave and return to the ship. He did this several times until he learned an ex-junior recruit named Berry worked in the ship's administration office. That evening Kurt was on shore leave with a green card.

Time on Duchess was cut short having served five months of an expected nine month posting. Kurt had reoccurring pain in his left kidney that intensified and became more frequent. After seeing the ship's doctor, he was immediately transferred to the Naval Hospital at HMAS Penguin in Balmoral, Sydney. He was bed ridden for several weeks and then released and assigned to Penguin's Ships Company. A number of medical board interviews followed, and four months later Kurt was honourably discharge on medical grounds.

Chapter 2
Discovering Sales

At 18 Kurt was discharged from the navy. He had little in the way of money and was unemployed. Finding a job, any job, took months.

The employers did not want to hire him because they thought he was too young and lacked experience. One potential employer stated he did not want to hire an ex-sailor. It was not until Kurt changed tactics applying for a storeman role—ignoring the advertisement instructions to phone and make an appointment. Instead, he got up early the following morning, drove to the suburb and waited outside the business until it opened. The company was TF Stewart an electrical wholesaler.

When the manager Mr McKenzie arrived at work, he was somewhat surprised to see an applicant waiting for him. Nevertheless, he decided to interview Kurt and in a short 30 minutes later hired him. It was not until months later Kurt learned Mr McKenzie valued initiative and honesty.

The business was part of a network of branches. The Wollongong branch consisted of seven people who had a diverse set of skills and backgrounds. The stand-out person was Mrs McLintock, the Administration Manager. A wonderful person whose fiery Scottish

Initiative and honesty—a valued trait for an applicant

no-nonsense approach put fear into anyone who crossed her. Mrs-McLintock had incredible numeracy skills—being able to add columns of numbers quicker than anyone could using a calculator.

The product range was extensive with dozens of brands and thousands of product lines, each with its own identifying catalogue number. There was much to learn. After several months at the branch Mr McKenzie moved Kurt into stock control and serving sales-counter customers. Mr McKenzie hired a younger person to fill Kurt's previous role.

18 months at Wollongong branch evolved to being offered a role at a larger branch in Sydney's Rydalmere. Stock control held no interest, and the new role was telephone and counter sales. It was considerably busier with a greater number of customers to deal with. Learning was on-the-job.

Pushing forward

Kurt resigned and joined a competitor. The business was only streets away and aptly named Rydalmere Wholesalers. One of the directors, Len Smith offered Kurt the same role, with the promise of experiencing external sales. There were two directors, each managing a customer base, both rarely came into the office. Both directors saw existing customers and appeared to have no time or interest in business development. This was the opening Kurt was looking for. He managed to convince Len to let him work externally one day a week. He had no skills only a deep-seated passion to do the job.

Kurt drove along Parramatta Road, Parramatta in Western Sydney, and noticed car dealerships on both sides of the highway. Not to waste time, he walked into the first car yard, a small dealership that stocked second-hand vehicles. He introduced himself to Sam, who said he was the sales manager. Kurt then took a quick glance at the cars before turning to Sam and asked, 'How do you showcase a vehicle overnight, one that you want to shift?' The sales manager responded in a grumpy-vocal tone, 'It goes on the ramp'.

Sam appeared to be waiting to see how Kurt would respond. It felt like a test. At that moment, he did not know what to say. His brain felt as if it had frozen. Then finally he said, 'Would you be interested in having a coloured fluorescent unit placed on the front seat of your display vehicle to attract potential buyers?' Sam did not hesitate, 'Yes'. Kurt let him know how much it would be. Payment was cash on delivery and assured Sam he will have it that evening. Sam agreed.

Kurt should have continued to the next dealership. Being inexperienced and feeling excited to have made his first sale, instead he returned to the warehouse to make up the unit. The unit included the electrical cable and plug. Kurt returned later that day to deliver the product. All before seeing other dealerships.

The one day a week external sales did not last long because the internal workload increased dramatically. The directors refused to hire an additional person leaving Kurt with a decision to make. Kurt felt no value could be gained staying under those circumstances. So, he gave his notice without having another job to go to—a behaviour he repeated often in his career. Learning and growing professionally grossly outweighed any feelings of insecurity or lack of employment in the short term.

The wholesalers did not offer further education or any formal training, so Kurt started a journey of self-development—a journey that continues to this day. His main areas of interest have always been and remains is sales and business, personal development, psychology, and marketing. Sources include, but are not limited to universities, TAFENSW Colleges, short-term private courses, seminars, books, and online.

Learning and growing professionally grossly outweighed any feelings of insecurity or lack of employment in the short term.

Australian companies at one time believed a salesperson's success hinged on product knowledge and therefore did not invest in developing sales skills. Forward-thinking companies sent their salespeople and sales managers to seminars to meet their training needs. In hindsight, seminars served as information sharing. International charismatic speakers provided entertainment, motivation, sold their books, audios and videos. The excitement for attendees wore off in a matter of days, and the generic content was rejected. Salespeople thought it sounded good at the time but saw it as high-pressure selling and not suitable for their product, service or industry. Other reasons were:

- Salespeople did not try to apply what they had learned
- Salespeople lacked the skills to transfer the seminar context and content to their selling environment
- Fear of change
- Low self-worth and lacked the confidence
- Seminar content was incompatible for the needs of the salesperson: typically, sales strategy was required but only sales skills provided
- Usually there is no follow-through by sales management
- Knowing the limitations of what was available at the respective companies where the salespeople worked.

A breakthrough opportunity came for Kurt when an industrial chemical company advertised for a salesperson—no experience required, sales training and sales coaching provided. The organization appeared to have a strong sales culture offering promotion to sales management and general management, based on sales performance and aptitude.

Lessons learned

- Setbacks are part of life. They provide opportunities, time to think, feel and re-assess a current situation.
- There is always a reason why a door needs to close—it allows other opportunities to be revealed.
- Opportunities will always be discovered, it is a matter of patience, time and timing.
- A new opportunity may appear uncomfortable, but that is where growth and progress is.
- Have the confidence to be yourself. Don't follow the crowd.
- Observe and learn from others as well as your own experiences, even those perceived as negative, build on these and go forward.
- Take control of your career, invest in yourself, do not rely on an employer or others.
- Have the courage to step out of a present comfort zone. You will learn about yourself and feel grateful you did.

Chapter 3
Sales Role:
Industrial Chemicals

The company manufactured and sold industrial chemicals and lubricants direct to industry. A global organization with their head office in the United States. The Australian operation was managed and staffed by an Australian team.

Securing an interview for the salesperson role was easier than Kurt had anticipated. What was unexpected was the number of interviews. The first interview felt low key, with questions centred on getting to know Kurt's interests, hobbies and his understanding of the company and the position he had applied for. The Australian General Manager, Francis Bidston did the interview. He was a tall heavyset individual with a constant smile.

Kurt was invited back for the second interview and after the initial polite conversation, was led into an adjacent room and given a product brochure to read. He was given ten minutes to prepare for a mock sales meeting. After trying to digest as much as he could, Kurt knocked on the general manager's door where he was met by an additional person, Gavin Cornwell the Sales Manager. Kurt felt nervous because he only knew what he read about the product, and he did not know how to sell. He gave it his best shot, which quite frankly was terrible. As he progressed through the presentation, he wondered why the two managers kept interrupting and asking questions. At the time it was quite off-putting, but on reflection Kurt believed they were trying to help him.

The third interview was another uncomfortable experience because Kurt was asked to critique the mock-sale he did several days ago, including the skills applied or not-applied. The general manager did the questioning whilst the sales manager was mostly silent. Although Kurt was a complete novice at sales, he did what he could to answer the questions. The general manager paused after listening to Kurt, then proceeded to give his evaluation. It was extensive and critical, spoken in a polite manner. Feeling out-of-his-depth and somewhat embarrassed, Kurt responded by nodding in agreement. When the general manager completed his assessment, he told him to wait in the reception area.

The Most Unlikely Salesperson

After 15 minutes the sales manager called Kurt back for what was a short-final interview. The general manager had a serious manner about him. He told Kurt, *'To your credit you have courage, but I have reservations'*.

He continued, *'You are 24 and the youngest person to applied for the role. The job is tough, so we prefer to hire people who are 30 or older. Most of the work is cold calling; the products are one of the most expensive in the market and it is highly competitive'*.

Again, Kurt kept eye contact and nodded to show he understood.

The general manager paused and then continued, *'You look the part, but I don't know if you have what it takes'*. Kurt did not ask what he meant by, 'look the part' because he was trying to digest what he had said.

The general manager paused again then said, *'You can start but, it is on a three-month trial basis'*. The sales manager shook Kurt's hand and welcomed him to the company. They walked to his office when he let Kurt know he would be reporting to him and outlined the employment terms. It was a sales-commission role that paid an advanced weekly payment against future commissions earned. If commissions were greater than the draw amount, an additional payment was made. There was a defined timeline of employment if commissions did not meet the draw amount.

The company sold an extensive range of products including water treatment, fertilizers, bug and weed killers, disinfectants and heavy-duty cleaning products. Customers ranged from small to medium businesses, government and mining organizations.

The learning curve and challenges would be steep because:

- Two successive salespeople had failed in the sales territory Kurt was assigned to
- There were 40 products to learn. Most had to be demonstrated to prove-quality performance and to engage with the customer
- In the short term, Kurt needed to sell enough product to stay ahead of the draw payments, and selling was a skill he had yet to learn and master
- Customer records would not be released until the end of the trail period. Management wanted to see what he could do developing new business and not rely on existing customers.

The greatest attraction for Kurt was the intensive pragmatic sales training provided by management. The trainers were all previous sales award winners—a pre-condition of the company before entering management. The managers also had the ability to transfer their skills in accordance with the company's methodologies.

The first four days were with Gavin Cornwell selling in Kurt's sales territory. To get a sense of what he could expect on the Monday, Kurt spent Sunday afternoon driving around one of the industrial estates taking note of business' names he thought could use industrial chemicals. This was pure guess work.

Kurt met Gavin at a predetermined address at 8:00am Monday morning. Gavin had won several company sales awards. He had a pleasant disposition, in his early thirties, extremely fit and health conscious, and a family man who loved spending time on the beach. He was success driven and totally focussed on the job-at-hand.

Strict protocols were discussed prior to the first sales call of the day. These were sales call objectives, set prior to going into a potential customer. When Gavin did the sales call, he was responsible for the outcome. Kurt's role was to observe and learn. This created a respectful buyer/seller sales environment, allowing the prospective customer to feel comfortable dealing with one salesperson. There were occasions when the prospective customer was curious and wanted to engage Kurt in conversation. He politely answered any questions and as soon as the opportunity presented itself redirected the conversation back to Gavin. This was part of the agreement and it worked both ways.

Gavin did three sales calls in succession, whilst Kurt observed how the company's sales process was applied. It was now time to switch roles. Kurt saw a large fruit shop and asked Gavin what types of products they could use? According to Kurt, he thought these were very imaginative, but who was he to comment—he had his training wheels on. Gavin was not concerned about getting a sale but wanted to see how Kurt was going to handle the sales call.

Apart from the introduction Kurt made a complete hash of it. At one time he was so nervous he temporarily did not know what to say. Gavin did warn him that if he struggled during a sales call he would not step in. This sounded tough, and tough enough in front of a potential customer, but it was particularly painful making mistakes in front of Gavin his manager. However, it turned out to be a blessing because Kurt never forgot those hard-earned lessons developing sales competence.

Regarding the fruit shop experience, he somehow managed to get through it less a sale. As they both left the fruit shop Gavin suggested they have a coffee and a coaching debrief session. Gavin controlled his anger and had quite a bit to say as Kurt sat there and listened. It was an unpleasant experience, but they both agreed to move on and continue to work together.

Gavin decided to divide the skills associated with the sales process into smaller learning units. It made a huge difference to understand what to do, when, why, and how it all fitted together. The planning prior to the sales call helped the implementation of the sales process to flow easily. On the

The Most Unlikely Salesperson

completion of the fourth day Kurt was able to complete a sales call from the introduction through to the close whilst Gavin observed.

The following weekend Kurt decided to divide his sales territory into four zones. The aim was to concentrate on a smaller area and connect with a greater number of potential customers. The cycle would be repeated so relationships could grow with new customers. He felt excited and tense at the same time. Monday morning and the first place he walked into was an automatic transmission business. He met the owner and introduced himself. From there Kurt made a number of selling mistakes. In hindsight he realized:

- He asked too few questions and ended up knowing little about the owner and his business
- He forgot to give the owner a company advertising novelty
- He provided an overview of the product range too soon
- He did not demonstrate how any of the products worked—the demonstration was a crucial step he completely missed
- He did not handle the sales objection, 'It is too expensive'
- It was as if Kurt had learned nothing the week prior.

He politely thanked the owner and left feeling annoyed with myself. If there was a positive outcome of the sales call, it was that Kurt clearly identified the mistakes he had made.

On his first day working solo, he walked into 20 businesses in Zone 1: West Ryde District, New South Wales and sold nothing. His closing ratio was poor: 20 sales calls/0 sales. Far from a good start, but it was a start.

Within three months Kurt walked into every potential business in the allotted sales territory and he kept detailed customer records. Though his sales results and skills were far from good, he thought the territory was too small and not viable. It could have been why the two previous salespeople had failed?

The trial period ended and Kurt expected a formal interview, but nothing was mentioned, so he assumed he still had the job and kept going.

Kurt had a theory about the size of the sales area being too small and limited. He met with Gavin to discuss why the sales territory needed to be larger and provided his own customer records to make his point. He also challenged Gavin to question him about any business he thought he may have missed. Gavin listened and reflected on what Kurt had said, then agreed to give him the adjoining territory. He handed over the customer records for the new territory and the one Kurt had been working in.

Sales were poor in the adjoining territory and salespeople lasted only a couple of months at best. Reviewing the records was depressing-reading

The Most Unlikely Salesperson

because the comments were negative and inflammatory. To Kurt's surprise whilst he reviewed the current territory records, he noticed he had converted a number of the previous salesperson's prospects into customers.

Kurt was glad Gavin did not provide the original customer records when he first started with the company because his thoughts would have been influenced by the commentary. Knowing the area history in the beginning, Kurt may not have approached those businesses. After reading all the notes he discarded them.

The advertising novelty was a small low value gift salespeople used mostly during business development calls. When given in a light-hearted and fun manner, it helped to gain the prospective customer's attention. The novelty created a relaxed atmosphere and built relationships. The key to connect emotionally depended on how the advertising novelty was introduced and presented. Customers were mostly maintenance engineers, so interruptions such as phone calls and people coming into their office were common. The advertising novelty worked well to minimize and, in many cases, stop interruptions because the engineer then focused and gave the directive to staff 'not to disturb'. They appeared to welcome the break, preferring to listen to a story about the advertising novelty.

A favourite novelty enjoyed by every prospective customer was a small pocketknife that fitted easily into one hand. It could be used to peel apples and oranges and had a concealed blade. Kurt's engaging story referred to the pocketknife as a blow knife. He stated, 'to release the blade you are required to blow in the top end'. The process was to hold the knife in one hand so it could not be seen, blow in the top end and at the same time gently push the bottom of the blade with the middle finger. This released the blade without the prospective customer noticing. Fully extended the blade was about 65cm long. Then, pause for effect before pushing the blade back into its sheath. Next hand the knife to the prospective customer. They would blow into the knife and naturally nothing happened. Timing was everything. Leave it too late and they could get frustrated and angry, respond too quickly and the curiosity and engagement were lost. After the prospective customer tried a couple of times Kurt would ask, 'Can I show you how it works?' An eager, 'Yes' was often the response. They were totally enthralled. He showed them what he had done which was met with a smile and laughter.

He then asked, 'Do you catch up with friends after work or on the weekend?' The answer was usually, 'Yes' so, he suggested, 'Try it on your friends and let me know how you got on when I see you next month'. This let them know Kurt will be coming back.

The follow-up sales call was met with a smiling face and stories of how the customer had fun tricking their family and friends with the blow knife.

The Most Unlikely Salesperson

Sales calls always got off to a great start, helped build the relationship and created many memorable moments.

The advertising novelty that took the most time to develop an engaging story was a pen that had the company logo on one side. A popular item for companies to promote their name and there was nothing special about it. Kurt introduced the pen by saying, *'This is a magic pen and can write in many colours. Let me show you. Can I have a sheet of paper?'* The prospective customer would tear a sheet from their writing pad and Kurt would ask, *'What colour do you like?'* The pen had black ink, and most would respond with black to which Kurt wrote in upper case, BLACK then asked, *'Another colour you like?'* The response might be, *'Blue'*. The word BLUE was written in black ink. It was amazing how many did not catch on, so he asked again, *'Another colour you like?'* Response, *'Red'*. He wrote RED. Then the penny dropped, and the prospective customer realized it was a joke and laughed. He handed them the pen and said, *'I hope you have a lot of fun with it'*.

The company had an extensive range of advertising novelties, and Kurt developed, practiced, and refined stories linked to each one. The focus was on having fun and engaging prospective customers as well as existing customers.

Kurt walked into businesses his failed predecessors had and copped abuse. There were days every sales call was met with an angry and aggressive individual. It appeared what had occurred was inconceivable behaviour by the previous salespeople.

One salesperson was terminated when it was discovered what he had been doing. This salesperson wanted his sales revenues to look impressive and receive huge commissions. He managed to get away with it for several months until it all came crashing down.

The first experience Kurt encountered was a boat maintenance business located in the Hawkesbury River about an hour's drive north of Sydney. The owner stood at the far end of a long pier that was part of his premises. He wore overalls, appeared to be two metres tall and weighed about 130 kilos. He had his back to the entrance as Kurt walked on the creaking-timber floorboards, attracting the owner's attention. He turned quickly and ran directly at Kurt yelling and screaming profane language. At the fast pace the owner was running Kurt had no chance of getting away, so he stood there fixed as if his shoes were glued to the spot. It is amazing what fear can do. At 24 years of age and of slight build, who was he to shape up to this mountain of a man. The owner literally stood over Kurt pointing his index finger and yelled at the top of his voice. Kurt had no idea why he was so aggressive, until a fleeting thought, the owner recognized the company's signature briefcase Kurt was carrying. He verbalized his frustration for what seemed an eternity but eventually ran out of steam and stopped.

Kurt responded by saying, '*I can see you are incredibly angry. I would appreciate if you would tell me what happened?*' A slight pause before adding, '*Could we sit down somewhere?*' The owner nodded in agreement and Kurt followed him to his office. This was the beginning of Kurt taking control of the sales call. The owner's demeanour did soften as they sat down. Kurt introduced himself and the man responded, '*Jim Stanton*' as they shook hands.

Kurt soon understood why Jim was so angry. He told him he ordered 25 litres of solvent from the previous salesperson and received 250 litres. When Jim phoned the office to sort the error, he was told the copy of the order was for 250 litres. The salesperson added a zero to the 25 after Jim signed the order. Compounding the problem an internal person within the company mishandled the situation by refusing to take the container back for credit. Kurt immediately arranged for it to be returned and a credit given. Though Kurt told Jim the other salesperson was terminated for unethical behaviour, Jim refused to continue to do business with the company. The problem was finally sorted, and Kurt left Jim on good terms.

The salesperson wrote fake orders for delivery in four to six weeks, and it was not until the goods were delivered that his actions became known and led to his dismissal. Alarm bells should have been ringing earlier because the salesperson's forward orders were in excess of 80% compared to the company's 5-8%.

It was quite a learning experience handling the problems left by the dismissed salesperson, and reinstating a relationship based on honesty and integrity. It took time but many prospective customers were won over.

The company developed and marketed new products throughout the year making the role exciting and requiring ongoing creativity to sell them. One that captured prospective customers attention was a two-part glue system. To test the glues' strength, Kurt mixed the two parts and bonded an old medicine bottle to a piece of wood. Once the glue had set, the two parts could not be separated. A boating company in Berowra, New South Wales were the first company in Australia to place an order for the product. They had several difficult repairs in their workshop and though the product was $150 per pack, it was significantly less money than replacing parts and the labour involved. Showing the bottle and glued wood model, then asking a prospective customer to try and separate the two, made sales interesting and easy. No one was ever able to pull it apart.

The Most Unlikely Salesperson

The sales territory had more bowling clubs than any other type of business, so it made sense to find out if there were any sales opportunities. The company's catalogue had a section outlining a range of fertilizers, weed and bug killing products. Kurt's knowledge of these was limited to what was printed on the pages, and he was keen to learn from a customer's perspective. The Ryde Eastwood Bowling Club was nearby, so Kurt walked in and introduced himself to the greenkeeper. He asked, *'Would you mind helping me out? I am fairly new to this job and would appreciate if you could tell me the difference between the two bowling greens? The grass looks different'*. The greenkeeper stopped his ride on mower and said, *'Sure, it is almost smoko time'*. Then he invited Kurt to his maintenance shed for have a cup of coffee.

Kurt formally introduced himself, the greenkeeper said, *'I am Jack Lawson'*. He continued, *'The green to your left is couch, and the other is bent'*. Kurt asked what the differences were. Jack explained in detail then immediately bridged into talking about a new type of grass introduced from the United States, Tifdwarf. He said it was recently laid at the Gladesville Bowling Club. Fortunately for Kurt, Jack liked to talk. Jack stating tifdwarf was hardier than bent, less prone to disease and lower maintenance. He gave Kurt the full background. There was a natural pause when Kurt asked, *'Jack would you mind giving me your opinion on products that relate to the maintenance of bowling greens and golf clubs'*. Though Kurt and Jack did not know how the products performed, Jack spoke highly of the range based on the literature information.

After seeing Jack, Kurt headed for the Gladesville Bowling Club and sold several products. The time and expertise so generously given by Jack and subsequent greenkeepers helped Kurt built a portfolio of knowledge he gladly shared with those interested. The stories and information were not of a confidential nature and often not connected to the products he was selling, but relevant to the greenkeeper. This created a smooth transition from the discussion to greenkeepers openly wanting to talk about their current maintenance problems.

> **To create worthwhile communication, build a portfolio of knowledge about your customers and their operations.**

A major difficulty at one time was bowling and golf club greens were littered with small holes created by a black beetle plague. The chemicals they had been using did not work. Fortunately, the product Kurt was offering knocked the black beetles over in no time. You can imagine a greenkeeper listening to a story about another club that had the same problem, what they did to solve it and the results achieved. Greenkeepers would often know the greenkeepers or club Kurt spoke about. It reached a point when Kurt walked into a new club and introduced himself, the greenkeeper had already heard about him. This trust and credibility generated sales, and referrals to club managers who in turn purchased cleaning products and referred Kurt to other clubs. Selling became effortless and a pleasure creating record sales for the range of products. However, whilst sales were good, product volumes were not high enough to win major sales awards.

After 14 months working the two sales territories Kurt decided to move to Perth, Western Australia. He asked the new General Manager Nigel Turner if he could work the central business district because it was not represented, and any area the existing state salespeople Robert and John were not operating in. Both were long term employees with ten and 15 years' service and number one and two respectively for sales in Australia. Robert worked the mines in the north of the state and John went wherever he pleased.

With a third salesperson about to start in Western Australia, the general manager divided the state into defined sales territories. There was considerable pushback from Robert and John but in the end, they accepted the new structure. Kurt was allocated the Perth Central Business District. The company had no customers in Geraldton, four-hours north, and Kalgoorlie, a mining town 6½ hours east, these regions were also added.

Kurt began by working the central business district. In the last month he managed to exceed expectation and won the 50-orders in a month sales award. The next award was the 150-order sales award, achieved by producing a minimum of 50-orders per month for three consecutive months. He was a third of the way but did not reach the second month's target. This meant he had to start over.

Kurt was determined to win all the company's sales award, including the prestigious 8000 litre volume award. He told Nigel he intended to achieve it during June, July and August. Nigel reflected on what Kurt said and then highlighted the difficulties including, June was the end of the financial year and businesses held back purchasing during this period, and August was the federal government's budget announcement that caused businesses to react in the same manner.

Kurt felt disappointed in Nigel's comment and spoke before thinking, *'If I do not achieve it, I will resign'*. This did not go down well with Nigel and for Kurt there was no turning back, he made a public statement and now had to deliver.

It was mid-May, Kurt decided to review what he had done to-date, what worked, what did not work, and was there an optimal way to manage a sales territory? The four-weekly selling cycle had worked well in the past,

The Most Unlikely Salesperson

but it was not an effective model for the large sales territory he wanted to cover. He decided to increase the cycle to six weeks and reduce his time in some areas that had limited potential and increase others. The goals were to minimize travel time by clustering prospective customers in smaller areas and close more sales. He would continue to keep thorough customer and potential customer records, forecast product usage, and adjust sales call intervals according to the business' potential.

Kurt had no previous data to go on, so he researched the companies in his sales territory and developed a list of businesses, semi-government and government organizations. He allocated each sector a geographical sales territory Area 1 through to Area 6. He then took a conservative estimate on what they could use. His objective was to assess if 150 orders and 8000 litres of product could be achieved within a three-month period. Perth was divided into Area 1 though to Area 4, and Geraldton was Area 5. There were no significant industries between Geraldton and Port Hedland 1400 kilometres north, where Robert's sales territory started. Area 6 was Kalgoorlie.

North of Kalgoorlie was Leonora, a 2½ hour drive. It had a hospital and a small motel. Continuing further north into the centre of Western Australia was Agnew Mining, another 1½ hours away. The mine had a camp consisting of modern portable buildings for workers and visitors. A small township formed part of Agnew.

Sunday evenings were dedicated to planning the coming week, and each evening fine-tune the next day's selling activities. Waking up in the morning knowing what needed to be done and why, set the tone for the day. There was no room for procrastination. Kurt had total autonomy managing six areas and could switch sales call cycles depending on where the greatest opportunities were. He phoned Nigel every Friday afternoon to report the week's activities and sales results.

A common misconception was rainy days and Fridays prevented sales success.

The first of June was a Friday, a day that was synonymous with hearing, '*What are you doing working on a Friday?*' This was followed by, '*You should be on the golf course like other salespeople*'. Potential customers in particular thought this was humorous. Kurt welcomed the jibes because it made the transition from the introduction to a conversation easy—providing an advantage.

Many companies had salespeople tied up in sales meetings on a Friday. There were salespeople and sales managers who falsely believe Friday is not good for selling, so they have a meeting. After the meeting salespeople appear busy with non-sales activities around the office.

Another falsely held belief is customers are not receptive to meet with salespeople on a rainy day. Kurt never let weather conditions prevent him from selling. When he walked into a potential customer's premises, at times somewhat wet, it was the weather that triggered the conversation. A receptionist would say, *'What are you doing out in this bad weather?'* Kurt's response was always upbeat, *'The weather is great because my plants are being watered'*. They probably thought he was a bit crazy, but a light-hearted conversation followed. The receptionist to Kurt's surprise would go out of their way to track down the maintenance person he wanted to meet. When he meets the person the subject of the weather would always come up, so it turned out to be a wonderful ice breaker.

The prospective customer having empathy would say, *'No-one goes out on a day like this'*. That was true for Kurt's competitors, because if it were not for the rain he would usually hear, *'You are the (they quote a number) chemical salesperson who has come here today'*. To lighten up the atmosphere whenever Kurt heard that statement, he responded with a smile and said, *'Well I am lucky because another chemical salesperson just pulled up in the carpark'*. For a few seconds there was a serious look on the prospective customer's face, before realising it was a bit of humour. The majority smiled and said, *'Well show me what you have'* as they both walked towards the workshop or office.

Another advantage competitors unwittingly gave Kurt was they selected prospective customers based on the size of the building and neglected the smaller businesses either side.

Kurt walked door-to-door. Reactions were either complaining about the number of chemical salespeople they have seen, or they had not seen a salesperson selling industrial chemicals in months. Both responses were welcomed to start a conversation.

Setting daily activities and sales targets will reduce feeling overwhelmed

Kurt felt exhilarated at the extent of the sales challenge that lay ahead. To avoid becoming overwhelmed he set a minimum daily activity and sales target. Smaller numbers felt manageable and achievable. His sales ratio had improved considerably since the first day in West Ryde. He knew on average if he walked into eight businesses, did five demonstrations, he could close one in two sales. To achieve the sales target, it was simply a matter of increasing the number of sales calls and demonstrations.

Perth's government and semi-government bodies had existing contracts in place with low-cost product suppliers. The products Kurt was selling were high-end and priced accordingly. The challenge was to convince line managers within government and semi-government organizations to purchase outside the contract agreement. To do this he would have to prove:

- The products outperform the contracted items in terms of speed and effectiveness. Proof by demonstration
- The products made their job easier
- Kurt had a greater breadth and depth of products to select from
- The unit cost of the diluted product was competitive.

From a prospective customer's point-of-view all chemicals do the same job. There is next to no difference, so they try to create difference through purchasing at a lower cost. It is their way to justify buying from one company rather than another.

Being aware of this when Kurt was asked, *'What makes your company and your products different?'* with a smile and somewhat cheekily he replied, *'Dealing with me'*. This created laughter and comments that led to customer interest—a closer connection was formed.

Selling high-end products to government and semi-government organizations without a contract provided its own challenges. The premier of the state at the time added to it by going on television advising consumers to, 'Look for the Birth Mark'. The 'Birth Mark' was a yellow logo of Western Australia with a red dot in the centre. It was printed on all products made locally. Though the advertisements were for consumers, senior bureaucrats sent memos to line managers instructing them to buy locally, even if the product was up to 10% dearer.

The industrial chemical products Kurt sold were manufactured in Sydney. To provide a quicker delivery service, a warehouse was opened in Osborne Park, an industrial estate in Western Australia. When questioned about the products, Kurt stated the products were warehoused locally and left it at that.

The month of June was off to a good start with 53 sales. It was time to head north to Area 5 and see what sales opportunities were there.

The remuneration package meant accommodation and travel costs were Kurt's responsibility and not the company. To minimize expenses, Kurt rented a caravan at the Geraldton Caravan Park. He drove a large vehicle with a generous boot to store the most popular products needed for demonstration. Also travelling vast distances meant he had to sell more product to cover the fuel bill. The goal from Monday to Wednesday morning was to generate revenues to cover all expenses. Wednesday afternoon, Thursday and Friday commissions on sales were his salary. It taught Kurt to totally focus on what needed to be done—with no distractions. He was amazed at how often the sales goal was achieved by late Monday or Tuesday. A great feeling to start the next day knowing all costs have been covered.

On his initial trip to Geraldton the first town Kurt stopped at was Eneabba, about 2½ hours north of Perth. He noticed a mine site, drove in and headed for the main office located just off the entrance gates. Opening the glass door to the office he made eye contact with the receptionist and smiled. She appeared to be in her early forties, well dressed and wore a multitude of gold rings on her fingers. Her fingernails were impeccably manicured and painted bright red. Her name tag on the left upper shoulder had Sue Waters engraved. Kurt looked at the name tag knowing she noticed then said, *'Good morning Sue, my name is Kurt Newman from the Industrial Chemical Company. I would like to see the maintenance engineer'*.

Sue informed Kurt he was in a meeting and there were two other salespeople waiting to see him, *'Thank you for letting me know. Do you mind my asking what his name is?'* The reply, *'Ken Stevens'*. She suggested Kurt take a seat which he did.

The two salespeople sat next to each other quietly, looking into space. After several minutes Kurt got up and went over to speak to Sue. He was fascinated by her jewellery and manicured fingernails and commented accordingly. Kurt had a small container of women's hand cream with him, one of the many company advertising novelties he had with him. He mentioned he does not sell hand cream but likes to give these as a promotional gift for his female customers and would she like to try it?

The response was an instant, *'Yes!'*, and at the same time Sue started removing her gold rings. Kurt applied the cream on her hands and told her a story about how fussy his mother is about hand cream disliking oily residue, *'This cream according to my mother leaves no residue'*. Within minutes of rubbing the cream into her hands Sue agreed and tried to leave her fingerprints on a sheet of paper. Kurt followed immediately with, *'Please accept the hand cream with my compliments'*.

Sue's phone rang and it was the maintenance engineer. Sue told him, *'Ken, Kurt from the Industrial Chemical Company has been waiting for you'*. Her vocal tone sounded as if she and Kurt knew each other. Kurt did not expect this and was pleasantly surprised as Ken walked past the two salespeople, then greeted him.

During the conversation he learned that Ken recently joined the mine and was becoming familiar with the site and his responsibilities. Ken did not know what industrial maintenance chemicals and lubricants he had or what he may need. The timing was out, but it was better to be too early

The Most Unlikely Salesperson

than too late. The relationship was off to a good start and Ken agreed to meet with Kurt on his next trip to discuss his specific needs.

To make the most of the sales call Kurt asked for a referral, *'Who do you think on the site might be interested in industrial maintenance products?'* Ken introduced Kurt to the chef, Jake Stone. Jake bought 25 litres of a water-based solvent to remove grease from the kitchen floor. Jake also insisted on giving Kurt a large tin of coffee.

Continuing to travel north, Kurt looked for opportunities in reasonably large towns—there were few. Geraldton was another two-hours drive away. New customers were mining companies, local councils, car dealerships and a monastery. The monastery came about because Kurt was curious, walked in and asked one of the sisters if she could let him know who looked after maintenance. The sister asked him to wait in the foyer, and within minutes Kurt was introduced to Declan and Mary Boyle. They were responsible for the upkeep and cleaning of the monastery. They were a delightful Irish couple. Kurt asked questions to uncover problems that needed solving, then demonstrated the appropriate products. On conclusion of their meeting, Mary withdrew, saw the Mother Superior and returned with an order number.

Curiousity can drive new sales opportunities— explore even what you think is a faint link

Kurt arrived in Geraldton late afternoon on the Monday, drove around the town listing the businesses he was going to see the next day, and then onto the caravan park. The following morning, he walked into the Geraldton Building Company, the largest building company in the region. The business supplied demountable buildings as well as stocked an extensive range of general hardware. Kurt went from department to department, eight in total, and asked to be referred after the first sale. By early-afternoon he left with five sales, and the commissions earned covered his expenses for the week.

The local water board, a government body was nearby. The Perth depot bought several products from Kurt. Using a referral from the Perth depot, Kurt was interested to see if the maintenance engineer at the regional workshop had similar problems to be solved. He introduced himself to the maintenance engineer who said his name was Peter. During the conversation Kurt mentioned Bill Kensington from the Perth depot. To Kurt's astonishment Peter was Bill's father. The connection was instant. He demonstrated one of the products Bill uses and secured an order for 60 litres. Peter bought other products on successive trips and became one of his best customers in Geraldton.

The Most Unlikely Salesperson

Area 5 turned out to be enjoyable to work and sales increased dramatically with successive trips. The six-week cycle was reduced to four weeks and Area 2 in Perth extended. Declan, Mary and Peter purchased products on every visit, as did several other customers. Products were reordered, additional products purchased, and customers were added regularly. Sales aside, the relationships, warmth and hospitality Kurt experienced will always be with him.

July finished with 56 sales and good volumes. One month to go. Area 6 was next. Kalgoorlie was an eight-hour drive west of Perth. Kurt left on a Sunday to get an early start on the Monday.

Kurt arrived in Kalgoorlie late Sunday afternoon and scouted the town to find and list potential customers. There was a gold mine with a huge mountain of soil inside its fenced area. A local told him this was about to be reprocessed to extract any remaining gold that may have been initially missed. The town had many small and interesting businesses that if pursued could have yielded more sales. Fortunately, Kurt was ahead of his sales target with the number of sales, but was aiming for more volume.

Monday morning came and he decided to leave Kalgoorlie and drive to Leonora three-hours north into the desert. When he arrived, the Leonora Hospital stood out as a prospective customer. Kurt walked in and asked for the matron, the person he asked said she was the matron. Her name was Sadie Canning. Sadie radiated kindness and humility, and mainly spoke about her community work. Along the entrance hallway were framed photos of Sadie being awarded an MBE by Queen Elizabeth II. It was an interesting sales call because there were constant emergencies and interruption, of which Sadie had to attend to. It got to the point there was no value continuing the sales call. Kurt thanked Sadie and suggested he leave so she could attend to her patients.

Kurt drove around Leonora, but the few businesses there were too small to be considered prospective customers. It was too late to leave for Agnew Mining, so he booked into the one-and-only motel. It had ten clean basic rooms.

He left Leonora the next day around mid-morning for Agnew Mining and planned to stay several days there. He booked into the Agnew Mining camp accommodation. This was the only accommodation for visitors. Arriving early afternoon, the town administrator's office drew Kurt's attention. He walked in and spoke with the receptionist. After asking a few questions he was introduced to the general manager Sam Bartholomew. Sam's role was similar to that of a local council general manager. He bought 480 litres of product and referred Kurt to the town's domestic garbage contractor, Jack Rowe.

Chapter 3 Sales Role: Industrial Chemicals **21**

The Most Unlikely Salesperson

Kurt left the office, sat in his car and as he pulled away from the curb, by coincidence was behind a garbage truck. When the truck stopped for the driver to pick up a garbage bin, Kurt stepped out of his car, walked up to the person assuming it would be Jack and introduced himself. Jack appeared relaxed as they both stood on the footpath. He told Kurt he owned a large and a smaller truck for the job. Kurt showed Jack a product that would clean and sanitize his trucks and offered a heavy-duty spray applicator with a 60 litre purchase.

Jack said, *'I'll have it'*. and then asked Kurt where he was staying. He said the mining camp accommodation. Jack immediately said, *'No you are not, I will call them and let them know you are staying with me and my family'*. Kurt felt deeply touched by his generosity and for a moment searched for words to thank him and to politely refuse, but Jack jumped in, *'It is settled. You are staying with us, and I will be organising a party in your honour'*. Kurt asked what he meant by, *'a party in your honour'*. Jack responded, *'You are a visitor and our guest, and I want you to meet our friends'*. Kurt felt a deep sense of gratitude and humbly accepted.

The number of people at the party filled the house and most of the backyard. He found it hard to believe so many people would come to see the new guy in town. It was more-than-likely an excuse to have a party. Whatever the reason, everyone was welcoming, sociable and had a wonderful time.

Four days in Agnew, it was time to leave. He started packing his gear on the last morning when Jack asked when was he coming back? Kurt replied, *'around mid-November'*. To prepare Kurt for what to expect, Jack mentioned the temperature that time of year can be 50°C.

Area 6 volume sales were equivalent to four months of Perth sales

Total volume sales were the equivalent of four months sales in Perth.

Arriving back in Perth early evening, Kurt had the next day to make up the shortfall, of two orders and 200 litres of product, to make-a-clean sweep of all the company sales awards. But where to find it? He had seen every business that could use industrial chemicals and lubrication products. The best option was to contact a large or several large existing customer/s with the aim of acquiring a repeat order.

The person who came to mind was Elson Watson, who processed purchase requests for the Perth Water Board depots. Elson was in his late fifties and had a fatherly manner. They enjoyed each other's company immensely. In Elson's office, Kurt spoke openly about the sales awards and asked if he could help him. Elson did not hesitate, *'Call me in an hour'*.

The Most Unlikely Salesperson

Elson contacted the maintenance engineers at each depot, most of whom knew of Kurt, and had stocks of various products. They placed purchase requests totalling four orders and 650 litres of product. Elson fast-tracked the purchase requests through head office administration, so these now became official orders. When Kurt rang Elson back, he was blown away by the details of each order—a huge weight was lifted and were replaced with exhilaration and feelings of gratitude. Their generosity touched Kurt deeply. He knew Elson liked Chivas Regal Scotch Whiskey and the maintenance engineers got together after work and had a beer. Kurt headed for the local bottle shop, purchased the items and then delivered each one. He let them know how much he appreciated what they had done for him, and it was personal and had nothing to do with business.

After doing the rounds of deliveries it was only 11:00am and a beautiful sunny day. Kurt ponded what to do next. He had worked long hours. Sales award targets had been exceeded on all accounts. He felt he deserved the rest of the day off, so he did. He grabbed his swimming trunks and towel and drove to Cottesloe Beach where he stayed until 3:00pm. He then phoned Nigel and told him what had happened, and that he was at the beach. Nigel did not comment about the latter because he was elated at the results. He informed Kurt there were two other sales award winners. One in Sydney, Jeremy O'Connor and the other in Brisbane, Grayson Burrows. Both achieved the 150-order sales award but fell short of the 8000 litre volume award.

The company had a strong sales culture and provided a salesperson was an above-average sales-performer and showed management potential, they had the opportunity to be promoted to sales supervisor. The primary responsibility of the sales supervisor was to train and coach salespeople new to the company through to salespeople who needed to get back on track. Their other responsibility when not coaching was to continue managing their sales territory and to grow sales. This as Kurt discovered, was quite a juggling act. Time management and the ability to adapt and transfer sales skills to salespeople who had varying backgrounds, experiences, skills and demographics was crucial.

To validate knowledge and skills had been effectively transferred the company kept detailed records and tracked the performance of the coached salesperson for two weeks. If the sales graph showed a huge reduction throughout this period, it was a red flag for management to ask questions. Could it indicate the sales supervisor did a poor job of coaching or did they do most of the selling? Whatever the reason, the sales manager would spend time with the sales supervisor to guide them in the right

Chapter 3 Sales Role: Industrial Chemicals 23

direction. If after the session the behaviour/s did not change the sales supervisor would be found unsuitable for the role and encouraged to go back full time working their sales territory. There were a number of great sales performers including Robert, who sold the largest volume of product but did not make an effective sales supervisor.

For those who put in the energy and produced the results, the company was quick to promote them further. From a sales supervisor role to state sales manager to country manager, then to an overseas posting. Promotion in the pipeline meant the individual had to find a replacement for their current role. This is why it was important to have at least one person trained and ready to take their next in-line place.

The promotion model had merit on many fronts, particularly for those who wanted to progress in the company. They respected the person ahead of them because that person had the ability to demonstrate sales and sales management competence. They walked-the-walk that young salespeople wanted to emulate.

Sales awards were celebrated at annual conferences. Winners were presented with a number of status-symbol clothing and other items to show their level of sales success. For some salespeople, it was an ego driven occasion. Kurt achieved what only three other salespeople in Australia had, and he was the youngest by far at 27 years.

To be presented with the sales awards by Nigel felt euphoric for Kurt. He persisted and finally made it after overcoming failure and setbacks the previous three years. He was surprised when Nigel said, 'Do you know prospects say no to you up to five times before saying yes?'

Kurt had no idea. In today's world, this would appear to be high-pressure selling, but it was not then. In the years Kurt sold products for the company, he had only one cancellation and one of the highest repeat sales records. He put this down to being himself and genuinely caring.

Accepting the awards, he thought back to day one walking into 20 businesses and no sales—a ratio of 20:0. The ratios improved dramatically to 3:1 and quite regularly 2:1 and remained at that level for the duration of his time with the company.

Lessons Learned

- The goal may appear impossible at first, but do not let your emotions prevent you from starting. If there is a path, divide it into manageable steps, then take action to create movement and movement will propel you forward.
- If you want something bad enough, you have a strong-restless yearning, then you have what it takes to get there. Expect obstacles and that your determination will be tested. It is a natural part of the journey. Keep focussed and see any challenge as a learning experience and as character building—yes character building—and you will get there. How do you stop a person who will not be stopped? The answer is you cannot.
- Success is to be acknowledged and celebrated. Do not categorize success as being small or large, success of any size moves you forward and will encourage you to keep going.

Shortly after the conference Leroy Jones the Senior Vice President of International Sales visited Australia. Whilst in the country he wanted to formally interview Jeremy, Grayson, and Kurt. They were not told what Leroy's intention were for the interviews. Kurt was the first to be called into Nigel's office where the interviews were conducted. The room was long rectangular in shape with a large round table at the far end where Leroy sat facing the door entrance. Kurt was asked to sit directly opposite him, and Nigel was on his left side.

The senior Vice President was in his mid-sixties and of slight build. His interviewing style was to ask an open question followed by closing his eyes as Kurt answered his questions which was followed by a long pause. This was done repeatedly throughout the 80 minute interview. Kurt noticed a wall clock directly behind the senior Vice President which made it easy for him to see the duration of the long silent pauses. These were often up to two minutes. Perhaps it was his way of testing Kurt to see if he would break the silence? He just sat there and looked at the clock or Nigel from time to time. Both smiled at each other because they knew Leroy was trying to make Kurt feel uncomfortable and put him under pressure. On one occasion when Leroy opened his eyes, Kurt asked him an open-ended question in an attempt to get him to talk. He sensed Leroy did not like to be asked questions because his answers were exceptionally brief.

The Most Unlikely Salesperson

To briefly side-track, for several months prior to the interview Kurt did infield sales coaching throughout Australia. This was part of an ongoing development programme and to assess if he had the attributes to be successful at transferring sales skills. Leroy reviewed the records of every coaching session focussing on sales achieved by each salesperson, sales by Kurt, and two weeks post-coaching sales results of individual salespeople. The post-coaching results were particularly important because it confirmed the level of coaching effectiveness. If a salesperson's sales dropped dramatically during this period time, it could be interpreted as the sales coach having done most of the selling and a poor job of transferring skills.

As the interview neared its completion Leroy stood up quickly, reached over to shake Kurt's hand and said, *'Welcome to sales management'*. He then realized why Leroy wanted to interview the sales award winners. Kurt was delighted and at the same time felt mentally spent after the intensity and length of the interview. Jeremy and Grayson's interviews were 20 minutes each and shortly after they became New South Wales and Queensland Sales Managers, respectively. Kurt's scope for the sales management role was not defined, and he found himself about to undergo further challenges and evaluation.

The following months were extremely busy with extensive interstate travel. Though he still lived in Western Australia, Kurt was in one region of Australia or another for two to three weeks at a time. The tasks and responsibilities were to induct and coach salespeople new to the company, turnaround salespeople who developed counterproductive sales habits, and guide top sales achievers to higher-performance levels. The ability to adapt to individual personalities, identify current skill levels, tailor the sales coaching accordingly, regional to capital city business development and account management skills were paramount. Kurt was 27 and often given a challenging time by much older experienced salespeople, but it was all in good fun. The national sales team consisted of 28 salespeople.

When back in Perth, Kurt was expected to maintain sales volumes in his sales territory. This was part of the company's strong sales culture and less than up-to-par performance was not accepted, so the pressure to achieve results was always present. Although a demanding workload, the learning and experiences provided a fertile ground for rapid personal and professional growth.

The diversity of salespeople Kurt worked with is highlighted by two examples, John Fenton and Kay Burman. John was a long-term employee with eight years of service and experience. Kay had recently joined the company. John was the second highest sales producer and did exceptionally well with repeat sales, but sales had slowly regressed because he did no ongoing business development.

Salesperson example 1: John was in his comfort zone and not motivated to change. Kurt's objective during the four days they were to spend together was to reacquaint him with the skills of acquiring new accounts. Kurt expected resistance—and it came sooner than anticipated. The evening before they were to start, John rang Kurt with a succession of excuses. He clearly felt uncomfortable at the thought of sales coaching. Kurt reassured him and then insisted it was going to happen. John finally agreed to meet him at 6:00am when they would travel together to a regional part of John's sales territory. John was 16 years older than Kurt, physically in great shape having been a body builder and worked part-time as a singing waiter. Kurt was to soon discover John had a brilliant operatic voice.

After hours of driving, John pulled into a mine site visitor's car park. He said the mine was one of his best customers. He got out of his car and started walking toward the workshop when Kurt stopped him. It was standard practice to prepare a range of sample products for demonstration purposes and a visual aid folder neatly packed into a specially made briefcase. Kurt asked John to open the boot of his car to get the briefcase. From a distance he said, '*I do not need it*'. Kurt insisted, so he returned reluctantly and opened the boot leaving Kurt to assemble what might be needed. The metal hinges and locks on the briefcase were badly corroded but still worked and spider webs were in and around the bottom crevasses. It showed that John had not used the equipment in a long-time and it was far from presenting a good first impression.

John refused to use the sales tools and turned to walk toward the workshop. Kurt took what he could and followed. As John entered the building, he started singing the opera, Figaro. This was the first time Kurt heard John sing, and he could not believe the strength and projection of his voice as it vibrated throughout the workshop. What an entrance! Everyone stopped what they were doing and listened. John sang for about 15 seconds before finishing with a huge smile that was met with cheers and enthusiastic clapping. He responded by bowing and kept smiling.

The maintenance engineer came out of his office and greeted John who introduced him to Kurt. His name was Derek Gallagher. Kurt followed the two back to Derek's office. It was John's sales call, so Kurt took a passive role only becoming involved if Derek asked him a question. This allowed John total control and responsibility for the outcome. Kurt watched how the two interacted and it was obvious they liked each other and got on well. Kurt listened to what John said and did. After the feel-good catch-up conversation Derek initiated the close by placing a repeat order for four of the six items normally stocked. He handed a hard copy of the order to

John who then started to get ready to leave. Kurt identified two products Derek might be able to use that John did not mention.

He politely asked Derek, '*Would you mind if I ask you a few questions about potential problems you might be experiencing?*' Derek nodded affirmatively, listened, and then acknowledged the problems. Kurt briefly stepped him through the two relevant product brochures and demonstrated one product he had in the briefcase. In closing, Kurt suggested volumes he might like to begin with. Derek agreed and then asked John for the order copy he had given him and added the two items.

As they headed back to the car John's demeanour was frosty. Kurt asked what was wrong? John ignored the question. Kurt let it go, for now, and suggested they have a debrief-coaching session once they left the carpark. When John found a safe area off the highway he pulled over and stopped. Kurt began by giving John credit for the quality relationship he had developed with Derek resulting in six products being stocked and four reordered. He tried to mellow John's attitude but gained no headway. Kurt reached over the backseat and grabbed a pad and pen. He thought by drawing diagrams, talking, and asking questions might encourage John to lighten up and become involved. He outlined the sales process, corresponding skills, the skills John had applied and emphasized the value of setting sales call objectives. At that point, Kurt left out what John had failed to do because it was part of the coaching process. He wanted to see if John knew what he had missed, so he asked, '*If you had the opportunity to do the sales call again, is there anything you would do differently?*'

John did not answer the question, instead responded with broad comments he thought Kurt wanted to hear. Kurt acknowledged the comments then decided to change tact by bringing up the subject of the two add-on items—this was the elephant in the car. He said, '*Let us look at what happened during the last sales call and tell me if you disagree. For years Derek had two problems that will be solved as soon as the newly ordered products arrive. You have eight products stocked instead of six, and you earned additional commission*'.

Kurt looked at John waiting for a response—that did not happen. John was sullen and appeared to be controlling his anger. Kurt had to dig deeper, '*Have I done something that has offended you?*' Still no response, '*Okay, we are getting nowhere so let's leave it and drive to the next sales call. What is your sales call objective?*' They discussed and agreed, then did two role plays to lock down key skills John needed to competently apply.

What triggered John was that a 'stranger' (Kurt) who Derek did not know bought two additional products he should have sold years ago. Having a large family to look after, John also realized he had missed out on considerable commissions for those years. Kurt would learn more about John's true feelings at the end of the four days.

Fast forward to the last day of the coaching. It was Christmas Eve, 24 December. They met in the morning and John said he never works on this day. Kurt asked why? It was not for any religious reason, only he passionately believed no-one buys on this day or on Friday afternoons. Kurt did not accept this premise, and suggested they work half the day and if they get three new accounts by 12:00 noon John could have the rest of the day off. He smiled and shook his head, as if to say this is unbelievable, but reluctantly agreed. As it turned out the third new customer signed an order two minutes before midday. It was a magical outcome Kurt thought, but John found it hard to accept.

After the last call they sat in John's car for a final summary and coaching debrief. Kurt asked what he had learned in their time together? John began by saying, '*I learned I need to prospect for new business regularly, use visual aids and do product demonstrations. I will try and not prejudge whether sales are possible based on the time of the year, week or day*'. He then paused and looked down to avoid eye contact and said, '*I earned more money in the last four days than in any other period. I now realize I have lost thousands of dollars in commissions over the last eight years*'. He appeared sombre but something was brewing and then his true thoughts and feelings surfaced. John looked intensely at Kurt, and his parting words were, '*I respect you, but I dislike you*'. Kurt thanked him for being honest, wished him a Merry Christmas and stepped out of the car.

To summarise, John had been selling in the same sales territory for eight years. He did well in achieving the No.2 highest-volume producer in the company, however he had become complacent. Sales were easy, so over time he took shortcuts in the sales process and relied on his charisma, operatic voice and the long-term relationships. By doing so, he forgot the basic disciplines of sales and the need for regular business development to keep sales growing. This prevented him from selling greater volumes, having a larger customer base, becoming No.1 in sales, and most importantly, earning more income to provide for his family.

John's complacency is not uncommon for salespeople who have been in sales for a long time. John had been in sales most of his life before joining the Industrial Chemical Company. Staying in cruise control and doing the minimum will eventually unravel. Salespeople need to continually look for ways to add value—value which is not necessarily related directly to selling a product or service. Customers appreciate it and return it in loyalty.

Customers appreciate value-add propositions and return it in loyalty.

The Most Unlikely Salesperson

Business development is integral to sales. If not incorporated regularly, sales erode because natural events such as the customer no longer needs the product or service due to internal changes, the customer contact has moved on and the new contact favours a different supplier, and business takeovers can change the nature of the company, agreements and relationships.

Salesperson example 2: Kay Burman was a different salesperson on every measure to John. The sales coaching objectives Kurt had planned were to provide product knowledge, transfer sales skills and create new customers.

Kurt landed in Brisbane late Sunday afternoon to prepare for the week ahead. The phone rang some hours later, and it was Kay asking to see him to learn more about the products. She wanted to get a head start. Kurt admired her initiative so agreed to meet. He covered the top five most popular products as Kay took notes furiously and asked questions.

Kay had done modelling in a previous career and wanted to get into sales. She was a single parent with an eight-year-old daughter. Kay was motivated to succeed. Kurt was impressed by her drive and enthusiasm. He felt Kay had what it took to be a sales award winner.

They met early Monday morning and Kay suggested a sales challenge whereby Kurt did one sales call to her two. Initially he thought she was joking but a cheeky smile on her face suggested Kay was serious. It sounded like fun, and it did not matter who won because Kay would be the winner with new accounts. The focus was business development.

It was a typical hot Queensland day as they headed for Ipswich industrial area, not far from Brisbane. There were truck repair workshops, light commercial and manufacturing companies all within a large complex. These businesses were an ideal fit for the products they were selling. The roads were wide and in some cases not asphalted, making it dusty when trucks or cars drove by. Kay pulled up at the first truck workshop. Kurt looked across thinking 'this will be interesting'. Kay was immaculately dressed wearing high-heel shoes and her dress was designed with a split on one side. A stunning outfit for a corporate setting but, how would Kay be received by prospective customers in a heavy industrial area?

Kay wanted to observe, so it was Kurt's sales call. They walked into the workshop, rock music played loudly, and profanity was heard from several truck mechanics as they worked on an engine. One of them shouted, '*Hey, shut up and check her out*'. This was followed by loud wolf-whistles. This type of behaviour would not be tolerated today—it never should have then either. The wolf-whistles suddenly stopped, the music turned off, stun silence. No-one did any work as they looked at Kay.

The Most Unlikely Salesperson

One of the mechanics approached them, Kurt introduced Kay and himself. The mechanic said his name was Allan. Kurt asked, *'Could you help us, we are looking for the person responsible for ordering industrial maintenance products?'* Allan said the workshop supervisor was Darrel Smith and showed them to his office which was up a flight of stairs. On their way, Kurt casually asked Allan about his work which kept the conversation flowing.

Allan had forgotten their names but introduced them to Darrel Smith. Allan left and Darrel gestured they sit in one of the two chairs he had in his office. Kurt asked Darrel about his background, general questions about the workshop, confirmed he does the ordering for the workshop and personal questions which he answered freely. Darrel appeared interested in what Kurt and Kay were selling.

To lighten the environment and create some fun, Kurt showed Darrel the blow-knife novelty and how 'magically' it opened. He went through the same spiel as he always did. Darrel thought it was a great trick and was going to try it out on 'the boys' during lunch time. It was pleasing to see the impact this small item had on Darrel and the anticipated fun he would have.

Although the office door was closed, Kurt could hear the mechanics back at work. The conversation with Darrel gradually moved to some of the problems he was experiencing in managing a workshop of this size and the daily maintenance issues. This allowed Kurt to bridge into a brief company story linking it to industrial maintenance. He then used a visual-aid brochure to highlight a popular water-based industrial solvent. The product was one of the top-five best sellers for the company.

Kurt asked, *'Would you like to see how it works? ... Show me a difficult area needing cleaning'*. They followed Darrel down the stairs and into the workshop where one of the truck bays had thick grease on the concrete floor. It was near a walkway and obviously a safety hazard. Kurt sprayed the diluted solvent on the grease, waited a few minutes and then lightly scrubbed it before removing the combined grease and solvent with a cloth. The product not only removed the grease quickly but left a flat non-slip matt finish that made walking on the surface considerably safer. Kurt looked at Darrel for his reaction. He immediately asked, *'How does it come'* which made closing the sale easy.

> When a salesperson receives a positive response verbally or non-verbally as a direct result of what they discussed or had shown, it is referred to as a buying signal or an expression of interest.

The Most Unlikely Salesperson

To close the sale Kurt said, *'The product comes in three drum sizes 250, 120 and 60 litres. What size would suit you?'* He bought 60 litres and Kurt supplied a large spray applicator at no charge.

On their way out, the workshop noise stopped again followed by multiple wolf-whistles. Kay politely smiled, and they kept walking. First call and a sale. What a wonderful way to start the day.

A product's best attributes can be shown through demonstration selling: Kurt saw a pattern with long-term experienced salespeople where they tended to overlook this important phase of the sales process. Why? Because having completed dozens of demonstrations over many years they know the product so well, they unconsciously assume the customer has the same level of understanding. Yet, it is the demonstration that can create the buying signal, which in turn can make closing the sale effortless.

When discussing a recommended product based on customer needs, it is important to validate your statements about that product. This makes it believable from the customer's perspective. Validation can be customer testimonials either in writing or if appropriate video, and include one or more of the five senses of sight, sound, touch, smell and taste.

Darrel was convinced the water-based solvent did the job because he saw how quickly it cleaned the grease and the bonus was it left a non-slip matt finish. He witnessed this as it happened. He became emotionally involved which led him to ask, 'how does it come'. Kurt could have taken this to another step by letting Darrel spray the solvent on the greasy floor and wipe the solvent and grease with a cloth.

Selling intangible products such as professional services, can be more challenging in terms of client involvement. Salespeople generally do a good job of engaging the client mentally but not emotionally, yet it is the emotions that trigger the initiative to buy.

For an intangible product showing a video of how other clients express their thoughts and feelings, including any fears and the results achieved by the service, can create an emotional connection with your prospective client. It is also easier for the potential client to feel they have made the right decision if they know others are using or have used your services/s with great success. Unless a client is an early adopter, someone who is the first to go ahead and buy, clients generally are guarded and slow to proceed with an unknown or unproven product or service. Use videos rather than a written testimonial because people prefer to watch a two or three-minute video. It is more interesting, and quicker to digest information.

While with Kay, Kurt would complete three sales calls before undertaking a coaching debrief which summarized what happened and why. This would give Kay the opportunity to see the sales process and key skills applied in a variety of sales situations. However, he decided to use a different strategy and continue beyond the three sales calls encouraging Kay to asked questions about each sales call as they walked from one company to another. Questions such as, *'What did you learn? What do you think I could have done different?'*

The reason for taking a different strategy is, he believed it would fast-track her development, and Kay had the aptitude to do incredibly well in sales. It was a matter of adopting the sales coaching to maximize value in the timeframe. With a competition in play between Kay and Kurt, he wanted to complete as many sales calls together as practicable, but not lose Kay's learning and skills development in the process.

The next sales call was Kay's. They walked into a machine workshop that had two large parallel buildings with a walkway in the centre joining the buildings. It looked like the letter 'H'. Kay led the way, introduced herself and Kurt to the receptionist, and asked for the person responsible for maintenance.

Kay Burman and Kurt Newman at a sales training conference

The receptionist said it was David Jenkins. They waited and within minutes, the side door opened and a man in his early thirties walked confidently toward them. Kay did the introductions and asked if they could go to his office. This was a good question to ask because speaking with a prospective customer in their office or workstation creates the right selling environment. The prospective customer will tend to be more relaxed in their own workspace. Presenting in a foyer places the salesperson at a psychological disadvantage. The scenario is they are closer to the entrance/exit door, the prospective customer in many instances stands and listens, and is not always fully engaged. There is no privacy, and the distraction of other people arriving and leaving, and the noise makes this a most unsuitable place. The chance of securing a sale is close to zero.

As they walked from the reception area to David's office, Kay asked him qualifying questions and he confirmed he was the person who made the decision to purchase for the factory. The factory was large with a high ceiling, rows of lathes and associated machinery. It was noisy and busy. Kurt noticed lathe operators look up from the job they were working on, saw Kay, and stopped whilst leaving the machine running. They did not say anything because no one would hear them due to the noise and perhaps because David was their manager.

They sat in his office, and Kurt took a chair that was further away from David allowing Kay to have full control. She asked many probing questions, spoke briefly about the Industrial Chemical Company, and showed the brochure on the water-based industrial solvent. This was the same product the trucking company had purchased. David could see its value throughout the factory and maintenance areas. Kay did not suggest a demonstration and went straight for closing the sale. David agreed to buy a 60 litre drum. So why did it work without a demonstration?

As a sales coach there are many things to look for during a sales call from listening to what is said, and how the sales process and skills are applied, partially applied, or missed completely. Reading the body language of the salesperson and the prospective or existing customer can provide valuable information. It can show the point in time when rapport was developed or when things went off the rails, and why. In this sales call a demonstration would have been desirable but not mandatory because David's body language and multiple buying signals allowed Kay to successfully close the sale. Although this was Kay's first sales call it showed a solid understanding of how the sales process and sales skills are applied. The coaching strategy worked.

After completing the order details, Kay asked for a referral. Again, a great move because a customer is most receptive to referring someone else when they have just purchased the product. The referred person by all accounts may have similar values, like attracts to like, and can dramatically shorten the buying and selling cycle. David suggested his counterpart, Lou Johnston in the parallel building across the walkway. David showed them part of the way.

When people feel preoccupied or uncomfortable, they use excuses not to buy.

It was a sunny day, so they decided to walk via a grassed area rather than use the walkway. The factory windows were wide open to allow a draft of air through the building. Factory workers crowded around the windows, some with their necks extended as they looked at Kay. Jokingly she commented, '_They are perving at you Kurt_'. That said 'tongue-in-cheek' showed Kay's sense of humour.

As they entered the parallel building, a factory filled with more machinery and lathe operators, they heard someone shout, 'Shut up'. This was followed by silence and the only sound were the electric motors operating the ceiling fans. Kay asked the person who did the shouting where they could find Lou's office. He took them to Lou's front door. Kay knocked and presumptively opened the door. It was plain to see he was stressed with paperwork all over his desk, phone in hand and he had a frazzled look on his face.

As a sales coach there are many things to look for during a sales call from listening to what is said, how the sales process and skills are applied, partially applied or missed completely.

Kay did not miss a beat, introduced herself and calmly said, *'David referred us to you, and I would like to arrange a meeting. Would Friday at 11:00am suit you?'* Lou agreed.

If Kay had persisted to meet with him there-and-then, Lou at best would have superficially paid attention. The chance of developing the relationship and securing a sale would have been impossible. When people feel preoccupied or uncomfortable, they use excuses not to buy. Lou could have said no thanks or call me, but by agreeing to an appointment he made a commitment, and in turn will be prepared for Friday's meeting.

On their way out, Kurt suggested they have a coffee break to discuss the sales call with David Jenkins. He began by complimenting Kay on the sale and highlighted the skills she had applied starting from the introduction through to the close and how she asked for a referral. He then asked if she agreed with his summary, followed by did he miss anything?

The response was no, so he then asked, *'If you had the opportunity to do the sales call again, what would you do differently'*. Kay thought for a while then said, *'I cannot think of anything'*. Nor could Kurt. They chatted for a while and then prepared for the next sales call.

From a sales and coaching perspective much had to be achieved in four days. Kurt was conscious of his natural tendency to be overly serious and task orientated, which can be counter-productive when aiming to maximize sales and transfer skills. The sales coaching experience had to be light-hearted and enjoyable for the learning to have a positive and lasting impact.

The goals were:

- Transfer product knowledge and demonstration methodologies across the most popular products
- Identify and validate Kay's sales competencies

- Prioritize sales competence to be developed
- Prioritize sales competence objectives
- Agree on sales objectives prior to Kay's sales calls
- Implement debrief-coaching sessions to ensure understanding and provide sales competence feedback.

Regarding the sales challenge, the four days resulted in 12 new accounts. Kay opened more accounts than Kurt did which validated her sales competence. She achieved great sales volume that contributed to her monthly sales and bonuses. Although Kay had not been in sales for long, their time together demonstrated she had an acute knowledge of the sales process and associate skills. Kay was a quick learner and had the ability to apply new skills effortlessly. Kurt was not surprised to learn that in a matter of months Kay underwent further training for a sales supervisor role.

A key indicator of successful sales coaching is when a new salesperson can demonstrate how to apply sales skills resulting in landing new accounts and developing customer relationships. It is at that moment they believe it is possible because they just did it. This also has a motivating impact on the new salesperson.

Sales coaching is the balance between skills transfer and generating sales revenue because there is a commercial reality to the task.

Sales coaching is the balance between skills transfer and generating sales revenue because there is a commercial reality to the task. Two people working together is costly in the short term, but a good investment once the new salesperson becomes independent and productive. The Industrial Chemical Company kept detailed records of every coaching session including the conversion rate from the number of sales calls to demonstrations and sales closed. The commitment to sales training by the organization is to be commended.

To the credit of the salespeople Kurt had coached, they had the highest and most consistent sales. The organization was realistic and expected sales to drop slightly post-sales coaching. However, if the ratios were lower than the acceptable norms, the sales supervisor or the sales manager would discuss this with the salesperson, then spend one or more days with them in their sales territory. When the expected improvement in sales did not happen, Nigel sent Kurt. Although sales managers were responsible for the sales performance of their teams, they saw Kurt as a threat despite his best effort to be supportive.

Kurt's time in Perth managing existing and developing new accounts was ending. It was quite a challenge to find the time to service existing customers in the manner they deserved. Throughout this test period Kurt exceeded his quota every month. This was thanks to the relationships and mutual respect he had with his customers. They were receptive to ordering new products, reordering current stock, and bought products they normally sourced from a competitor. It made Kurt's task easier but more importantly, reconnecting with his customers was most gratifying.

Before taking on the general manager role, Nigel was a successful salesperson. He won the 150-order sales award. He would regularly go on sales calls with salespeople to get to know them and check on their progress.

During a conversation with Kurt, he shared his observation of the salespeople he had coached, *'The people you trained have been Newmanised'*. Kurt asked what he meant by that? Nigel continued, *'They use the same phrases and facial expressions you do'*. It was thoughtful of Nigel to give Kurt the feedback, so he thanked him and left it at that.

> **The people trained by Kurt were known as being 'Newmanised'**

Copying a coach's gestures and their manner of speaking is natural and part of developing competence. As the salesperson practices the skills and becomes confident, they will introduce their own personality traits. The starting point for the salesperson is to have the courage to get out of their comfort zone and be willing to make mistakes and learn from them.

As the company grew, more salespeople were hired increasing Kurt's workload. Top-sales performers were left largely to their own accord, and although the majority of his time was consumed with new salespeople and mid-level sales performers, he made sure they were not neglected. Kurt felt privileged to be able to work with and observe top-sales performers. Because of their level of sales competence, the challenge was to uncover skills needing to be refined in order for them to progress to the next level. An example was the questions they asked a customer did not drill down to get to the real cause of a problem. Their questioning, to use a metaphor, was like seeing a flat rock skimming across a lake. This was addressed by demonstrating an alternative approach called vertical questioning.

Top-sales performers put Kurt through tests to see how he would handle a sales situation, and with prospective customers they failed to convert to customers. The salesperson knew beforehand it was going to be a difficult sales call, but they did not forewarn Kurt during the pre-sales call

The Most Unlikely Salesperson

discussions and when objectives were set. They thought it was a practical joke, however their pranks were all in good fun. It was their way of evaluating if they could learn from him or whether they were wasting their time. Top-sales performers tend to have little in the way of patience.

Kurt managed to demonstrate what they needed to learn, and in the process gained their respect and reignited their passion to drive sales. They witnessed first-hand how skills were applied in live-sales situations, and during the coaching debrief were given the opportunity to compare what they had learned to what they had been doing. Following this, their sales call required them to apply the new skill.

At advanced level sales coaching Kurt would purposely apply a skill poorly or not apply it at all. During the coaching debrief, the top-sales performer would be asked to identify the skill and the effect it had on the outcome. Although achieving sales is important as outlined previously, the overriding objective is for the salesperson to achieve a higher level of sales competence, that-in-turn created more sales.

Salespeople who perform consistently at a top level only need minor tweaks in sales competence or attributes. These sales athletes actively seek feedback and are keen to immediately apply and internalize what they learn. They do not have a 'know it all' or 'been there done that' attitude. Thinking in this way closes learning and expansion. Another trait of the top-sales performer is they do not block out information because they have heard it before. They see it as an opportunity to refresh their memory or to relearn. However, average or poor sales performers do not share these attributes. They automatically assume they know it all, because at one time they had heard or read it. Because a skill is understood does not mean it is known. 'Known' happens with successful application and competence.

Nigel decided to come to Perth and spend a day with Kurt. Nigel did the first sales call and sold a 25 litre drum to the local council. Next it was Kurt's turn. They walked into a large car dealership where Kurt sold two 60 litre drums of solvent to the workshop manager. It was close to midday, so after the coaching debrief they decided to have lunch.

During the afternoon they walked into a drive-in movie theatre and Nigel asked Kurt to do the call. It was eerily quiet in the reception area with no-one in sight, until a man appeared from an adjoining office. He introduced himself as Bill Tompkins the General Manager. A small person in stature and he looked a lot like the actor Danny DeVito. They followed him into a conservatively decorated office. Bill responded to the questions Kurt asked. He mentioned he had two sites and a problem with cockroaches

The Most Unlikely Salesperson

and added he was dissatisfied with the local pest control company. This was an opening for Kurt to demonstrate an insecticide product that was dispensed by an electrically operated fog machine. Bill was most impressed.

Then came the fun part of the sales process, and a memorable one. Bridging into the close Kurt said, *'The product comes in bulk and in 250 litre drums and is dispensed by this machine that can be supplied at no charge with either order volume. What size do would suit you, bulk or a 250 litre container?'*

In sales this is known as the choice close. Kurt looked at him and waited for a response, but Bill looked at his desk then up at Kurt briefly, then back at his desk. He appeared to be avoiding eye contact but when their eyes connected, he smiled and then looked away. The silence felt like the Leroy interview. Kurt waited quietly for an answer. He noticed a clock on the wall and the time. The last few moments of the conversation replayed over and over in his mind, had he missed anything? He glanced at the clock again, it was five seconds before two minutes of silence had finally ended. It was a long wait for an answer.

Bill could not contain himself any longer. He leaped out of his chair, with a huge smile on his face, came down with his fist firmly clenched and thumped the table shouting, *'I'll have the 250 litre drum'*.

After the tranquil silence his loud voice and action was quite a shock. Bill said he had a sales background and wanted to see if Kurt would break the silence. 'Old-school sales' taught if you ask a closing question when closing the sale, then shut up. It meant to put pressure on the customer to decide and in most instances, they will say yes. However, Kurt believed if you ask a question and the other person has clearly heard and understood, it is a matter of courtesy to wait for an answer. Bill appeared to enjoy the experience.

An example of 'old-school sales', Kurt recalled going on

Facilitating at the company's sales conference

The Most Unlikely Salesperson

sales calls with an executive manager who was temporarily transferred to Australia from the United States. He told him, '*When a customer says no, they do not mean no, they mean k-n-o-w*'. He spelt the word, '*They need to know more…*'.

He continued with how to turn a customer around that showed complete disrespect for the customer and clearly is high-pressure selling. Sadly, whatever Kurt tried to say to change this executive's mindset was rejected outright. Nigel had a similar experience, and it was not surprising the executive was transferred back to head office and shortly after his services were terminated.

The organization had a strong culture of promoting from within. If the salesperson met the standards of performance—they are a sales award winner and have the ability to transfer skills—they were considered for promotion. Their behaviour had to exhibit leadership qualities. Before the transition to another role could take place, the salesperson had to find and develop their replacement. This was the situation Kurt found himself in. He needed to find someone in Western Australia. He looked forward to moving back to Sydney because the distance traveling from Perth to capital cities and towns throughout Australia was demanding both professionally and personally.

Kurt worked with Graeme Mogridge a salesperson he hired several years earlier and thought he would be a perfect fit. Graeme was a consistent sales performer and had a warm kind nature. He approached Graeme who agreed to take on the job. Part of the transition required Kurt to introduce Graeme to key customers including those in regional areas. It was a pleasant time thanking customers for their business and letting them know Graeme was taking over.

Many customers responded with, '*Go and show those Eastern Staters*'. Eastern States was a common term used by locals to describe Queensland, New South Wales and Victoria. They were not aware he was from New South Wales.

Kurt felt sad to leave the Western Australian Sales Team, particularly Graeme because they had become close friends. The evening before heading back to Sydney, Gay Mogridge, Graeme's wife arranged a get-together with the sales team and their partners. This turned out to be an emotional time for everyone as individual feelings were expressed. Gay spoke openly of the tough time her family had prior to Graeme joining the organization and the delight she felt receiving flowers Kurt had sent her. The flowers were to congratulate Graeme for being the successful applicant and to welcome Gay to the organization. Kurt believed the best sales manager is a salesperson's partner, and if times got tough in the role, the

40 Chapter 3 Sales Role: Industrial Chemicals

partner would be the first person to support and motivate them. This was also his way of getting to know more about the individual salespeople he worked with. Gay told Kurt she burst into tears of joy when she read the note that was attached to the flowers. Apparently, Gay received the flowers before Graeme arrived home to let her know he landed the role. Kurt invited them to dinner the Saturday evening before Graeme started on the Monday. Gay said she burst into tears again when she received the invitation. The farewell get together was a most humbling and touching experience.

The organization had many divisions within the group. Around the time of transferring back to Sydney, there were plans to launch a second division in Australia. Kurt could have taken on the divisional general manager's role which would have been a great career move, but he decided not to pursue it. He felt it was time to explore other industries and different sales environments. He spoke with Nigel who understood as Kurt gave his one-months' notice.

When the sales team heard he was leaving it created a domino effect with many wanting to resign because of the loyalty they felt toward him. Kurt spoke with every salesperson and let them know why he was leaving, and encouraged them to stay, but resignations still happened. Leroy returned to Australia in damage control, met Kurt and made an offer to continue with the organization, but Kurt had made up his mind to leave.

Weeks later, Kurt discovered the majority of salespeople who gave notice to leave did so despite the organization's efforts to retain them.

Lessons learned

- Multiple obstacles need to be overcome to succeed. It is never a smooth or a straight-line journey.
- If someone says it cannot be done or has never been done before, does not mean you cannot do it.
- Accept that you will make mistakes as you learn and develop new skills. It is a natural part of the process.
- Keep moving forward, even if the road ahead appears bumpy and uncertain.
- Have the courage and continue to give it your best despite setbacks.
- Obstacles and outright failure are a blessing, although this can be tough to accept at the time. These provide lessons and skills to be developed. Although emotionally painful the greater the pain, the greater the lesson and progress.
- Listen to your intuition and override what your conscious mind tells you cannot be done.
- Have the courage to speak to the person who can change whatever needs to be changed, improved or fixed.
- Customers will tell you almost anything if you ask them in a polite and respectful manner.
- Customers know the practical application of your product, perhaps better than you do, so why not ask them to expand your understanding?
- Be the bearer of interesting and useful information to customers. As a result, they will look forward to seeing you and will share more about themselves and create a closer bond.
- Be yourself and let prospective and existing customers get to know the 'real' you. If it means showing your emotions, do so. It builds trust, relationships and loyalty.
- When you have to choose between making a sale that does not feel right because you doubt it will deliver the promised value or to walk away, do the latter.
- Loyalty is earned by giving loyalty, being honest and trustworthy.
- When you have thoroughly considered all the options, reflected and decided to proceed, then go ahead.

Chapter 4
Sales Role: Publishing and Advertising Industry

Only two weeks after leaving the Industrial Chemical Company, Kurt started to look for a new sales management role. He scanned through the *Saturday Edition* of *The Sydney Morning Herald* Newspaper—popular at the time for job advertisements. While scanning, he noticed a position for a sales and marketing manager. The position was in a magazine publishing company and appeared interesting. So, Kurt called and spoke to a Geoff McLaughlin who was screening applicant enquiries. The phone call went well, and they agreed on the day and time for the first interview.

Geoff was friendly and asked numerous questions about the chemical industry. What captured Geoff's imagination was how sales and business development were implemented. He asked Kurt several times to repeat part of the sales process—to ensure he had heard correctly.

Kurt said, '*Salespeople walk into a prospective customer's business with no prearranged appointment to meet and qualify the decision maker...*'. Geoff smiled and raised his eyebrows when he heard, '*no prearranged appointment*'. He nodded his head as he listened and remained in a forward-lean position.

> *A common misconception is the person doing the talking is in control, when in fact the person who asks the question, is in control.*

Geoff was not aware of his body language showing keen interest.

The conversation was one sided, with Kurt doing most of the talking answering Geoff's questions. Kurt was becoming increasingly conscious of this and intended to balance the dialogue. A common misconception is the person doing the talking is in control, when in fact the person who asks the question, is in control.

There was an opportunity when Geoff paused between questions, so Kurt asked, '*Geoff do you mind if I ask you a few questions?*' Geoff replied, '*What did you want to know?*'

Kurt, '*I would appreciate knowing a little about your background, and the attributes of the sales and marketing manager you are looking for?*'

Geoff stated, '*I am the general manager and have an accounting background. We have contracts to produce magazines, and the advertising generated within the magazines is our revenue source. I am looking for someone who can motivate the sales team to sell more advertising space*'.

Geoff began to appear distracted, and instead of continuing he asked, '*What would you do on day one if I were to hire you?*'

> **Sales is about active listening—particularly how words are used, tone, and the context.**

This was quite personal, '*...if I were to hire you?*' In sales, a question like this would be an expression of interest, and a step closer to a conclusion or sale close. Geoff did not ask, '*What would you do on day one if you were hired?*' Sales is about active listening—particularly how words are used, tone, and the context. It can provide insight into how a person is feeling that can lead to understanding what they might be thinking. Intuition or gut feel can be a reliable guide. Geoff's question was framed in a manner that indicated he saw Kurt in the role.

Kurt nodded to acknowledge he heard and replied, '*A great question. Subject to the company's induction procedures, I would briefly meet everyone in the sales team, and then allocate a day with individual salespeople to jointly attend sales calls*'. At that moment, Geoff's facial expression changed to a perplexed look, so Kurt asked, '*Do you have a question?*'

His eyes dropped temporarily to gather his thoughts, then in a questioning manner asked, '*You would meet customers on the first day?*' Kurt responded, '*Yes. Is that a problem?*' With the same look on Geoff's face, '*No, I thought you would spend the first week in the office*'. Kurt paused then said, '*If you want me to stay in the office I will, but having responsibilities for the sales team and sales, I believe it is a priority to get to know every salesperson and identify how I can be of greatest value*'.

Geoff nodded as if he understood, but Kurt felt he needed to provide greater clarity, '*Geoff, my aim is to create a relaxed, easy-going sales environment so every salesperson feels safe, encouraged, and motivated to excel. To achieve this, I would like to understand who they are as individuals, what motivates them, what are they looking for personally and need professionally. By spending time with them from day one, I will also learn about your market and competitor activities*'.

Geoff sat back as if to reflect on what he had just heard. Kurt was expecting a second interview to be scheduled. Instead, Geoff lent forward and offered Kurt the job. Kurt started the following Monday.

On the first day, Geoff introduced him to the team then left. Kurt spoke openly to minimize any apprehension they may have been feeling, then set dates and times with every salesperson. He encouraged them to do what they normally do in managing their sales territories and customers.

The company's sales structure was divided into two divisions:

1. Advertising agencies and large corporate sales.
   This had a sales manager and two account managers; and
2. Small to medium business sales.
   A sales team of five. This was now Kurt's responsibility.

The week working with individual salespeople passed quickly. It was clear there was a cultural pattern-of-behaviour resulting in time and productivity loss.

When people within an organization share similar values and beliefs, their behaviour over time becomes the norm. In this current situation, no-one was accountable for achieving sales results. The sales team did the best they could and in good faith, but weekly sales call numbers and sales revenues were stagnant. As one conscientious but frustrated salesperson put it,

'I feel like a mouse peddling harder and harder on an exercise wheel and getting nowhere'.

The core issues were:

– Salespeople spent two to three days in the office arranging sales meetings
– Sales generated revenues were as low as $150 per sale
– Prime selling time was not on sales, but wasted on administration tasks. Prime selling time in this case was 8:30am–5:00pm
– Hours were lost travelling distances between appointments, limiting the number of sales calls per day.

Prioritising efforts

There were a number of initiatives Kurt recommended. The first being to hire two tele-salespeople to concentrate on potential advertisers in the small business sector. This was to free up the sales team to pursue larger accounts.

Tele-sellers would be able to connect to more businesses in a shorter timeframe resulting in greater sales volume, and in turn increase revenues and profitability. Within weeks Kurt employed James Spilling and Julie

McCarran. Although the sales team were not barred from selling into the small business sector, they knew their role was medium to larger businesses.

Julie and James had opposite personalities. Julie was reserved and started her daily activities within minutes of arriving in the office. She was friendly but preferred to keep to herself. James, a 19 year old person, let everyone know he had arrived by proudly strutting around the office telling everyone what he did the previous evening. He was extroverted, a lovable character and enjoyed life immensely. James often arrived late-to work, appeared dishevel, tidied himself up, and as soon as he picked up the phone a professional serious side emerged.

The introduction of tele-sales was a great success. Julie and James became an integral part of the team, increasing sales revenues and regularly passing on leads of larger companies they came across.

Prioritising methods

The other change to be introduced was how the sales team worked—excuses to avoid change were expected. Administration tasks such as sales reports, where possible, were to be delegated, and if not, to be done outside normal business hours. This was surprisingly accepted without much pushback.

The number of sales calls per week had to be significantly increased through effective-time management—clustering sales meetings in close proximity to reduce travel times. Decision makers were typically the business owner or manager, making the job of meeting them unannounced easy. This was a different market when compared to large corporates, where setting a prior appointment is the norm.

The mean sale value of $350 made spending days in the office on the phone or email financially unsustainable. Video conferencing had not been developed at this point.

Fear of the unknown when change is proposed is a natural reaction.

Kurt suggested the team select an area or suburb where potential advertisers were and go from business-to-business to maximum the number of sales calls and sales. He then asked how they felt about that? One salesperson could not contain himself, angrily shouting, '*It might work in the industrial chemical industry but not in publishing*'. Kurt was glad the salesperson said that because more-than likely others had similar views. Fear of the unknown when change is proposed is a natural reaction. Emotional blocks to their buy-in for change, needed to be addressed.

Kurt, '*I appreciate where you are coming from. How would you feel if we developed a theme for an up-and-coming issue and printed a mock example that showed available advertising spaces to potential advertisers?'* The room fell silent, the reservation and apprehension could be felt when unexpectedly Maria De-Angelo, one of the salespeople, expressed in an uplifting-vocal tone, *'We could try this for the up-and-coming Royal Easter Show'*. Others still remained silent, but Maria's enthusiasm and willingness to give this a go was welcomed. Kurt, *'Great idea Maria'*.

Kurt scanned the room looking at every salesperson then continued, *'What if we developed a sales process and practiced the skills prior, to ensure we feel comfortable and confident in what to do? How does that sound…Is it doable?'* To get a response felt like extracting teeth—slow and painful. At that moment, again it was Maria, *'I would be prepared to give it a go provided you show me how this works'*.

Kurt was glad Maria was in the room, *'I would be delighted Maria. Is everyone else onboard if I work with each of you?'* Although their answers were far from overwhelming the wider team did agree, and it was the beginning of a new era in sales for the business.

Maria was responsible for generating revenues for the East West Airlines Inflight Magazine. She asked the art department to develop a double-page mock spread with a Royal Easter Show banner across the top of the pages. This popular annual event was in six weeks—the timeline was tight. The airline serviced regional New South Wales towns, so the Royal Easter Show was a perfect choice. The exposure for an advertiser's product was excellent because businesspeople and families read the magazine during the flight to Sydney. Once in Sydney they would often go sightseeing and shopping.

Maria was in her early thirties, dressed impeccably and had a flamboyant personality. Her prepared mock-double page had photos of animals and crowds-of-people waiting near various rides, representing families and fun times. There were rectangular slots drawn amongst the photos, each represented future advertisements. Maria included copies of past editions to show advertisers the quality of the magazine. She also included statistical information to validate readership figures. The fee was $150 per slot, and there were 20 slots to be filled across the double-page centre spread.

The objective was to sell all slots in one day generating $3,000 in sales. Maria chose Sydney's Double Bay retail shopping district. Only 4 kilometres from the Royal Easter Show, this beautiful Sydney suburb was close enough for people to explore.

The Most Unlikely Salesperson

Old South Head Road, Double Bay retail district

On the road

Teaming up, Maria and Kurt arrived at 8:45am when the shops started to open. Being somewhat methodical, Kurt suggested they start at one end of the strip-shopping centre and work their way along. The first business they walked into was a jewellery store. To demonstrate the sales process and associated skills, Kurt did this first sales call.

A short bald gentleman with a thick-Hungarian accent came from behind a screen. Kurt introduced Maria and asked the gentleman his name and if he was the owner.

The business owner said, *'Gustaf and yes'*. Kurt engaged in small talk then bridged into asking if he did any advertising? He had hardly asked the question when a definitive, *'No'* was received.

Kurt paused, then in the same relaxed vocal tone continued, *'Do you mind my asking why?'* Gustaf, *'It is a waste of money'*.

> **Kurt was conscious to not waste time, and with Maria standing next to him observing, he had to move this along. The situation felt unnecessarily serious.**

Kurt responded by saying, *'I appreciate your honesty. Would you mind if I showed you an opportunity that could attract more customers to your business?'* Gustaf nodded affirmatively. Kurt briefly showed Gustaf copies of past editions, outlined readership statistics, and then presented Maria's double-page spread. Watching closely for any changes in Gustaf's body language, he highlighted the best slot to place his advertisement. Gustaf changed from a defensive-mindset to what appeared amenable—so it was time to close the sale.

Kurt asked, *'If you were to advertise, what slot would you prefer—one on the left or right side of the page?'*

Gustaf looked up, *'Who in the shopping centre has advertised?'*

He said, *'You are the first business we have seen today'.*

Gustaf, *'I might be interested if other businesses advertise'.*

Perhaps a glimmer of light? To confirm what Gustaf had just said, *'So, to clarify my thinking, if I were to show you other businesses participating in this edition, you will go ahead and book a slot? Is that right?'*

To Kurt's surprise an instant, Gustaf responded *'Yes'.* Kurt, *'Okay, thank you. I look forward to seeing you later today'.*

Maria and Kurt both left and headed for the next retailer. Kurt aimed to do three sales calls in succession so Maria could see a sales process pattern and sales skills in action. The second sales call was a café and Kurt struck out.

The third was a menswear store and the owner confirmed a slot. He said people look at the right side of a page when they open a magazine, which is true, so he chose that position. Kurt wrote the name of his store in the slot.

The first sale was the most challenging to fill, but the ice had been broken. Maria and Kurt celebrated the first sale by going for a coffee and discussing the three sales calls in detail. Maria was keen to give it a go. She sold a slot on her first sales call and beamed with confidence. They were on a roll so kept going and missed very few sales. A short lunch break at 12:30pm then back into it.

At 2:30pm, two slots were left to fill. They walked back to see Gustaf in the jewellery shop. Kurt showed him the double page with the local business names. It looked impressive. Gustaf took his time as he read the names, and then wanted a slot that had already been sold. He said he liked the position. After some verbal jousting he bought one of the two remaining slots.

The last advertising slot was located at the bottom left-hand side of the page near the centre fold, not an ideal position. They did four consecutive sales calls, and on the fifth it was sold. Their persistence paid off.

Maria's sales improved dramatically and within months was promoted to selling page and multiple page advertising space to marketing directors and advertising agencies. This was a different sales environment Maria was used to, so walking in off-the street would not be appropriate. Kurt assisted

The Most Unlikely Salesperson

Maria to develop a phone script she felt comfortable with to make her appointments.

There were many enjoyable and challenging times selling and coaching the sales team.

Geoff asked Kurt to attend The Gunnedah Ag-quip Show to sell advertising space in a new magazine the company wanted to launch. Being new, there were no previous editions to show and no circulation figures. What he had was a mock version of what the company envisaged the magazine would look like including photographs, editorials, allotted advertising space and blank pages to bulk it up.

The Gunnedah Ag-quip Show was an annual event for exhibitors to display their latest farm and agricultural equipment to farmers. It is a huge event that attracted thousands of people locally, interstate and overseas. Gunnedah is located in north-west New South Wales about an hour's flight from Sydney. Kurt knew nothing about farming or machinery—but then at one time he knew nothing about industrial chemicals. The plan was to ask a lot of questions, and then outline what the magazine could do for advertiser's products.

He flew to Gunnedah and drove a rental car about 20 kilometres to the event. To gain a sense of the physical size, the type and number of exhibitors Kurt walked through the grounds. It would have been impossible to see every exhibitor in the allocated two days, so it was a matter of prioritising potential advertisers—the larger exhibitors and high-profile brands.

The objective was to sell half and full-page advertising space. A major brand tractor distributor caught Kurt's attention, he walked into their marquee. The person who greeted him was James Chandler, Sales and Marketing Manager, so his name tag read. Kurt introduced himself and asked, 'Could you help me out, who would be responsible for buying media in your company?' James said it was part of his responsibility.

Greater clarity was needed, 'Part of your responsibility? Would you mind my asking, does that mean you share it with someone else or is it part of your marketing role?' He answered, 'Part of my marketing role'.

Kurt casually pointed to the bales of hay near one of the tractors, 'Do you mind if we sit over there so I can show you what I have and to see if it interests you?'

The reason for suggesting sitting down, is it creates a more favourable selling environment with less interruptions, and it took James away from mainstream visitor traffic. 'James, would it be okay if I ask you some questions to get a greater sense of your business and what you are aiming to achieve at the show?' James, 'Sure, go ahead'.

He answered Kurt's questions and often expanded in detail, including sharing information about his personal life and hobbies. What Kurt uncovered, helped tailor what to say as he showed James the mock magazine. James did not hesitate and ordered a full page. Kurt thanked him for his business and asked, *'Do you know anyone at the show who would be interested in advertising in the magazine?'*.

Working with referrals can significantly reduce the selling-cycle time. James provided names of several other exhibitors. Kurt again thanked him and proceeded to ask about Joshua Brown, one of the referrals, *'Why do you think Joshua would be interested in advertising in the magazine?'*.

James spoke of how Joshua and he had worked together in a previous company, and believed Joshua—in his new role as sales manager—would want to see the magazine. Kurt went through the same process with the other referral names James provided, then thanked him a third time. It was a wonderful way to start the day—first sales call and a confirmed sale as Kurt headed for Joshua's stand.

> **Working with referrals can significantly reduce the selling cycle time.**

The reason referral selling works so well is the client who has given the referral, often shares similar values and perspectives as the referee. When contacted the referee will listen to the salesperson because the credibility of the referrer will unconsciously be transferred to them.

The results of the two days of business development were beyond expectation. Five full pages and two half-pages were sold. Four referrals were followed up in Sydney adding an additional two pages. The new magazine was shaping up to be a winner.

Sales revenues were growing progressively each month and the sales team worked well. There were no plans to increase the sales team and nothing new on the horizon. Kurt felt he was cruising along—which he could have continued to do, but that was, and still is, not in his nature. He wanted to keep expanding his experiences in sales, perhaps another industry.

It was time to move on, so he gave notice to leave without having another job to go to—a pattern he would repeat often.

The Most Unlikely Salesperson

Lessons learned

- When being interviewed for a position let your potential new employer see the real you.
- Ask questions during the interview, so you do not fall into the trap of talking most of the time.
- Be fully present during the interview, do not allow yourself to be distracted. Actively listen to the words, vocal tone and context during an interview or sales meeting.
- Have the courage to be different—to do what you know in your heart-of-hearts is right, even if it is not the organization's norm. Try the untried.
- If you see or feel a negative reaction, ask questions to uncover what is beneath. Do not ignore the reaction, because it will turn into an obstacle or worse a roadblock. Obstacles like sales objections can be overcome, but roadblocks mean you are stuck.
- Understanding what and why there is an obstacle can create a breakthrough.
- Persistence and thoughtful action generate breakthroughs, and with breakthroughs there is progress.
- Progress, no matter how small, provide the fuel to continue.
- When you connect with a referee, the referrer's credibility is automatically transferred to you.

Chapter 5
Sales Role: Long Service Leave Funding

Kurt took time out to reflect on what to do next. He had always sold tangible products, and decided to switch to an intangible product like a service. The industry, company or service were not important, but integrity and creditability were. He was also open to the idea of being self-employed and contracting his services.

An opportunity presented itself at a business network function when he met Peter Nathan. Peter had an introverted manner, spoke softly and was a chartered accountant. The conversation was personal as Peter expressed being divorced, having five adult children, living in Sydney's Rose Bay and being an enthusiastic collector of rare Matchbox-branded cars. He appeared to be in his mid to late 50s. Without notice he changed the subject and wanted to discuss an idea he thought might interest Kurt. They agreed to meet the following morning in a nearby café. Kurt asked if Peter would bring examples of his rare Matchbox cars. Peter's huge smile said it all.

Peter brought three replica 1940s delivery vans and lined them up end-to-end on the café table. He then proceeded to highlight the minute variations in a quiet but enthusiastic-vocal tone. Kurt was amazed at his depth of knowledge and the history of each vehicle. Peter's presentation was interrupted briefly when the waiter delivered their two ordered coffees. The interruption for Peter was like a trigger because he paused slightly then launched into, *'All companies have a book entry for their employee's long service leave obligations but, in my experience, it is only an entry. Small to medium size businesses usually do not have the cash funds available when needed'*. Peter continued, *'The obligation, can easily amount to tens of thousands of dollars'*.

He had Kurt's attention. The problem was understood, although he did not know the answer or what his involvement would be? Peter then slowed up his speech rate, *'Insurance companies selling long service leave policies, in my opinion, sell passively, and for businesses that buy the policy, they do not get an actuarial projection of their financial liability'*.

Kurt listened and then responded, '*Peter, this sounds like a wonderful opportunity, but I am not an accountant and with the greatest of respect, I have no interest to learn*'.

Peter had done his homework and methodically thought through how this could come to fruition, '*Kurt, you do not have to be an accountant. I will be reviewing the actuaries' figures prior to any meeting presentation. I see us working as partners selling the service and splitting the commissions equally. Imagine long service leave funding sold proactively, actuarial projections of the financial liability provided to business owners and CEO's. Imagine the shocked look on their faces when they realize the extent of their current and future liabilities?*'

Peter presented a powerful business case and Kurt felt they would work as a good team, so he reached out and shook Peter's hand to confirm they were now partners.

The next step was to convince a large well known insurance company to come on board. The brand recognition and credibility would be an added bonus during business development. Peter knew what he was looking for in terms of service and had two companies in mind to approach.

Realistic growth opportunities of the sector were there, provided it is sold differently.

He expected the insurance company's actuary to provide a 48-hour turnaround. He knew this would push boundaries, but it was not negotiable. The plan was to return to the prospective client within seven days of receiving their figures, so Peter needed time to review the actuary's forecast, make his own notes, and prepare the proposal. If this worked, it would be impressive.

They jointly agreed on the sales process:
- The initial client meeting to be with the business owner or CEO
- The company's financials received within two days
- The client's financials to be emailed to the actuary
- The actuary to complete calculations within two days
- Peter to review the figures
- Develop the proposal and sales strategy
- Arrange a second client meeting, present and close the sale.

Peter had senior level contacts within the insurance companies, so he organized two back-to-back meetings. The first was with two executives and the company's actuary. Once the introductions were made, it was down to business for Peter. He opened the discussion with an overview of long service leave funding, how it is currently marketed and sold, outlined the risks, liabilities, and obligations businesses face. He spoke from a chartered accountant's perspective, firmly establishing his professional credibility—and he did not miss a beat. He was in his element. There were regular nods-of-agreement from the executives. Peter then paused, and in a lighter-vocal tone, emphasized the realistic growth opportunities of the sector, provided it is sold differently.

He then metaphorically gave the menu—not the recipe—for how it needs to be sold to medium to larger businesses. The executives could see the impact this would have on their business and openly expressed interest. Peter looked at the actuary when he said a 48 hour turnaround was required. The actuary thought the turnaround for the financial projections could not be done and wanted a minimum of seven days. One of the executives interjected and suggested a test run to see if 48 hours was possible. Peter agreed and handed the reluctant actuary a set of figures to work with.

Realistic growth opportunities of the sector were there, provided it is sold differently.

Peter followed the same presentation with the second insurance company. Their actuary was in Melbourne and participated via a phone hook-up. The executives and the actuary were quick to see the value and engaged with comments and questions. Peter handed over the same set of figures to test the turnaround time.

The results were, the first company took five days and stated this was the best they could do, whilst the second company went all out and met Peter's criteria. Later that week a formalized written agreement was signed by all parties. The second insurance company provided them with a furnished office at 1 York Street Sydney rent free on the condition they met their financial performance conditions. Peter and Kurt accepted.

Peter and Kurt both reviewed a number of potential industries to approach and decided on the New South Wales Club Industry. The reason this industry ticked all the boxes was because it was one of the largest employers in Australia and individual clubs ranged in size from small, medium to large organizations. Also, Kurt had got to know the industry well when he sold industrial chemical products. He had a profound respect and admiration for the community work achieved by the people and the industry as a whole, whether it was helping ex-military personnel, children's sport, or the elderly.

Peter lived in the Eastern Suburbs of Sydney and close to the heart of the city, whilst Kurt at that time was in the southwest. Using their locations, it seemed natural to divide the business development into the two respective regions. Accordingly, they made appointments with club CEO's and in smaller clubs the general manager. Securing appointments was surprisingly straight forward, but getting the financials did require multiple follow-up phone calls.

Peter did an outstanding job analysing the figures given to him by the actuary. His depth of knowledge and ability to answer a question including the most complex from a club's Chief Financial Officer was impressive. The financial monthly commitment to meet long service leave obligations was considerable, requiring board of directors' approval.

To make the job seamless for the CEO or general manager, Kurt offered to attend the board meetings to present the club's proposal, answer questions, and then leave. This would allow the board to discuss the proposal with full knowledge, value to the club and allow them to make an informed unimpeded decision. One-in-three CEO's who saw the figures and listened to the presentation felt so confident, they politely refused Kurt's offer to address the board meeting. They insisted on doing the board presentation themselves. With the politics of a board to contend with, no sales skills, an inadequate depth of knowledge of the product, they would not be in a position to answer questions let alone convince their board. A majority, 'No' vote was the outcome, which was difficult although not impossible to change at a later date.

It was important to ensure the clients were making an informed decision based on facts.

When a CEO insisted on presenting the proposal, Kurt had not much of an option but to agree. However, he did so on the condition the CEO did not to take it to a vote, instead to postpone the decision until the following month's board meeting. Kurt explained this was to, '*Allow a representative to attend and respond to questions*'. Every CEO agreed. The procedure for Kurt to address the board the following month was:

- Long service leave funding is the first item on the agenda
- Introduction of the representative by the CEO
- Overview to refresh the board of the previous month's presentation
- Respond to questions, then leave the meeting.

Leaving the meeting and contacting the CEO the next morning worked well. It demonstrated respect and allowed the free-flow of discussions, debate, and a vote based on facts.

Kurt had one extreme but amusing case. Sue Bellows the CEO of a mid-sized RSL club made two attempts to get the proposal approved and was unsuccessful each time.

The first follow-up call, Sue sounded flat, '*The board knocked it back*'. He asked why and it turned out Sue did not know the answer to several questions. That was no surprise. When Kurt gave her the answers her

The Most Unlikely Salesperson

vocal tone changed and said, *'Leave it to me. I know what to say this time. Call me next Friday'*.

No matter what Kurt said or tried to do, Sue was determined to do it herself. She arranged a special board meeting to discuss the proposal. Before hanging up the phone Kurt reiterated, *'If for whatever reason the presentation does not go as planned, please do not let it go to a vote. Leave the door open for me to attend the next board meeting'*.

Sue agreed. He called as instructed and the proposal was rejected again but Sue let him know, *'It is okay, I rescheduled for the 15th at 6:00pm for you to address the board'*. He confirmed and then asked, *'Do you have a few minutes? Could you give me a sense of every board member particularly those who objected?'*

There were nine board members. One board member Brian Johnstone vehemently objected. He was so vocal, he created doubt in three others who initially supported the proposal. Kurt asked Sue for his name, to ensure he knew who to look out for. Sue did not know what his motives were.

The 15th came around quickly. Kurt prepared for the board meeting and headed for the club. Sue introduced him to everyone and during an overview presentation of long service leave funding Brian interjected with a question. Kurt paused, listened to what he had asked. Before answering Brian, he made sure there was good eye contact, and then briefly looked around at individual board members before finally back to Brian. Kurt did this to include everyone before providing the answer. Once answered, to ensure Brian understood, Kurt asked *'Brian, have I answered the question to your satisfaction?'*

Brian avoided eye contact and merely grunted. Kurt remained composed and continued with the presentation. Brian maintained his aggressive vocal tone with questions and outlandish statements about the insurance industry. There were occasional whispers between board members, and just about everyone appeared uncomfortable. The chairman tried to encourage other board members to ask questions to reduce Brian's dominance. To lighten the atmosphere and create involvement, Kurt posed several commonly asked questions, paused, and then provided the answers. This was well received.

Brian came out with a statement that was one too many as far as the board were concerned. The Chief Financial Officer Alan Ullman, calmly and politely, followed the meeting protocol and asked

Posing questions to a client, pausing and then providing the answers, can assist in managing as well as changing the tone of an uncomfortable situation.

to speak through the chairman. Alan was composed before telling Brian to, 'Shut up'.

Alan looked at Kurt and said, 'On behalf of the board, I apologize for the way you have been treated'. Alan's two words to Brian were welcomed by everyone, including Kurt. Kurt thanked Alan, told him it was not necessary to apologize, and then concluded the presentation. The meeting finished on a reasonable note.

Driving home he wondered how the board voted? Based on their body language, Sue's background information, and the questions, he assumed five definite 'Yes', three not sure, and one definite 'No'.

Kurt rang Sue in the morning and felt her verbally beaming through the phone. With delight Sue said, 'We are going ahead'. I congratulated Sue and thanked her for her persistence and the business.

Kurt asked, 'If you do not mind, what was the result of the vote?' It was 8-1 better than expected by far. The sale was worth $500,000 over the duration of the term. The club had the monthly cashflow to afford the payments and now were assured of funds when an employee went on long service leave.

Peter was most comfortable analysing figures and joining Kurt on second client meetings. They enjoyed each other's company and did well as a team. However, on his own Peter made few sales appointments and only one sale. Working together the conversion rate was close to 100%.

They only missed one sale. A club general manager agreed to provide the financials for the actuarial calculations but used excuses every time he was followed up. Something outside of Kurt's control was going on, so he wished him and the club all the best.

In hindsight, Kurt felt the partnership should have been structured so all business development was his responsibility and Peter to do the figures and attend second client meetings.

After two months, the insurance company informed them there was a sales competition that started five months ago. The prize was ten days in Hawaii for the top 20 sales agents. Because the dollar value of each sale was substantial, they came in seventh place, an incredible result considering other agents had a five month start. They travelled to Hawaii, Maui then back to Hawaii for a conference. There were formalities at the conference and specific dinners to attend but by-and-large their time was their own to relax and go sightseeing.

When they returned from Hawaii, Peter seemed somewhat distracted and made no sales appointments. Kurt had a strong sense their time was over. He called Peter and suggested they catch up. They met at a pier in

Rose Bay and walked the length of it as they talked. Kurt would normally have asked about Peter's Matchbox cars, but instead thanked him for meeting and his friendship. He did not want to disappoint or hurt Peter's feelings, but he had to let him know how he felt. Peter's response was one of understanding and acceptance. They had an incredible time, a wonderful experience, and both learned from each other. Kurt asked what he was going to do, and he said he planned to open a store in Sydney's Chatswood Shopping Centre selling collectable Matchbox cars. Peter literally had several hundred model vehicles. Kurt visited Peter from time to time, and it was pleasing to see how happy he was immersed in his hobby that turned into a business.

Lessons learned

- Do not stay in a job that has no potential for your ongoing personal and professional growth.
- Security is not in a job, security comes from within. Do not live in fear of losing your job.
- Have the courage to change jobs even if you do not have another one to go to. Things always have, will and continue to work out.
- Try and work in a different industry if you can. It may create expansion and the opportunity for an exciting new career path. 'Nothing ventured, nothing gained'.
- Aim for a face-to-face board meeting and only accept a video conference meeting if there is no option.
- Always do your homework and pre-plan before a sales call, particularly with a committee or a board of directors. Develop a profile on every stakeholder so you know who is on your side, who the fence-sitters are, and those who could be against your proposal.
- Remain calm and courteous if a client behaves aggressively. Show empathy whilst standing your ground.
- Be integral and always do what you say you will do.

Chapter 6
Sales Role:
Electrical Switchgear

In the pursuit of more change and more experiences, Kurt looked to other industries. He took on the New South Wales Sales Manager role for an electrical switchgear manufacturer. The company manufactured and sold a comprehensive range of industrial and domestic switches, power outlets and a limited range of domestic exhaust fans. The products were stocked and distributed by electrical wholesalers.

To introduce Kurt, Robert Stanton (Bob) the State General Manager arranged a sales meeting with the team. The atmosphere was flat, although some tried to sound upbeat. On completion Bob asked where he would like to start? Kurt's response was pre-planned:

- *'Spend a day with every salesperson in their sales territory*
- *Uncover difficulties internally and externally that prevent better sales performance*
- *Ask for the individual salesperson's thoughts on how sales can be improved*
- *Identify the sales competence of every salesperson*
- *Develop a plan on how to move forward'.*

Bob agreed and asked for a report on completion.

The sales team consisted of two electrical sales engineers responsible for the company's products which were specified by architects, designers and engineers. Five salespeople managed the electrical wholesale accounts throughout the state and four internal customer service personnel who also provided technical back up support.

Kurt reported to Bob, who in turn reported to the newly appointed CEO, Albert Larsons located in Melbourne, the company's head office. The company was founded in the 1930s and had a proud history of producing high-quality and reliable products. At one time the products were market leaders.

The company had become complacent, did not innovate to develop new products, and had ongoing stock outages. This created an opportunity for a competitor to enter the market.

A large manufacturing company, firmly entrenched for decades in the industry, had a range of domestic switches and accessories decided to expand into industrial switchgear. To their credit the products looked robust, were promoted well and available within 24 hours of the wholesaler placing an order. The impact on the company Kurt had just joined was profound.

Stock outages had a substantial effect on revenue and cashflow. Employee morale was low because of the fear of losing their job. The constant frustration of not being able to supply stock and listening to angry customers and end users—who at times were verbally abusive—was wearing them down. Despite the stock issues and low morale, Kurt was instructed sales had to increase.

> *Complacency, coupled with the lack of R&D for new products, left an opportunity for competitors to enter the market.*

He started with the electrical wholesale team because they were directly responsible for generating revenue. A day was booked for the one-on-one sales territory sessions. Jim Speers, a salesperson with decades of industry experience, was the first salesperson Kurt would spend time with.

They started the day by meeting for a coffee and chat 45 minutes before the first sales call. Jim was in his late fifties', married with two adult children and worked in the industry his entire career. He radiated kindness, was down-to-earth and had a no-nonsense approach. Kurt's impression was Jim would not suffer fools lightly. Within minutes of sitting down, Jim spoke passionately as he offloaded his frustrations.

He said, '*I am sick-and-tired of losing business because of stock outages and deliveries made weeks after the due date, then customers cancelling the order*'. Kurt listened as he took notes. Jim spoke for some time, expressing in great detail the problems he had encountered and eventually sounded exhausted. He paused, took a deep breath and in a pleading voice said, '*Fix the factory*'.

That was a logical directive, except manufacturing was not Kurt's responsibility or skillset, but he needed to find out why these problems were not being rectified. He nodded to acknowledge what Jim had said and then responded, '*Jim, thank you. I appreciate your frankness about the issues and for letting me know the effect these have on yourself, your wholesalers, and their customers. After I have spent time with everyone in the team, I will come up with suggestions of what we could do. Is there anything else you would like to tell me?'* Jim was brief, *'No'*. They then prepared to leave for the first sales call.

The first sales call was a wholesaler in Artarmon NSW. Jim greeted Shane Delaney who was the branch manager and then introduced Kurt. Shane invited them into his office. When the door closed Shane's demeanour changed from being pleasant to an explosive rant using the most colourful language as he waved his arms around expressing his anger. He threatened to return the stock he holds, cancel back orders, and close the account. The number of back orders created his greatest frustration.

> **At all times maintain eye contact and respectfully and actively listen when a customer is angry.**

Jim and Kurt respectfully listened as they remained standing. When someone is this angry maintain eye contact and actively listen. They will calm down once they have expressed what they need to express. Shane did eventually calm down—this was reflected in is vocal tone, reduced volume, and his speech rate slowed. He then asked Jim and Kurt to take a seat. Shane must have felt exasperated.

Kurt felt for where Shane was coming from and was about to respond when he added in a subdued vocal tone, *'You seem like a nice bloke, what the &%^$#@ are you doing working with this mob?'* Kurt nodded his head to acknowledge he had heard him.

The experiences with Shane were almost identical on every sales call for the duration of Kurt's time with the sales team. There were no remotely-pleasant sales calls, only sales calls highlighting the difficulties the salespeople experienced daily, and the severity of the product outages. As the industry realized a new sales manager had joined the company, the abusive phone calls from specifiers, electricians, developers, wholesalers, and situations salespeople could no longer tolerate, were transferred to Kurt.

Although unpleasant, Kurt was grateful customers cared enough to take the time to express their anger and frustrations. It would have been a considerably greater problem if customers stopped trying to buy the products, return stock and close their accounts. The emotional buy-in of the brand was still there—thanks to previous decades of quality, reliability and availability—despite the continuous stock shortage problem getting close to breaking point. There was not much Kurt could do in the interim until he completed the one-on-one sessions and uncovered more relevant facts.

He responded to phone calls with empathy by saying, '*Thank you for taking the time to let me know the impact our stock situation is having on your business. One of the reasons a new CEO and I were hired was to address this problem*'. Kurt as yet had not met the CEO, so what he said was 'tongue-in-cheek.' The responding comments from callers were, '*It is about time*' or, '*We will see*'. The latter sounded somewhat sceptical but understandable.

Kurt had no idea what the drivers were that caused and continue to cause stock shortage problems, let alone how to solve it. The sales team were in constant damage control, so the only competence Kurt saw repeatedly being applied was how they handled conflict—this they did extremely well. To assess the full range of sales competence was impossible under current circumstances.

Companies under stress are difficult to assess for sales competence and performance.

Time spent with the sales engineers was sedate when compared to the wholesale team. The architects, designers and engineers did their project-product reviews and recommendations years before going to tender. This meant they were not exposed to the day-to-day company stock shortages. The brand was well-known and had a reputation for quality and robustness, as a result they felt comfortable writing the specification accordingly.

Kurt interviewed the customer service team and was not surprised to learn their issues were a carbon copy of the wholesale sales team. After almost two weeks with the sales and customer service teams, Kurt discovered the root cause of the stock crisis. The company's Customer Relationship Management software (CRM) was incompatible with the manufacturing plants Enterprise Resource Planning software (ERP).

Apparently, the ERP was purchased because it was low cost, but no one asked the obvious question, is it compatible with the company's CRM? The mismatch of the software platforms meant two software programmes operated independently. To try and overcome the problem, part of the customer stock order process was done manually. This was more of a temporary band aid, but not a long-term solution. The outcomes validated the process' ineffectiveness, regardless the manual component was kept. The manufacturing system was riddled with errors—the mistakes were significant and costly.

An example of the ineffectiveness and errors was when a customer purchased 124 brown power outlet bases at a hugely discounted price. These were the last of a discontinued line. Within three weeks, the same discontinued stock was replenished at the Sydney warehouse from the Melbourne Plant. No-one in manufacturing took responsibility—in itself this was a problem. Shifting blame was an everyday occurrence between manufacturing and sales.

Finding a solution for the CRM/ERP problem rested squarely with the new CEO and needed to be a top priority. The cost in implementing a new platform would be substantial, but far less than the current mounting problems of poor-customer relationships and order cancellations, a resistance to placing orders, and the damage done to the brand long-term.

In addition, the greatest internal issue was low morale that was intrinsically linked to what was happening and the frustration of the company's inaction. This created employee tension and tempers irrupted regularly. The daily volume of angry customers and electricians who were instructed by their wholesaler to contact the company directly was taking-its-toll. Wholesaler managers increasingly admitted to convincing their customers not to buy the company's brand and instead to purchase the competitor's product.

During the review process, Kurt gave Bob a daily update and was ready to write his report. They met for a morning coffee at the local café. He provided a brief recap of the current situation and discussed recommendations to lift morale and improve sales. Bob listened intently and then stated outright, *'A copy will be going to the CEO'*.

The report used standard headings: introduction; objectives; findings; and recommendations. The findings were validated with facts quoting specific instances, customer names, dates, and the impact on those involved.

To keep the report concise, issues were placed under two headings: those sales and customers service had control over; and those they did not. The top two on the control column were attitude and morale. Despite the current situation a shift in attitude would positively influence morale, and in-turn provide the mental and emotional energy to tackle sales. However, sales and customer service had no control over the stock shortages and the flow on effect created by the CRM/ERP software.

The issues in both columns included recommendations. For immediate action to reduce the divide between sales and manufacturing and get stock into the hands of customers, Kurt proposed the sales team develop a six-month projection of product sales. Manufacturing would not be wasting time analysing false information and data from the CRM/ERP nor be side-tracked checking for accuracy. The sales team were in the best position to know what customers want. Therefore, manufacturing would be focussed on producing the right products at the right time—that was the theory. The report was presented to Bob, and he accepted it in its entirety. Kurt proceeded with the implementation.

The first action was to address the sales team to gain buy-in of the findings and recommendations. Everything went well until the team were asked to develop a six-month sales projection based on specific products. They said it was a manufacturing responsibility and not the type of work they wanted to do. However, the thought of having stock available for customers motivated them to start the projections.

Next was to contact Paul Rodgers the Melbourne Plant Manager whose reaction was unexpected. His ego got in the way, and he refused to accept the idea of receiving a product forecast from the New South Wales Sales Team. Although it would make his job easier, focus resources and reduce stress all round, in a reactionary vocal tone he said, '*Sales are not going to tell me what to do!*'

Kurt paused then politely responded, '*We are not telling you what to do. We want to work in with you. Do you mind my asking, do you have an alternate plan to produce stock customers need?*'

> *Sales projections for stock quantities can sometimes be met with resistance from manufacturing:*
> *'Sales are not going to tell me what to do!'*

This must have been like lighting-a-fuse to a bomb because the phone went instantly dead. He had hung up! One could only assume he had no alternate plan and felt threatened by the phone call. Kurt left it at that, then spoke to Bob giving him an outline of what had happened. New South Wales operations was Bob's responsibility and for Kurt this pushback was of concern.

Kurt's main priority was to improve sales and lift morale. It was somewhat of a chicken-and-egg situation, what comes first?

He decided to start with morale by introducing some light-hearted fun. The first opportunity came one morning as Kurt headed toward the office from the car park. He greeted one of the customer service team in an uplifting tone of voice, '*Good morning Jenny. How are you?*' Jenny reciprocated, '*Good*', then asked, '*And how are you?*' Nothing unusual so far until he responded enthusiastically, '*Fantastic!*' Jenny appeared somewhat bewildered and may have thought he was a somewhat crazy, and simply gave an insecure smile in reply.

Consistency was vital so he kept this up for weeks until Jim decided he had heard enough. Kurt had been in the warehouse and walked toward the office when Jim headed in the opposite direction. They greeted each other and after Kurt's usual, '*Fantastic*' Jim shouted at the top of his voice that echoed throughout the warehouse, '*Fantastic! Have you lost your mind? You must have no idea how serious the situation is. Are you in Lala-land? We could all lose our jobs, and you are going around saying you are fantastic*'.

> To achieve the desired response from others, the following behaviours were integral when Kurt stated he was 'fantastic', he:
> - Used upright body posture when walking or seated to project confidence
> - Listened actively and used good eye contact so the other person felt valued and respected
> - Spoke using language to reassure and leave no room for doubt, *'I can... It will be done... Leave it with me...We can do this'* and dropped vague language, *'Possibly...Probably...Maybe...Not sure'*.
> - Stayed consistently true to his word—what he said, will do, and did.

Jim eventually settled down and when he did, Kurt asked in a calm voice, *'Could I shout you to a coffee to give you an explanation for what I am trying to achieve?'* Jim agreed, and they walked to the local café. Kurt showed him the list of issues sales and customer service had control over and could change. Then said, *'Lifting sales is important for our job security but we need to start by changing our attitude and lift morale. In that case, this is a pleasant place to work'*.

Jim nodded in agreement. Kurt paused then continued, *'My intention is to put a smile on everyone's face by responding in a manner they do not expect. By saying something outrageous like fantastic, stops them in their tracks. You will be surprised at how often it has led to a conversation, and they walk away with a different perspective'*.

Jim apologized for his outburst, but his frustrations were understandable. By coincidence, the next morning they crossed paths again in the warehouse, Kurt greeted him. Jim asked how he was and before Kurt could respond, Jim shouted in a loud voice with a smile on his face, *'Do not tell me. I know you are bloody fantastic!'*

They both laughed as they went on their way. It was great to hear Jim laugh. It was only a matter of weeks before Kurt discovered the sales team told their customers he was 'Mr Fantastic'. Although no harm was intended, it fuelled the anger of some customers.

In one case, a property developer from northern New South Wales rang and told the receptionist, *'Put me through to Mr Fantastic. He won't be fantastic by the time I am finished with him'*. You can imagine this and similar phone calls.

There were critics and sceptics voicing their opinion at every opportunity, but this did not deter Kurt from what needed to be achieved—a change in attitude, morale and increase in sales. There were times he did not feel remotely 'fantastic', however he kept it up and in doing so noticed an emotional shift—a sense of well-being.

These behaviours slowly but steadily began to impact on the customer service team. The first noticeable change was the customer service team arrived 20 minutes early in the morning and stayed back to complete tasks before finishing for the day. This was in vast contrast to arriving just in time, preparing to pack up at 4:50pm and out the door by 5:00pm.

Within two weeks of the new behaviour, they approached Kurt to have positive affirmation statements they had selected to be printed on large, framed posters and hung on their office walls.

Alternatively, the sales team needed to get their house in order before a shift in attitude could be expected. Their company owned vehicles were poorly maintained, rarely washed, and internally filthy. The rear seat and floor were littered with rubbish. Kurt gave them a week's notice to get their vehicles up to an acceptable standard and to prepare for spot checks until he was convinced they had developed a new habit. Vehicles were spotless after only two spot checks.

The sales team needed to get their house in order before a shift in attitude and outcomes could be expected.

To develop the sales team's sales competence, Kurt initiated two-hour sales training sessions twice a month. No-one had been through structured-sales training previously at the company—it was met with caution. The first session was to learn about words and the emotional impact of words.

The sales team had been greeting customers in a mono-vocal tone and their responses were, *'Fine... Okay... Reasonable... Not bad...'*. This only added weight to how they were feeling. The replacement words they chose to use were, *'Great... Wonderful... Brilliant... Excellent...'*. They role played customer scenarios using the alternate words in line with an uplifted-vocal tone. Although they initially felt uncomfortable their self-confidence soon grew.

Sales training sessions were scheduled from 1:00-3:00pm every two weeks. The day before the first session, the sales team were asked to phone Kurt at 8:00am to be given a sales challenge that finished at 12:00pm sharp. The challenge was to instil fun, creativity and sales for the products— preferably products in stock in the New South Wales Warehouse.

The salesperson who achieved the highest number of orders would receive a surprise gift.

Sales team started coming in at 11:45am with four orders each. Orders had two-to-eight-line items. This was an incredible achievement compared

The Most Unlikely Salesperson

to the norm. Jim came in with five orders and assumed he won the challenge. It was two minutes before 12:00pm and the last salesperson, Patrick Townsend, a young ex-electrician, came in and dropped seven orders on Kurt's desk.

Jim protested in a loud aggressive tone stating it was impossible to call on seven wholesalers and get seven orders, in a morning. That was true. The sales team listened and waited for Patrick's response, *'Jim, who said anything about going to see wholesalers? I phoned and asked if they could help me win a surprise gift by giving me an order. I made seven phone calls then quickly drove around and picked up the confirmations'*. That was being creative and out manoeuvred everyone.

Patrick won a beautifully presented bottle of port wine elegantly placed in a wooden box. It was valued at $70. A small investment by the company for the huge increase in sales, lifting spirits, their paradigm, and aspirations of what is possible. The excitement and anticipation of the surprise gift made the sales challenge a lot of fun for everyone, except for Jim.

He protested again, but this time Jim took Kurt to one side stating how unfair he thought the challenge was. Kurt repeated the criteria: *'the salesperson who achieved the highest number of orders would receive a surprise gift. How this was to be achieved was up to the salesperson'*. Jim was the consistent top sales producer, and he did not want to accept that Patrick won the sales challenge by thinking outside the box.

After several months, the sales team increasingly embraced the sales training and diarized appointments months ahead. Changes could be seen in their demeanour and way they spoke. It was pleasing to see the two sales engineers replace their cardigans with business suits after a dress and appearance session.

The company's sales needle moved from the red zone into the black, just by selling the products in stock.

During the third month, the company's sales needle moved from the red zone into the black. This was the first time in two years New South Wales sales revenues generated a profit. A sense of determination within the sales and customer service teams became apparent as they focussed on selling stock that was available. If it was not, they would let the customer know within minutes. This reduced the volume of back orders and customer complaint calls.

Kurt put in strategies that changed how the sales and customer service team were approaching a problem. They could no longer tell Kurt about a problem without having thought through at least two possible solutions. Being the closest to the problem, they were in an ideal position to come up

The Most Unlikely Salesperson

with the most appropriate solution. Kurt would listen to the problem and their alternate solutions, then asked, *'In your opinion, which solution do you think will give you the outcome you need?'* They were then encouraged to go ahead and action their chosen solution. Their confidence and competence grew despite having to deal with the ongoing manufacturing stock shortages.

Generating sales revenues had its challenges. One specifically was how to shift $245,000 of obsolete stock held in the New South Wales warehouse. The Warehouse Manager Sam Malik gave Kurt a list of the products and quantities he costed at current trade price.

One of the company's customers, an independent electrical wholesaler was the largest in the industry. The business was founded by Bill Trundle. Kurt knew Bill had a passion for wheeling-and-dealing, attending auctions to secure a bargain, and sell it at a profit. Kurt had heard Bill started his day at 6:30am, so he rang his direct landline, *'Good morning Bill, my name is Kurt Newman of the Electrical Switchgear Company. Have I caught you at an okay time?'* Bill, *'Yes. What do you want?'*

Kurt, *'I would like to arrange a meeting at a mutually convenient time to show you a list of obsolete stock you might be interested in? Perhaps you might like to look at it over tea or coffee?'* Bill's voice changed, *'Make it 6:30 tomorrow morning'.*

Kurt arrived on time and was greeted by Bill who had a jug of hot water ready to pour in a tea pot. Slices of fruit cake were on two plates. Apparently, he had a sweet tooth! To get to know Bill whilst they relaxed and had their tea, Kurt asked about his personal life and how he got started in the business. Bill told him he had been in the industry since leaving school, he had four adult children, and three of them worked as branch managers in the business. Bill was in his late fifties and had an incredible work ethic.

Kurt handed over the stock list and told him candidly the age and condition of the products, then sat back and was quiet while Bill scanned through the pages. Kurt's description of the stock didn't seem to faze Bill. Each item had a trade cost next to it and at the bottom of the last page, in large font, 'Total $245,000'. He studied the list, took a sip of tea, looked up and said, *'I'll give you $30,000'.*

Kurt knew Bill liked to drive a hard bargain and if he responded too soon the wrong signal would be sent. Bill might think his offer was too high and change his mind. Kurt thought the $30,000 was a fare offer but remained silent, slowly shook his head reaffirming he had heard him and was

> **One of the rules of negotiation is, if you agree, ask for something in return.**

The Most Unlikely Salesperson

contemplating the offer. It was obvious they were both enjoying the negotiation game.

One of the rules of negotiation is if you agree, ask for something in return, but what could Kurt ask for? How far could he push the negotiation boundary? He wanted Bill to feel pleased he had struck a great deal and agree there and then. Kurt, '*If I were to agree, you would have to give me a cheque now, arrange to have the stock picked up, and throw in the 1972 rusted utility in back of your yard*'.

Payment meant instant revenue, the company would be rid of obsolete stock providing room for more current product lines and the company would save money by not having to deliver the products. The rusted utility was a 'tongue-in-cheek' request that Kurt expected to be rejected. Bill stood up and shook Kurt's hand sealing the agreement. Bill gave him a cheque, the utility was dropped off later the same day, and the stock picked up in good time.

Within hours of leaving Bill's Office, Kurt received a phone call from an angry executive in Melbourne Head office stating his actions will harm the brand because the market would be flooded with obsolete products. Kurt rejected his statement and responded by saying the transaction on all accounts was exceptional for both companies. The flood of obsolete products never eventuated.

Sadly, several years later Bill had a heart attack and passed. He was a kind-hearted person and a character the electrical wholesale industry will miss.

Jim and Kurt had their differences, but Kurt respected his honesty and work ethic. Prior to the first sales training session Jim said, '*I have been in the industry 40 years, have product and industry knowledge and do not need sales training*'. Kurt responded, '*I appreciate your extensive background. In today's competitive sales environment, experience, product and industry knowledge are great assets, but it is not enough. We need a thorough understanding our customers, their businesses, their issues, and ability to communicate in a manner that differentiates us from our competitors. So, there are many skills to learn and apply*'.

He paused then added, '*Jim, could I ask you to keep an open mind during our training sessions and being the most senior salesperson and top producer, there are young salespeople in the team who look up to you. I am sure they would appreciate your valuable insights*'.

Kurt did not have to say more. Jim shook his head and agreed, sat down, and to his credit actively participated during every session. He took on board the sales training with pride and applied it verbatim.

70 Chapter 6 Sales Role: Electrical Switchgear

The Most Unlikely Salesperson

Regularly, Kurt spent time coaching individual salespeople in their sales territories. On one such occasion Jim was greeted by a customer rebuttal, *'I have enough stock'*. Jim responded, *'I appreciate you letting me know. David, I would like to introduce you to Kurt Newman, who is the New South Wales Sales Manager. Whilst I am here would you mind if I show Kurt the product range you stock?'*

David was about to serve a customer and appeared distracted but nodded agreeing to the request. Jim found product lines below the wholesaler's minimum stock level, made a note including suggested reorder quantities, then approached David with the list.

David was finishing up with the same customer and instructed Jim to write up the order for him to sign. Jim wrote up the order, however front-of-mind was to sell products that were in stock.

He showed David the order then said, *'David, you currently have the ten pack exhaust fans in stock'*. These were ten individual fans packed in a large carton allowing electricians who were the wholesaler's customer to purchase one unit at a time.

Jim continued, *'What I would like to suggest is to get a carton of the four pack because the three-pin bases are supplied at no charge, a saving of $11.40. Would it be okay to add this to your order?'* This meant the electrician would be purchasing four units at a time, increasing the dollar-value of the sale for the wholesaler.

David agreed. Jim walked away feeling proud of himself with an 8-line order including the additional product line—the four pack exhaust fans. Many salespeople in the same situation would have accepted the rebuttal and walked back out the door.

Regarding the four-pack exhaust fan. This was the one-and-only product line with massive stocks both in the New South Wales and Melbourne Warehouses. However, sales were almost non-existent despite the fact the product in the ten and four pack were the same. When Kurt discovered the huge stock number he asked the sales team the obvious question, *'Why are we not selling four packs?'*

Brian, one of the salespeople reacted, *'You see, when an electrician takes one unit out of the four pack the other three become loose and move around in the carton'*. Kurt, *'I understand there is no individual packaging just a divider, but so what? I thought the $11.40 saving would be a reason to buy?'*

The loose exhaust fans in the carton were not the real issue. After some discussion the real issue emerged, the sales team's perception was that it would be a problem for the electrician. They decided to take a fresh

The Most Unlikely Salesperson

approach starting by role playing how to sell the four pack and how they would handle any sales objection. Collectively they agreed on a sales target for the next month.

Kurt wanted to provide an incentive, so he asked, *'If we achieve this target what would you like in return for your hard work?'* The sales team were quick to ask for an evening with their partners at a Chinese Restaurant in Parramatta, a Western Sydney suburb. This was easy to get to for the majority of the team, and it was a fair request.

The sales team put in an astounding effort that resulted in the state exceeding the company's national five-year sales figure for four pack exhaust fans. The sales record was achieved under normal trading terms and no discount incentive. The months of persistent hard work, classroom sales training and one-on-one infield sales coaching had paid off with a substantial increase in revenue for the company. This was despite the ongoing stock shortages on most product lines.

Jim sold the greatest volume of four pack stock. To give him the acknowledgement he so-rightly deserved and to do something different, Kurt arranged to have a large bunch of flowers sent to Jim's wife, Julie. On the accompanying card, *'Dear Julie, we congratulate Jim for winning the greatest sales volume competition'*.

Kurt received a phone call from an excited Julie thanking him for the flowers and for recognising Jim's achievement. The following day Jim came charging into Kurt's office, aggressively slammed the door and let loose a tirade of abuse. Kurt sat in his chair and listened. When Jim finally finished, he asked why he was so upset? Jim, *'As soon as I got home Julie showed me the flowers and said Kurt sent me these flowers congratulating you on your sales win. The last time you gave me flowers was when we were dating over 20 years ago'*. This created quite an argument.

Kurt responded, *'I can see you are upset and angry and I apologize. My intention was for Julie to feel proud of your sales achievement and both of you to enjoy the surprise'*. In the end Jim settled down and they shook hands. As Jim opened the door a crowd of people from administration quickly disbursed. They had been listening to what had happened.

Later that day and prior to going to the restaurant, the office was a buzz with excitement celebrating the record-breaking success. As they were about to head home to get ready and pick up their partners Kurt was called away to take a phone call from Paul Rodgers the plant manager in Melbourne. He blurted out, *'We are out of four-packs, and I have quite a back log of orders, so I am now forced to put on an afternoon shift'*. Kurt responded, *'Paul, what a great problem to have, and I will leave you with it'*. He then politely hung up the phone.

The Most Unlikely Salesperson

As Kurt left the office he thought about the uneasy relationship between sales, administration, and operations. What if individual salespeople were paired with an operations or an administration person and they went on sales calls? The aim would be to create empathy for the challenges the individual teams face and develop a sales and customer service culture.

Kurt outlined the plan to Bob including the value to employees, customers and the company. To minimize disruption joint customer visits would be in half-day units and implemented over 12 months. The department heads rejected it outright. The excuse was they could not afford the employee time. This highlighted the narrow and inflexible thinking of middle management, that in itself was a problem.

Sales for the industrial switchgear range progressively dropped. The competitor was making solid inroads selling their new range. As the sales team began to increasingly believe the stories they were told by wholesalers, their morale plummeted to the point where they accepted sales objections. They had lost confidence in the company's product switchgear range. The situation had to be addressed head on.

Kurt borrowed the competitor's top five most popular switchgear products from a nearby wholesaler. He then took the company's direct equivalent product, so like-for-like could be compared. A sales meeting was scheduled, centred around assessing which brand provided the greatest overall value from an electrician's perspective. Remember, electricians were the end user and bought from wholesalers.

Using a whiteboard, Kurt drew a vertical line down the centre. On the top left-hand side, he wrote the company's name and catalogue numbers of the top five products. On the right side the competitor's name and their products. Kurt, *'As you know I am not an electrician and do not have your level of product knowledge or expertise, but I do trust your integrity and ask that as we go through this process we do so with complete objectivity. I do not know how this will turn out, but whatever, we will handle it'.*

He took the first pair of products and asked the sales team about physical size, weight, sturdiness, ease of wiring and installation. There was next to no difference in cost, so it was not discussed. Every feature was discussed and the benefit/s for an electrician. Their contributions were written verbatim on a whiteboard and numbered for both brands. The process continued until they completed assessing the five sets of products. The numbers on each product comparison were tallied. Although the sales team had been heavily influenced in favour of the competitor product, the final score ranked the company's individual products 25-40% higher. This was not expected by any stretch of the imagination.

The Most Unlikely Salesperson

In summary, the competitor switchgear range looked good because of the modern design and had several advantages over the company's products. However, from an electrician's perspective, the company's range had considerably more going for it—particularly greater robustness. The competitor lacked the depth and breadth of product range, so on a large project to keep uniformity the company's industrial switchgear was an obvious choice.

Having started the exercise with much trepidation, Kurt felt relieved it turned out the way it did. The sales team left the meeting with a new outlook and refreshed. They felt motivated to sell product and handle any sales objection.

Although the company's stock shortages continued, the sales team's work ethic was admirable. They did whatever they could to supply stock to their wholesale customers including borrowing stock from one wholesaler to help another. Stock arrived twice a week at 6:30am from Melbourne. The sales team were there ready to sort through products they thought could be supplied to their most desperate customers. It was not the most productive use of a salesperson's time and costly, but it kept customers buying. The sales team were acutely aware of the cost of their time, so when they delivered the products, they treated it as a sales call and sold more product. To maximize their time and secure more sales, they walked into other wholesalers in the area.

Stock returns occurred from time to time and were handled by Sam the warehouse manager. However, when he received a request for a $50,000 credit dated five months earlier with no corresponding product, he immediately contacted Bob. The transaction had been authorized by Kurt's predecessor. Bob delegated the task of fixing the problem to Kurt. Reading the document, it was signed by Brian Johns the CEO of the largest wholesale group in the industry. The amount of money involved, the fact a CEO signed the documentation, particularly on behalf of an organization of this size, something did not feel right. Kurt had to find out what was going on, and a face-to-face meeting was paramount.

Kurt, *'Good morning Brian. My name is Kurt Newman the New South Wales Sales Manager of The Electrical Switchgear Company. The reason for the call is two-fold. I have not met you as yet and would like to, and secondly to discuss the request for a $50,000 credit'*. Brian replied, *'It is about time'*.

Brian had a reputation for being bullish and getting his way with suppliers. Kurt aware of this asked, *'Depending on your availability, would next Tuesday or the Friday at 10:00am suit you?'* Brian, *'Next Friday at 10:00 is fine. See you then'* and hung up the phone.

74 Chapter 6 Sales Role: Electrical Switchgear

The Most Unlikely Salesperson

Kurt introduced himself to Brian and sat across from his large desk that was filled with manila files and documents. He was in his early fifties, overweight, appeared stressed and sweaty. Within seconds of meeting Brian, he handed Kurt his copy of the request for credit and decreed what he thought will happen.

Kurt asked to see the products, to which Brian pointed to the far-left corner of his office. The products were stacked neatly and in the original packaging. The items were 'bread and butter' stock that turned over quickly, so why the credit request and why was the stock in his office?

Although Brian did not admit it, he wanted to replace the stock with the large competitor's products. He was so motivated by the thought, he had it all delivered to his office ready to return. Kurt's predecessor had caved into Brian's bullying and told him he would give him a credit.

Kurt was not going to be intimidated. Kurt, *'Brian I appreciate where you are coming from, but I will not authorize the credit because there is nothing wrong with the products and they are quick moving lines'*. Brian's vocal tone became aggressive and threatened to close the account. Kurt remained calm and tried numerous times to convince him to keep the stock, but this only enraged Brian further.

It was time to leave. Kurt, *'It was great to have met you, and I thank you for your time'*. He extended his hand and Brian ignored it, so Kurt got up and left.

Based on Brian's threats Kurt expected considerable fallout, but nothing happened. Despite the ongoing stock issues, the brand had a long-term history of function-reliability and continued to be specified for projects. The account was never closed and his wholesale branch network continued trading with the company.

To the sales team's credit, from the third month Kurt joined the company the New South Wales branch made a profit every month. They proved what was possible with innovative selling practices, going beyond the norm serving their customers, and despite the obstacles achieved a sales record. Two years had passed, and it became clear the CEO was not going to invest in, or was not allowed to invest in, a new CRM/ERP system. Although Kurt felt a deep connection with the sales team, it was futile to stay—as he had done previously, he gave notice without having another job to go to. It appeared Bob was also thinking the same, he had a state manager role for a large winery lined up and was about to leave. Within next 12 months the company was sold to the large competitor.

Years later Patrick reached out to Kurt on LinkedIn, and they caught up over a coffee. He spoke fondly about how he won the port wine and enjoyed the classroom sessions, the one-on-one sales coaching, and quoted examples of what he learned and still uses to this day. Patrick left the company shortly after Kurt and accepted a role as a senior sales engineer for a major German switchgear manufacturer.

Lessons learned

- There will always be people who will tell you something cannot be done. That does not mean it cannot be done. It means they have not done it or are incapable of doing it. It is essential to push past negative objections.
- For every problem there is at least one or more solutions. As more information becomes known, so do possible solutions.
- When inundated with problems voiced by others, identify the facts of a problem, not the interpretation or symptoms of the problem. Keep a clear head and do not allow yourself to be overwhelmed.
- Problems can present setbacks and bumpy progress but keep going. There is always a lesson to be learned, and with final success comes a great sense of achievement.
- Avoid acting on the first possible solution to a problem. Finding multiple and part solutions provide choice that can lead to a better outcome.
- If there is a major problem and you do not have the authority to solve it, then look for other ways of being productive to achieve your goals.
- When communicating, aim to lift others through your words and vocal tone.

Chapter 7
Sales Role:
The Scholarship Trust

Eric Sorenson, a salesperson in Kurt's network, worked under contract at The Scholarship Trust. Eric invited Kurt to apply for a role at the Trust. He introduced Kurt to Kevin Atkin the Regional Sales Director. Kurt was invited for an interview. Kevin spent most of the interview talking about the organization, his background and how good he is in sales. Kurt started the next day.

The Scholarship Trust was a savings plan for parents to enrol their children before age ten and matured when they turned 18 and started university. The fund was designed to provide an allowance, paid directly to and giving the young adult some independence. The fund was managed by a not-for-profit friendly society.

Engagement at the Trust was different to the usual. This time, Kurt signed a Contractor Agreement with the sales and marketing arm, which was contracted to The Scholarship Trust. At first, the role appeared to be similar to selling long service leave funding, but the differences soon came to light and were:

- High-volume sales were required because the commission per child enrolled was low
- Selling in a domestic as opposed to corporate setting
- Predominately evening and weekend work.

Kurt had never worked in domestic sales but had an open mind to its possibilities.

The title for the role was not negotiable. Everyone in sales was referred to as a Counsellor, perhaps it sounded better to parents than salesperson? There were three levels of counsellors:

- Level 3: upon joining
- Level 2: 50 sales achieved
- Level 1: additional 50 sales.

The Most Unlikely Salesperson

Each sale was referred to as an enrolment and commissions increased with each progressive level.

Kurt asked Eric and other counsellors how many children they enrol in a week. The average was eight. The sales record held for ten years by the founding director of the sales and marketing arm was 29 and no-one came remotely close to topping it. There was quite a gap between 8 and 29, so what would be a realistic number to begin with?

Kurt decided on what he thought was conservative. By seeing two families four evenings a week, and five on the weekend to generate 18 enrolments—one enrolment per family during the week and two enrolments per family over the weekend. However, the potential final number could be a total of 26 enrolments if every family had two children and Kurt had a 100 percent conversion—that was unrealistic. Allowing for some families with one child, people cancelling and others genuinely not being able to afford the instalments, 18 appeared to be achievable. It felt right.

The company had a one-page promotion brochure Kurt folded in two and dropped it into letterboxes and walked kilometres doing so. He encountered aggressive dogs but fortunately was never bitten. It gave him an appreciation for the those who deliver mail for a living. The letterbox drop activity resulted in only two enquiries. He initiated several shopping centre promotions, and the results were also poor. Too much time was consumed for these results.

The most effective business development activity was to be referred from one family to another and to address family groups who shared a common interest.

After losing time trying different approaches, he still managed to achieve Counsellor Level 1 in just under two months. Kurt quickly discovered the most effective business development activity was to be referred from one family to another and to address family groups who shared a common interest. To accomplish high sales numbers, this was the preferred way forward.

The breakthrough came when a family referred him to two families in Canberra, Australia's Capital Territory (ACT). Although a 3½ hour drive each way from and back to Sydney, it was worth exploring. Kurt phoned the two families and secured back-to-back appointments with a two-hour time gap between. This allowed extra time for the appointment if needed, and travel time. The appointments were booked for Saturday morning. He did not know anyone in the ACT and had nothing lined up for the afternoon or Sunday but was determined not to return to Sydney after a morning's work. His objective was to enrol the two family's children and

78 Chapter 7 Sales Role: The Scholarship Trust

ask to be referred to their friends who had children. This approach would fill the afternoon as well as Sunday with appointments.

Upon arriving at the first family Bill and Sue Donovan, tea, coffee, cake and biscuits were prepared. The reception felt warm and welcoming. Bill asked Kurt, *'Have you ever been on a sheep farm?'* Kurt replied, *'This is my first time. The scenery once I left the highway was wonderful to take in'*. Bill and Kurt stood at a lounge room window as Bill pointed to various sheds and tried to give him an appreciation of the size of the property.

They then sat down as Sue poured the tea. The conversation flowed effortlessly about family history, the school their children attended and the aspirations they had for them. Bill and Sue had a good understanding of the trust because they had spoken to the family who referred Kurt. They decided to enrol their three children.

The process for enrolment was quite cumbersome involving completing a one-page document per child. It was time consuming filling in the forms and asking questions to avoid awkward quiet moments. Without a second thought Kurt asked Bill and Sue, *'Could you help me and complete some of these forms?'* There was no hesitation as Bill and Sue reached out and took a form each.

Once completed and the administration fee was paid, Kurt congratulated them on enrolling their children. As he packed the enrolment forms away, he showed them the referral form. This was a single page with 12 framed rectangular boxes for names, addresses and phone numbers. The top of the page was reserved for the name of the family and a statement directly below, 'Please contact the following families so they may have an opportunity to know the benefits of The Scholarship Trust.' Kurt held the form in front of them as he read the statement and asked, *'Do you have family, friends or work colleagues who might be interested?'*

Both Bill and Sue looked at each other and started discussing the people they knew. Sue took the form from Kurt and started filling in names, addresses, and contact phone numbers. Bill went to the kitchen and came out with an old-fashioned Teledex full of business cards. He rotated through it and quoted names for Sue to write down. They completed the form with 12 referrals. Kurt thanked them both as they handed the form back to him.

Kurt concluded, *'I will be staying in Canberra this weekend and whilst I am here is there a family or families you would like me to see?'* They looked at each other and in agreement and said, *'Yes'*. Kurt continued, *'That's great. Would you like to call them, so we can arrange a mutual time?'* Sue walked to the kitchen, took the phone off the receiver, started dialling and stretched the long phone cord so she was visible from the lounge room where Bill and Kurt sat.

The Most Unlikely Salesperson

Sue called Belinda Elks, a close friend whose name was on top of the list. Sue gave a glowing recommendation and then handed the phone to Kurt. After the greeting he gave a summary overview of what to expect and then agreed to meet Belinda and her husband Fredrick at 2:30pm. Kurt thanked Bill and Sue again expecting to leave, when Sue arranged another introduction. Kurt repeated the process and secured another appointment.

On subsequent appointments the same process resulted in the weekend and the following week being fully booked. He finally headed back to Sydney the following Friday afternoon. The days were long, exciting and gratifying meeting families of different backgrounds, religions and cultures. Some families were exceptionally hospitable offering dinner and alcoholic drinks, which he politely refused. Kurt would often return to his hotel room well after 10:00pm.

The referral process ran smoothly, except when enthusiastic parents phoned their friends to introduce Kurt and started to tell them every minute detail in the shortest possible time before handing the phone over. It made the job of decluttering the overload of information quite a challenge.

From then on, asking parents to phone their referrals was done sparingly because it was easier for Kurt to phone. There were some parents so excited they wanted to tell their friends immediately. To avoid or at least minimize them creating confusion, Kurt would ask, *'Is it okay if I ask a favour of you?'* An enthusiastic, *'Yes'* followed.

Kurt, *'Would you mind keeping the introduction brief. The reason I respectfully ask, is it has taken us 30 to 40 minutes to fully understand the trust and the value for your children. I find some parents try to tell their friends everything in a three-minute phone call. You can imagine the confusion?'* The response was one of understanding with every parent. They then asked what they should specifically say.

The week in the ACT resulted in 26 children enrolled and the conversion from the appointment to the enrolment was 100 percent. It was an incredible outcome and from a sales perspective, it was utopia.

Convincing both parents to enrol their children had its moments. Mostly, the mother of the child or children saw the value in the programme well before their husband or partner. A common objection from the husband or partner particularly in more affluent areas was, *'We will have enough money to provide an allowance for our children'*.

Kurt followed the objection with, *'I appreciate you letting me know. Do you mind if I ask you a question? How do you think your children will feel, as young adults, having to ask Mum or Dad for pocket money for three or more years whilst at university?'*

The Most Unlikely Salesperson

Kurt would pause, allowing the parents to reflect on what he had said. This question had an incredible impact as they mentally visualized what it would be like for their children. There was the odd parent who stuck to their original statement, but the vast majority nodded their heads acknowledging their future adult children would want some financial independence. He then continued, *'We found the greatest benefit for a young adult is the payments are regular and coming from an independent source is good for their self-confidence'*.

The mother would be the first to express why she wanted the children enrolled. Her husband or partner would then eventually agree.

Contacting a parent to arrange an appointment was straight forward, but frequently the obstacle was to see both parents. One in four phone calls resulted in one parent not being available due to their employment including shift work, away on business or on military exercises. The response from one parent Kurt phoned was usually, *'I can see you and will let my husband know what we discussed'*.

> **To generate acceptable revenues in this business meant volume sales were mandatory.**

Kurt had no doubt they were sincere and would talk to their husband or partner, but he politely declined to make the appointment. Both parents needed to be present to make an informed decision. To expect a parent to have the same level of understanding in a 30-minute presentation that took Kurt weeks to develop would be unrealistic and place them in a difficult position. Parents were not trained salespeople and how would they respond to questions they had no answers for?

If it were possible a parent did convince their husband or partner to proceed, Kurt would have to go back a second time. Two sales calls, for the one sale made the transaction financially unviable. To generate acceptable revenues in this business meant volume sales were mandatory.

There were situations however, when one parent did make the decision, but this required a second qualification over the phone. Kurt always asked, *'To make sure I understand, if you like the programme you would make a decision without your husband/partner being present?'* The reactions ranged from an immediate, *'Yes'* to an indignant, *'It is my decision! I do not need my husband's approval'*. Sure enough when Kurt met with them they enrolled their children.

> **There was a pattern emerging regarding customer social status that related directly to sales.**

The Most Unlikely Salesperson

The great majority of sales in the ACT were people employed in the public service sector. Kurt learned they were status conscious and quoted what he understood to be a public service pay scale number. This meant, if a public servant knew another public servant's number, they knew how much they earned. Those on an eight or nine scale were on a higher income and quoted this with great pride. Kurt noticed a pattern emerging that related directly to sales.

When a parent on a high pay scale referred him to a parent on a lower pay scale, the appointment conversion was 100 percent. There was never a sales rebuttal. The appointment was accepted as soon as Kurt mentioned the person who referred him. This led to a 98 percent enrolment—an incredible percentage. The two percent short fall were parents who genuinely could not afford the instalments.

It was a completely different scenario when the pay scales were reversed, starting with the phone call to set the appointment. He was given excuses, a succession of sales rebuttals and sadly condescending statements about the person who provided the referral. One parent stated, *'He is on a much lower pay scale, so he needs it'*. The arrogance was breath taking.

In this case, there were few appointments confirmed and those that were, few sales resulted. Kurt would always leave on a high note by genuinely wishing them well. It was not unusual for these parents to offer to refer him to parents they thought might be interested, but Kurt respectfully declined. If the referred parent were to ask, *'Did (name of the referrer) enrol their children?'* Kurt would have to honestly reply, *'No'*. Credibility would be lost in an instant. Why would they enrol their children if the referrer did not?

The referral business development strategy worked exceptionally well. It never ceased to amaze Kurt how many parents tried to complete the 12 names and addresses on the referral form. Perhaps because there were 12 rectangular boxes? Some parents asked for a second sheet and discussed amongst themselves who and why the names should be included. Acquiring so many names per sales call had a compounding effect, particularly with groups who share a common interest and communities of the same nationality. The strong bond and the sense of responsibility to each other could be seen and felt. Meeting and interacting with these communities and learning about their lives was enlightening.

A couple originating from India, Mani and Anita Narrandera, enrolled their two children and asked Kurt if he would address their evening school. The school was for children of their culture to learn about the country they came from and to develop closer ties with each other. There were 38 families in this community. Mani listed the contact details on the referral forms on the condition Kurt address the parents before he approached them. This was done the following week with many parents asking to set an appointment with Kurt at the conclusion of the presentation. Those that did not book that evening, Kurt phoned the week after. The closing ratio was 82 percent enrolments from this community.

A similar situation happened with Brett Johnson, a Naval Commander, and his wife Gillian who enrolled their three children. During the interview, Brett mentioned he was the head of a religious sect. Brett and Gillian completed two pages of referral names. Kurt was surprised that everyone he contacted on the lists expected his call. Brett told them about the programme and recommended they enrol their children, and they did.

Selling in this manner felt like sales were on steroids. Pages upon pages of referred names was a business development dream.

Selling in this manner was most enjoyable and it felt sales were on steroids. Kurt had pages upon pages of referred names to contact, a business development dream. The ACT became so busy he did the trip every second week. To reduce overhead costs, he stayed at a hostel that was a converted motel.

Enrolment numbers were increasing every week and that was noticed by other counsellors during weekly meetings. It motivated them to go to the ACT because they thought it was a gold mine for sales. They stayed at the same hostel and during breakfast Kurt tried to help them where he could. They soon realized it required commitment, skills, empathy, and long hours. After several trips they gave up and ultimately left the organization due to poor sales performance.

During his time in the ACT, Kurt broke the ten-year old sales record of 29 enrolments increasing it to 38. What was interesting, the very next week 64 children were enrolled in Tasmania creating another sales record. This was achieved by a married couple who worked appointments separately, then combined their enrolments under the one name. Although it was not comparing apples with apples, it was a great effort.

As the numbers climbed two weeks in a row, it created pause to reflect. Why did the original record of 29 enrolments stand for ten years? The founding director told everyone no-one would be able to surpass that number—they believed him. This became a self-limiting belief. It was not until a new paradigm was created, that everyone realized it could be beaten.

Within two weeks of enrolling 38 children, Kurt was asked to establish a larger office in West Ryde, north-west Sydney, to further build the sales

The Most Unlikely Salesperson

operation. The office was massive, taking up half the second floor of the building. A plaque was ordered with adequate space for the next 12 months of names for the top counsellor sales awards.

When Kurt took over the New South Wales Team, there were 34 counsellors. He began by interviewing each one and reviewing their performance—mostly well below unacceptable. The primary reason was they saw the role as part-time and did not take it seriously. He let them know if they wanted to continue their contract with the organization it was a fulltime sales role. A large proportion of the counsellors did not accept this. As a result, Kurt terminated their services.

He advertised for counsellors and attracted mostly teachers who were looking for a career change. The role had many benefits Kurt outlined, but he wanted to make sure they understood what was involved by stating possible negatives from their perspective. Kurt, '*This role has nothing to do with teaching or your background. It is pure sales. It is a contract role, so you are not an employee, hence the reason why the job advertisement was in the self-employed section. Seeing parents is predominantly in the evening and weekends, the days can be very long. The role requires you to develop new skills and a different mind-set. How do you feel about what I have just told you?*'

Many applicants appreciated his honesty and bowed out. Other applicants showed the determination and commitment Kurt was looking for and they joined the organization. The most successful counsellors were women who did not want to be tied down to a 9-5 job.

Unfortunately, months after opening the new Sydney office the trust decided to cancel the sales and marketing arm's contract, so all contracts were terminated.

Lessons learned

- Opportunities requiring change can appear uncomfortable because you have no past reference, but that does not mean it is not right for you.
- Step into your discomfort, that is where growth happens.
- Be open-minded about working in a different sales environment: corporate to domestic; private enterprise to government; and government to corporate.
- If you want to stand out and achieve great success, be prepared to swim up stream and against the tide, and not follow others who are heading the easier downstream path.
- When the unexpected happens like a job termination, shift your attention to what you will do next to open new opportunities.

Chapter 8
Sales Role: Computerized Motion Signs

One of the most memorable characters Kurt worked with selling The Scholarship Trust was Noel Strange. He originally came from Ireland, a generous and kind nature, and outgoing. Given a choice to have a drink with friends or to go on his scheduled appointments, he would cancel the appointments and end up in a local Irish pub. Noel was in his late 50's, smoked several packets of cigarettes a day and somewhat overweight, however none of this slowed him down— he burnt the candle at both ends.

About a week after the trust contract was cancelled, Noel rang Kurt sounding extremely excited. Noel said, *'I am working for an Australian family business selling computerized motion signs. I told them about you and the owner is interested to see you'*. Noel continued talking at a 'rate of knots'. Kurt did not interrupt, just listened to absorb as much as he could. Noel was firm in his conviction as he emphasized:

- The signs were the future of advertising
- A family-owned business with six employees
- The business started in their garage and now operate in a factory complex
- Australian design and quality manufactured signs
- The main competitor was a national company who imported signs that broke down regularly and their service was poor
- The business owner had been selling the signs, but was now full time in operations and manufacturing
- The sales team was Noel and another person who split his time between sales and operations
- The owner wanted to hire salespeople to grow the business.

Noel had an incredible talent for language, he could make the ordinary sound amazing. He did not lie, it was his interpretation and he truly believed what he said. Kurt enjoyed working with him so agreed to meet the proprietor, Peter Williams.

The appointment was for 5:00pm at Peter's home in Lilly Pilli, a beautiful suburb south of Sydney. Kurt was told Peter had a home office and the interview would take place there, but it turned out to be quite a family affair. He was introduced to Peter's wife Margaret, two adult daughters, a son-in law, and two other relatives. They all worked in the business in a full or part-time capacity. Being a family business, it was apparent they wanted to make sure whoever they hired fitted in. They were all in the lounge room that had been set up with plates of finger food, tea, coffee, wine and beer.

Although Peter was the proprietor, it was his wife Margaret who financed the business and was the real powerhouse behind the scenes. Margaret was friendly but had a no-nonsense manner. Peter had a sales background, in his early 60's, thick white brushed-back hair, dressed impeccably and spoke eloquently. The interview was low-key and relaxed with the majority of questions being personal.

There must have been signals between each of the family members that Kurt was not conscious of. Peter all of a sudden stood up, smiled and asked Kurt if he would like a guided tour of the property to which he agreed. As they walked around the yard Peter suggested they go to his office that was in a separate building located at the rear side of the house. Whatever happened earlier Kurt must have passed the interview.

Peter's demeanour changed as he dropped the personal conversation and got straight down to business. He spoke openly about the industry, background of the business, his challenges, and what he wanted to achieve. His primary concern was cashflow stating it was tight because large sums of money were needed for research, development and manufacturing. Peter was proud and committed to making quality value-for-money signs. He had one of the smaller units in his office and gave Kurt an overview of how it was programmed and its functions.

Peter emphasized, as did Noel, other products on the market were imported, made from low-cost materials and did not operate reliably. His company's product range was limited to the most popular sizes suitable for internal or external use. The customer service responsibility was left to one of his daughters Gail, who provided customers with the training on how to programme the signs. This value-add differentiated the business by providing a service competitors did not.

Peter covered every detail, and then bridged into the terms and conditions of the job. It was a self-employed role that paid 20 percent commission on sales and there were no restrictions in terms of selling in a geographical area or an industry. The high dollar value of each unit, 20 percent commission and paid on sales made the offer attractive. There was no formal written contract, so they shook hands and Kurt agreed to start the following Monday.

On his way home, Kurt thought about possible sales processes and industries that would gain value using the signs. The sales environment was complex because the signs were a high-ticket item, required a senior management decision involving multiple people and potentially long selling cycles.

To generate regular cashflow, sales needed to be confirmed in the shortest timeframe. Although Kurt considered numerous industries, he kept coming back to the club industry. The reason was he knew clubs heavily promoted events and entertainment that changed weekly. These were outside the club building and internally as members and guests entered the premises. He had sold industrial chemicals and long service leave funding to the industry, so he was familiar with club culture and how it operated.

The easiest thing to do would have been to go and revisit the clubs he had dealt with in the past, but he decided not to. He always wanted to spend time driving down the New South Wales south coast to take in the beautiful scenery. Following some research, he discovered there were a good number of clubs scattered from Wollongong to Ulladulla. He listed the clubs in a logical sequence, starting from the most northern club in Wollongong. To ensure he had the correct name and title of the most senior manager, General Manager or Chief Executive Officer (CEO), he methodically phoned every club and checked. This turned out to be straight forward as he updated and completed the list.

Kurt then asked, *'Do you mind if I ask, in your opinion when would be the best time to contact (the manager's name)?'* The consistent response, *'Not before mid-morning'*. The reason was managers worked well into the evening, therefore started later the next day.

Kurt anticipated the cost of the signs would be greater than the amount a club manager could sign off—this meant the decision needed board approval. Kurt was familiar with club boards. His plan was to meet individual club managers, develop a trusting relationship and outline the advantages the sign had for the club, their members and guests. He did not want the manager to address their board on his behalf. Instead, it was hoped the manager would become an advocate who would introduce him. His aim was for the presentation of the sign to be the first item on the board's agenda.

The Most Unlikely Salesperson

After contacting the first six club managers, four were curious and agreed to a meeting. The appointments ranged from 9:30am to 5:30pm. Kurt allowed ample time to drive from one meeting to the next.

He tried to phone Peter to keep him updated and ended up speaking to Gail. During the conversation, Kurt mentioned he had meetings lined up with clubs on the south coast. He was glad he did because Gail said she had a customer service call in Mollymook, a town just north of Ulladulla. These two towns were close to each other and were next on Kurt's list to contact.

Gail said she had always been interested in sales and could they combine the trip? He agreed because he wanted to learn the finer points of how to programme the signs. The letters and words in the sign could be programmed to scroll, move from left to right and right to left. The acrobatic actions of the letters and words were designed to gain attention.

Kurt arrived at Gail's home at 7:30am and they placed three signs in the back of the car before heading off. The trip was hectic but most enjoyable getting to know the people who live and work in the region. A relaxed lifestyle and easy-going compared to the city dwellers. Club managers invited their senior employees to attend the meetings, making each appointment longer than planned.

Gail's role during the meetings was passive. She simply looked on and took mental notes of what was happening. Driving between towns to the next appointment they discussed and analysed the previous sales call. It provided a learning opportunity for Gail and drew Kurt's attention to what he could have done differently or better. The four appointments resulted in two board presentations, one immediate, and the other a confirmed future time and date. No progress with two bowling clubs because they were struggling financially.

Gail and Kurt headed for her customer service call. Gail was in her mid-30s, had a warm predisposition, and as Kurt soon discovered, was an incredibly skilled communicator. She could make customers feel comfortable within minutes and made the learning of the programming easy to understand and apply. Customers felt reassured by her manner and the way Gail gave her business card, drawing their attention to her mobile phone number.

Kurt's reservations about working for a small family company faded as he got to know everyone in the business, and as he experienced the professionalism and genuine care Gail had for her customers. Their personalities and individual skills dove tailed in perfect harmony.

Gail and Kurt worked well as a team, and they decided her entry point in the sales process needed to be at the board meeting. They both played

The Most Unlikely Salesperson

specific roles to ensure the presentation captured the board's attention and flowed smoothly—well mostly. There was the odd technical glitch, and when it occurred, Kurt was grateful Gail was well versed in how the signs worked and could fix just about anything.

Gail keenly observed the behaviour of every board member as Kurt addressed the meeting. She noticed those who were quiet and kept to themselves or projected negative body language. When Kurt handed over the demonstration phase of the presentation to Gail, it was shortly thereafter Gail singled out the individuals who needed to become actively involved. Gail did this by asking them questions in a direct manner. This was the right thing to do. Not to address any concerns or objections would risk those board members voting against the purchase of the sign. Voting was generally done when Kurt and Gail left the meeting.

Gail looked at the individual board members and asked, *'If your club had a sign, what would you like programmed?'* The question was not, 'Do you have any questions?' This would have attracted a 'No' response. Her question was brilliant, *'If your club had a sign, what would you like programmed?'* It created involvement.

By seeing a club event promoted live on the sign meant no board member had to rely on their imagination. It removed doubt and created an emotional buy-in that most often led to a purchase. Gail waited for an answer after asking her question. It was not surprising board members responded quickly by referring to an impending event.

> *Questions create buying signals—ideally use open questions inviting involvement.*

Gail then asked, *'How would you like me to word the event?'* Again, they responded. Finally, Gail asked, *'What would you like the words to do? Scroll, go from left to right, or right to left?'* Each of these questions increasingly engaged the board members.

The questions created buying signals, *'Would this sign be best suited to the foyer? Can this sign be used externally? Is there a sign larger than this one and how much is it?'* These questions came from a cross section of board members and provided opportunity to close the sale.

The majority of board presentations resulted in immediate confirmation of a sign, whilst others were followed up with a phone call the next day.

The largest sign was bought by a club in south-west Sydney. The unit was 3.5 metres long or 12 feet. It was a memorable presentation because it did not go smoothly. Multiple technical glitches happened in succession and had to be overcome. The challenge was to keep the board's attention and interest while each glitch was being attended to by Gail. The board were empathetic and relaxed, probably thinking, '*I am glad it is not me up there*'.

Once the problems were resolved, Gail did an impressive demonstration that motivated the Chair of the Club Max Stanley to say, '*Thank you Gail*'. Then he turned to his fellow directors, '*I think we have seen enough. Let us put it to a vote*'. The board decided to vote whilst Kurt and Gail were in the room, and it was a unanimous, '*Yes*'. The unit was positioned on the front fascia immediately above the entrance doorway allowing patrons and guests to see impending entertainment as they entered the club.

Sales conversions for the signs ranged from 50 to 70 percent and grew steadily. Despite this, there were ongoing cashflow problems that affected the company's ability to manufacture and deliver the product. The constant stress caused tension and arguments between Peter and Margaret that spilt over into the day-to-day management of the business. It became an uncomfortable environment to work in. After only six months selling signs, Kurt resigned.

Noel's partner Marianne phoned Kurt to let him know Noel had a heart attack and passed the previous evening. Noel's body finally gave out after years of heavy drinking, smoking and a poor diet. He was a genuine friend and a fun person to be around. May he rest in peace.

Lessons learned

- When a sales presentation does not go according to plan, a client will understand and give you some leeway. Your attitude during this time is vital. Simply lighten up as you go through what you need to get back on track. It makes your job of turning an uncomfortable situation around easier.
- When people become emotionally attached to the idea of buying a product or service, they will want to own it, therefore go ahead and purchase. When questioned about the purchase they will defend it logically. An example is when 'the cost of a sign' is questioned, answer is 'it will attract more members and guests, creating more revenue'.
- Family businesses have unique challenges due to relationships that create greater bonds or feelings of separation, therefore impacting viability of the company.

Chapter 9
Sales Role: Training & Development Consultant

Again, leaving without another position secured, Kurt looked and explored possible and alternate industries. With sales training as part of so many previous positions, Kurt was offered a sales role in the training and development industry. This new role had the opportunity to develop skills in consulting, training programme design and facilitation skills. The primary role was to sell the company's training services which included customer service, sales training, management, leadership, and team development. The courses included a mix of public and in-house training.

The company's founder was Patrick Hanwell, an ex-religious minister with a charismatic personality. He was an excellent keynote speaker and salesperson. Patrick had four children and was married to Martha. He had a natural deep baritone voice which drew attention from any audience. He had successfully sold various products, the most recent was a high-profile American sales trainer's video and associated audio programmes. Patrick was image conscious, dressed well and drove a red two-door sports car. He rented an office that was a converted two-story townhouse in Glebe an inner Sydney suburb.

Abby Kelly was the other member of the team. Abby was in her mid-twenties, intelligent, extroverted, and had a great phone manner. Her primary role was research and to write course content for Patrick.

Kurt's first day on the job was phoning small to medium businesses to convince them to attend a public sales training course. He promoted Patrick as the facilitator. Patrick's credibility for teaching sales was based on his experience and what he had learned from the American sales trainer's products.

Kurt read through the course content, and thought it was relevant, but it bordered on being outdated. Sales skills were changing subtly, and he saw an opportunity to rewrite and update the programme—this would have to be planned and at the right time. Abby and Kurt managed to get 30 participants to attend.

The three became a solid team, learning from each other and appreciating the different skills everyone contributed. Patrick was a big picture individual and enjoyed business development. He was not one for details, loose ends were always followed up by Abby, and later it was Kurt. Abby had good people skills and could consume large volumes of information from various sources, then rework it into manageable learning modules.

The second course was months later and held at a motel in Camperdown, inner-west Sydney. It was a three-day sales training course for 15 participants. Patrick rang Kurt the evening prior stating he could not make it, and would he run the course? This was the first of many occasions Patrick pulled out of a commitment at short notice and delegated the task. Self and time management skills were not his greatest strength.

Kurt felt excited and anxious at the same time. He needed to learn the course content, and structure the timing of each session to ensure it flowed effortlessly. He also familiarized himself with all participant's products and services so specific and relevant examples could be given. It was going to be a late-night reading and memorising the content of the leader's guidebook and aligning the overhead slides with the designated pages.

The makeshift system he used was to place a large red dot on the pages where a slide was used, and a post-it-note on the relevant page showing the time allocated for each session. The post-it-notes were extended just outside the appropriate page, easily seen at a glance.

A lesson he learned, and still uses to this day, was to plan the estimated times as a guide only. The timing of each session changes depending on the participant's rate of learning and skills development. There were times participants were 45 minutes behind the estimated time. When this happened, Kurt asked participants if they agreed to shortening their lunchbreak or stay back after the standard 5:00pm finish. There was never an objection to the request, in fact the response was appreciation for caring to ensure the development of their sales skills.

Participants waited as Kurt entered the room. The desks were arranged in a horse-shoe shape, allowing facilitator access in the centre. Kurt was about to approach the group and introduce himself when Patrick came in offering to do so before heading out again. The introduction went well, but Kurt felt apprehensive as he stepped forward and thanked Patrick. To establish creditability, he began by providing an overview of his sales background. He then stated, *'You have my total commitment to develop your sales skills'*. A slight pause before, *'Would you mind introducing yourself, your company and let me know at least one thing you would like to gain from this course?'* He turned to the closest participant on his right side, *'Let us start with Ashley'*.

As every salesperson spoke, Kurt wrote their name and their objective on a large pad clipped to an 'A' frame. The list was quite extensive with many quoting multiple skills they wanted to develop. This gave him insight into the knowledge and skills he needed to focus on. To lighten the atmosphere, after what felt like a serious start, Kurt used a slide that created smiles and laughter.

As they progressed through each session, Kurt shared a variety of examples to help their understanding and validate the learner manual content. Participant role plays were in small groups of three consisting of a salesperson, a client, and an adjudicator. Kurt walked from group to group briefly listening to the interactions.

The adjudicator's responsibility was to ensure the role play followed the objective of the exercise. If not, to intervene and restart just before it went off track. The three roles rotated regularly giving everyone an equal opportunity. The structure maximized learning and minimized discomfort when compared to a role play on stage where everyone looks at them. The written comments and ratings on the course evaluation forms were positive, highlighting what they had learned and were committed to implementing.

Patrick uncovered an opportunity for a multi-six figure project with a major telecommunications company. It required working collaboratively with a management consultant who won the contract. The role was to research, design, and facilitate sales and management training programmes throughout Australia. Prior to the final confirmation the telecommunications company wanted a demonstration on how individual trainers would facilitate a session. A panel of three assessors was formed, consisting of two women and a man from the learning and development department.

Kurt was the first to be evaluated and as he walked past their desk, he noticed they each had a clipboard with typed notes and a square on the right-hand edge of the document for ticks or crosses. The room was sparse, apart from a whiteboard that had a small shelf with several whiteboard-coloured pens. One of the women, Kurt assumed to be the most senior, asked him to show them how he would facilitate a session on questioning. He began by introducing myself, outlined the objectives and the expected outcomes.

He then addressed the panel as if they were participants, *'What are some of the difficulties when not enough or the right questions are asked?'* The response was, *'That's fine what would you do next?'*

The Most Unlikely Salesperson

Kurt stepped closer to the whiteboard, picked up a whiteboard pen, and wrote the heading Open and Closed Questions. He then proceeded to list the different characteristics, provided examples, and tried to engage the panel. The panel continued to be reserved, stern, and at times just nodded their heads. As Kurt proceeded with the session, they wrote notes and ticked boxes before leaning into each other and whispered. Kurt was about to progress to advanced questioning when the person in the centre thanked him and told him he would be one of the trainers. Patrick and a contracted consultant, Bob Simpsons were next and also accepted.

The learning and development department emailed a list of subjects that needed to be researched and the content structured in a competence-based format. Patrick delegated the task to Abby and Kurt. The timeframe for completion was one week, totally unrealistic, nonetheless Patrick had agreed to it. The starting point was to give each subject a title and list the required content. They scanned through articles, bought and read books. This was before the days of Google, the process was cumbersome and timing consuming.

To complete the draft courses, they worked 19 hours the first day, 20 hours and 18 hours on days two and three. Day four, time out to recover, and the fifth day the final edit, and design visual aid slides ready for implementation the following Monday. Kurt and Abby felt a great sense of relief and satisfaction for having achieved what appeared to be impossible at the beginning.

Patrick, Bob and Kurt were given a schedule of training dates. Patrick was allocated South Australia and Western Australia, Bob to Melbourne, and Kurt to Sydney and Brisbane. The programme kicked off with a two-day course in Brisbane for executive and senior management. These were one and two levels respectively below the CEO.

The objective for this level of management was to understand the content and objectives of the total programme. Then they in turn could actively support their direct reports as they completed each course. The first group of direct reports were scheduled to start the programme later the same week. The executive and senior management team were intelligent and highly driven.

Kurt began the session with everyone introducing themselves followed by a slide that was a thought-provoking puzzle for them to solve. He used it as an icebreaker to lighten what felt like a tense environment. There were 15 participants. As Kurt outlined what they could expect over the next two days, one manager interrupted, 'We have been through similar training previously'.

The same manager sounded frustrated as he continued to let Kurt know about the internal politics of the company and the problems they have with their learning and development department. After listening and looking at the other managers, Kurt was curious to know how they all felt. Kurt, *'Thank you for letting me know. Let me ask, how do the rest of you feel?'*

This question opened a flood of complaints, negative comments and showed deep-seated frustration and anger. Another manager quickly stood up and said, *'It is not your fault. We are sick of having consultant after consultant come in and tell us what to do'.*

It appeared to be a long-standing problem that had nothing to do with Kurt, but he had to do something constructive. Kurt said, *'How would you feel if we substituted today's content and worked on a solution for the current issues?'* The feedback back was plain and simple, they were not interested.

This was the first time Kurt had experienced anything like this. It was 8:30am and he could not see any value in continuing. To ensure Kurt understood what they had told him, he summarized their statements which they confirmed. Managers at random apologized for the situation.

Kurt responded to the group, *'I really appreciate where you are coming from. To continue would only be going through the motions and we do not want to waste each other's time. Let's have a coffee break whilst I go and make a phone call'.*

Patrick could not be contacted, he was on his way to Perth. Kurt then called the management consultant who had the contract and told him what had happened. His initial response was scepticism, inferring Kurt had done something wrong.

Kurt returned to the management group, thanked them, and suggested they return to their office. An hour later the management consultant phoned Kurt sounding subdued and suggested he catch the next flight back to Sydney. Bob in Melbourne had a similar reaction from his group. Within a week the project was cancelled. The management consultant's contract was terminated. Whatever the reason behind this debacle, Kurt was never told.

Generally, Patrick tended to push the boundaries of his time management, this meant he was always behind schedule including meetings with clients and prospects. Kurt arrived up to ten minutes before a meeting, let the receptionist know of the appointment, and waited in the client's foyer for Patrick. The client came out minutes before the meeting was to start. Kurt introduced himself and they headed to the client's office. Patrick was nowhere in sight. The conversation was cordial, as he asked questions about the client and their business. The relationship was developing, everything was going smoothly, and then there was a knock on the door, Patrick walked in. He never apologized for being late and was insensitive to the fact his late attendance was disruptive. Patrick considered himself lucky to have made it at all, when in fact, he should have waited in his car. To recapture the mental and emotional connection, that had begun to develop prior to the interruption, could not be regained. The dynamics of having an extra person arrive when they did, changed the feeling of the meeting.

After experiencing three joint-sales meetings like this, Kurt let Patrick know he will no longer be going on appointments with him. He paused, then shook his head and acknowledged he understood.

Kurt was grateful for the professional development opportunities he had working with Patrick. To professionally mature and grow required taking on additional responsibilities and being accountable for the outcomes. It meant getting out of his comfort zone, because that is where the opportunity for growth is. There is no expansion remaining in-and-around-the-centre of what he perceived as his security zone, which was all the things he had done repeatedly and knew well.

> *To professionally mature and grow required taking on additional responsibilities and being accountable for the outcomes.*

Kurt was thrown in the deep-end when Patrick did a classroom training session for a large car dealership that did not go well. The dealer principal phoned Abby and said his service manager was dissatisfied with the training and wanted Patrick to call him. Patrick approached Kurt and told him to sort it. Kurt phoned the dealer principal Terry Donavan, *'Terry, this is Kurt Newman. I work with Patrick Hanwell. He asked me to contact you because he said your service manager was dissatisfied with the training session. Would you mind if I contact him directly to see what we can do?'*

Terry cordially said, *'Thanks for calling. Hans Johannsson is the service manager. He told me the training was too theoretical and did not address the issues in the workshop. You can call him directly on 9** ****'.* Kurt, *'Thank you Terry. I will call you back after I have spoken to Hans'.*

He contacted Hans who told him what Terry had said and added he did not appreciate being preached to. Patrick tended to bring religion into his sessions. Kurt met with Hans who provided details of what happened and what he expected from the training session. On completion, Kurt offered to redo the day's training at no charge. He also outlined the practical activities he would incorporate to make the session interesting and to develop the skills Hans wanted his workshop team to have. Hans replied, *'That sounds good. When can you do it?'* Kurt, *'How would next Wednesday at 8:00am suit you?'* The day and time were locked in.

Driving back to the office, Kurt rang Terry and gave him an overview of the meeting he had with Hans and what they agreed on. Terry was pleased with what he heard.

The workshop team were initially reserved but after multiple breakout sessions and interactive discussions they were completely onboard. At times, the room sounded quite rowdy and chaotic but the energy and commitment to learning was gratifying to witness.

Kurt met with Hans the following week and provided him with a detailed report, including the ratings and comments from everyone in the workshop team. On conclusion Hans sat back and said, *'The team gained much value from the session. I would like you to train my service advisers. When would you be available?'* Kurt, *'Thank you Hans. I would like to do that, but first let me ask you about their role, any difficulties they face and the skills you would like them to develop?'*

Kurt made notes as Hans spoke about the service advisors and was very particular about what he wanted to achieve. Hans felt comfortable booking a date without requiring a proposal. The following day Kurt met with Terry and gave him feedback on the workshop team session and outcomes. He started to mention the service advisor training when Terry said, *'I know'*.

He then reached over and grabbed a document, *'I have Patrick's proposal recommending training for the sales and management team. I want you to do it'.* Kurt, *'Okay. I'll let Patrick know and get back to you'*.

This was Patrick's account, and Kurt needed to let him know what had happened. He expected Patrick to agree for Kurt to do the training but keep the management of the account his responsibility. However, Kurt was surprised at his reaction. Patrick, *'You are a better trainer than I am. It's your account now'*.

Patrick never contacted or went back to the client. As the owner of the business, it would have been wise to do so. He decided to focus on sales, and let Kurt do the course design, training, and coaching. The partnership worked well.

The company continued to push boundaries, which meant Kurt found himself regularly in uncharted waters and out of his comfort zone. Experiential training was becoming popular for companies to develop leadership and team skills for their managers and employees. The industry consisted of individuals and small sub-contract groups providing rock climbing, adventure trails and abseiling but in the main, they had no business or corporate background. The feedback from companies that did

The Most Unlikely Salesperson

the training was, '*It was fun at the time, but now that we are back at work everyone has gone back to their old behaviour*'.

Before proceeding, Kurt, Patrick and Abby decided to evaluate experiential training by putting themselves through various outdoor challenges. Kurt was interested in how they could design tailored training and skills development based on client objectives, a balance of structured classroom theory and outdoor action learning. If this worked, newly learned behaviours would be transferred to the work environment and be the key point-of-difference between the training company and its competitors.

Patrick approached a mountaineering company that took individuals and small groups on outdoor activities. The business was owned by ex-army paratrooper Steve Hamilton and rock-climbing enthusiast Tim Edwards. Steve and Tim had a retail shop that was part of the business selling outdoor clothing and equipment. Their team included five sub-contractors.

The venue for the experiential training was a remote location in a mountainous region of Bundanoon in the Southern Highlands, New South Wales. There were eight people participating in the group. Patrick invited others to be part of the experiment. The outdoor company team had four including Steve, Tim and two of their sub-contractors. Everyone arrived at the motel on the Friday evening, so they could get an early start on Saturday. After breakfast they headed to the site in a minibus.

The objectives for the experience were to push themselves out of their comfort zone, to discover who they were under pressure, and identify how this learning platform could be of value to achieve client outcomes. The participants would have to face fears they were conscious of and discover fears that were subconscious. Kurt had a fear of heights for as long as he could remember—this was going to be quite a challenge.

Everyone in the team was fitted with rigs and harnesses, then proceeded to walk a kilometre along a narrow bush track to finally reach an escarpment. Kurt felt a rush of adrenaline as fear struck him. To distract himself and reduce his anxiety, he looked beyond the cliff edge and focussed on the blanket of tall gum trees gently swaying throughout the valley. Although this was a breath-taking view, its impact had minimal effect on how he felt as adrenalin continued to surge through his body.

The first task was to abseil down a 30-metre cliff. Steve and Tim went through the safety procedures, then checked everyone's harness to ensure it was fitted correctly. Tim asked for a volunteer. This was met with stunned silence. Patrick stepped forward which created a sigh of relief for those who were petrified of what was ahead of them. It did not take long for Patrick to go over the edge and out of sight.

The Most Unlikely Salesperson

Tim turned to the group and as he was about to ask for another volunteer, Kurt promptly raised his hand. He wanted to get this over with—the sooner, the better! Tim did the final harness check. Then walked Kurt with his back to the cliff edge, gave instructions to lean back and slowly step back. This felt a most unnatural thing to do, to walk backwards over a cliff.

Kurt's left hand gripped the rope in front of him, and the right hand was around his back near his buttocks to control the rate of descent. He looked straight at the cliff face as he descended. Half-way and everything was going well, until he looked down and noticed a huge crater in the cliff face directly below him. The only way to get passed this was to loosen his grip, push off from the cliff using both legs and free fall to the bottom outside edge of the crater. The distance was about four metres. The other choice, which was not much of a choice, was to crawl back up the cliff. So, he pushed off and reached the bottom of the crater. He was now about ten metres before reaching the bottom. He felt a great sense of relief when his feet touched solid ground.

Kurt looked up and a second parallel rope system had been set up. Abby was on her way down on the second set of ropes and appeared extremely nervous. Fortunately, the cavity in the cliff face did not extend to her ropes, so she had a seamless experience to ground level. Abby gave out a sigh of relief when the exercise was over. The rest of the team followed and managed to abseil down the cliff safely.

The next day everyone headed to the minibus to take them to a new location. The weather was sunny with a strong blustery wind which brought the temperature down to 2° Celsius. They travelled to a gravel car park. Then continued on foot, following Steve and Tim until an enormous gorge was directly in front of them. Steve said it was 200 metres wide and 1000 metres deep. It was an overwhelmingly beautiful sight, but unnerving for most who could only imagine what might be ahead of them.

The team was split into two teams of four each. Steve gave instructions. Both teams had ten minutes to agree on non-verbal signals they would use throughout the exercise. One team would then be transported to the other side of the 200-metre gorge. Although a challenge in itself to get eight people to agree on one system of non-verbal signals, it was easier than shouting instructions from one side of the gorge to the other. The process was hilarious with everyone shouting over each other trying to get their point across, then changing their minds and starting over again. It was pure chaos until there was only a matter of minutes left. Steve suggested to elect a spokesperson for each team to co-ordinate the ideas and agree on the signals. This was part of the learning experience. Considering the tight time frame this was the right process to follow.

100 Chapter 9 Sales Role: Training & Development Consultant

What the team had ahead of them was to construct a two-rope bridge two metres vertically apart spanning the width of the gorge, using non-verbal signals as the only form of communication. A two-hour time limit was imposed for the teams to relocate via the bridge to the other side. The challenge was to see how everyone coped with pressure that was physical, mental and emotional.

Initially, Kurt thought the timeline was generous, but it was soon discovered to be a difficult task. Each person had to cross the gorge by holding onto the top rope and shuffle one foot at a time sideways on the bottom rope. A safety harness and a karabiner were fitted, a high tensile oval shaped piece of equipment clipped to the top rope. The two ropes had a lot of flexibility almost like two rubber bands. There was plenty of bounce, and shuffling of feet along the rope was slow.

...an overwhelmingly beautiful sight, but unnerving for most who could only imagine what might be ahead of them.

An unexpected third challenge was the wind. It was gusting fiercely along the gorge valley. To get this terrifying experience over with, Kurt intended to be the first to volunteer, but Patrick decided he would. Looking at the team, everyone appeared pale with fright and stood well back from the cliff edge.

Once Patrick reached the other side of the cliff, an opposing team member came across from their side. As soon as their feet landed on solid ground Kurt walked up to Tim to be hooked up to the safety line. Kurt grabbed the top rope and placed his left foot on the bottom rope to begin the sideway shuffle. As he edged away from the cliff face, he felt the full intensity of the wind and adrenaline kicking in dramatically increasing his heart rate. Kurt is 185cm tall, the distance from the top rope to the bottom felt comfortable. He looked straight ahead as he shuffled at a consistent pace. This was going well until a quarter of the way across when a blast of wind hit him front-on, flipping him backwards—he now faced the sky. The turbulent wind then struck from behind. He spun in the opposite direction, forcing him to look down into the depths of the gorge—something he was desperately trying to avoid. There was the odd respite between gusts, but the wind persisted for most of the journey across. He kept heading in the one direction, shuffling steadily. It was like being on the high seas in extremely rough weather. Finally, he made it.

Kurt is almost across the gorge

Jenny Vella one of the team was next to cross. She was only 157cm tall and Kurt wondered how Jenny would reach the top rope. Fortunately, there was a lot of slack in the two ropes, and Tim was able to pull the top rope down enough for her to grab it. It was still quite a stretch for her to maintain though. Halfway across Jenny screamed as she lost her grip. She quickly descended until the two-metre safety line prevented her from falling further. Everyone's heart-was-in-their-mouth, so to speak, imagining this could be them. What would they do if it was? To her credit, she managed to crawl back onto the bottom rope, and after multiple attempts reached up and grabbed the top rope then continued to cross safely. It was a heroic effort.

The two teams managed to swap cliff positions in one hour and 59 minutes according to Steve. That was one minute within the allocated time. It was quite a scramble for the last person. That evening to commemorate the team effort over two days, Patrick handed out medallions to recognize individual contributions. The awards ranged from Jenny receiving the bravery award and Kurt for supporting others. This came as a surprise to Kurt because he felt a natural affinity for team members who clearly appeared scared, without hesitation he reached out and provided them with encouragement.

The Most Unlikely Salesperson

In the following Monday's meeting, a decision was made to include experiential training as part of the company's portfolio of services. To differentiate what others in the industry did the process was:

- Understand the client's challenges and requirements, the effects on the business and what needed to be achieved
- Agree on the objectives
- Design a classroom structured course
- Discuss the above with Steve and Tim
- Steve and Tim to tailor the outdoor component
- Ensure the classroom and outdoor content was seamless and connected
- Follow-up for client feedback one week after completing the course
- Follow-up for client feedback six weeks later.

The feedback during the follow-up would be crucial and include the team's thoughts and feelings of their experiences, shifts in employee behaviour, and skills transferred to the work environment. Kurt would provide feedback on every participant and recommendations to further their development.

The first confirmed project was a large window manufacturing company. David Tarento was the State Manager, a personable and highly analytical individual. The business was losing sales to competitors and the three departments of sales, administration and manufacturing operated in an adversarial manner. This affected productivity and morale. Within each department there were other problems that needed to be addressed. However, the priority was the three departments needed to work together in a respectful and co-operative way. Subsequent training and development would sort the other problems. David approved the proposal for a three-day experiential programme located in the scenic Blue Mountains of New South Wales.

The team of 30 people arrived at the venue late on Thursday afternoon. The programme completion was expected to be mid-afternoon on Sunday. Thursday evening felt relaxed and a lot of fun.

The first session on Friday morning consisted of learning in a classroom setting, followed by a series of outdoor exercises in the afternoon. The latter was to convert the theory into practical actions and experiences. The objective was to take the participants from knowing to understanding.

The tasks were not physically demanding, but required cooperation, asking questions, developing solutions to problems, learning through making mistakes, learning from each other, and being considerate of each other and at times apologize. They began to connect emotionally. This

The Most Unlikely Salesperson

formed the foundation for additional skills and, on the following day, trust to be developed.

The dinner that evening was filled with sharing stories about what happened during the day, telling jokes and laughter. The mood was light, and it was encouraging to see people from different departments reaching out to each other.

The day two had the same indoor and outdoor structure, and included content designed to build on the first day's outcomes. Day three involved overcoming several major challenges by applying what they had learned during the two previous days.

Kurt asked for a volunteer to take charge of the whole group and a support person. A junior from administration, Amanda Jones, raised her hand immediately and Gareth Smith from sales volunteered to be her back-up. Kurt briefly pulled Amanda and Gareth aside to provide them with the plan for the day and suggestions on how they might proceed, however the final decision was theirs. He let them know his role was to video the day's event, observe and provide advice whenever there was a safety issue.

Management would be placed in a situation which made them totally reliant on the team

Amanda took charge by organising the group into a variety of roles and responsibilities. They were then given an overview of the day's objective—the three departments had to work as one team.

Management would be placed in a situation which made them totally reliant on the team—to experience trust. Amanda emphasized the need to look out for each other because there would be safety issues. Management consisted of David Tarento, Brian Pullman Sales Manager, and Allan Ainslie Manufacturing Manager. The management were blindfolded for the day, and they needed to be guided by a volunteer team member through rough terrain and obstacles.

Amanda asked the three managers, '*Based on what we have learned so far this weekend do you trust the team?*' Without hesitation the answers were, '*Yes*'.

Amanda followed through, '*Would you trust the team to guide you through today's activities blindfolded?*' David instantly responded, '*Absolutely*'. This sent a strong message to everyone. Brian and Allan took their time to answer the question and seemed to cautiously agree.

The blindfolds were made of thick black material doubled over. Gareth made sure management could not see. Amanda directed four people to pair-off and walk-in front of and either side of each manager holding their forearms to ensure they walked safely. The rest of the team followed from

104 Chapter 9 Sales Role: Training & Development Consultant

behind. Guides were changed every 30 minutes. They did a brilliant job in drawing their manager's attention to impending rocks, logs, and tree branches that were in their way. After 2½ hours, including regular rest breaks, the team arrived at the site.

Team guides sat managers down on a fallen log. Then Amanda, who was quite the leader, proceeded to address the managers, *'There is a gorge ahead approximately seven metres wide and 50 metres deep. The team will be strapping two builder's planks together with rope, so we can cross over. One person will be allowed at a time and a rope will be tied to each person's waist and anchored around a tree for safety'*. Amanda paused slightly before asking, *'Do you trust your team to take you across the ravine safely?'*

David instantly reaffirmed his faith and trust in the team which showed great leadership under stressful conditions. Being blindfolded for hours would have conjured up the most frightening scenario. Brian's face changed to ghastly white. There was the risk he was about to take off his blindfold and fortunately, two of his guides noticed and were quick to reassure him. Kurt made his way to the other side to video individual managers as they crossed the ravine. As the managers crossed, he was then going to ask how they felt the instant their blindfold was removed.

David volunteered to be the first. The rope was tied around his waist, he then proceeded to crawl along the plank. There was some flexibility in the planks creating a bouncing effect in the centre where the two lengths were tied together. He made it across safely.

The moment David took off his blindfold Kurt asked, *'How do you feel?'* He replied, *'I am glad it is over. The team has been amazing. They came together and worked as one unit. It highlighted natural leadership skills of some team members, skills I was not aware of. I look forward to experiencing these qualities at work on Monday. Thank you'*.

Brian was next. David shouted words of encouragement from the other side. This however, had no effect because Brian was so frightened, his whole body quivered. As the team led him to the plank Brian placed his thumb under his blindfold and was about to pull it off when one of the guides stopped him. She reassured Brain was in very safe hands and the team were looking after him.

Brian took a deep breath, climbed onto the plank, firmly gripped it with both hands and began to slowly edge his way forward. Whenever there was the slightest movement in the planks he froze, and nervously screamed, *'What is happening?'* Eventually he made it across and as he took off his mask, Kurt asked, *'How do you feel?'* Brian was so nervous he could not speak for a while. Kurt suggested he take his time and a few slow deep breaths.

Kurt, *'Brian, as you are taking a few deep breaths, I want you know I admire your courage. You kept going despite how you felt. It says a lot about you'*. Brian eventually responding, *'If it were not for the guides, I would not be here. It made me realize I work with a great team'*.

The last manager about to cross was Allan. Weeks earlier, David told Kurt his greatest problem was Allan. Although a competent engineer, Allan had an explosive temper and did not hold back expressing his feelings. David's other concerns were the high employee turnover and number of accidents in the manufacturing plant. Allan's outbursts were not limited to his employees. When in the mood, he let loose on sales and administration personnel. David had multiple one-on-one conversations with Allan about his behaviour, the impact he was having on employees and the business, but nothing worked. David wanted Allan to learn humility and to realize he can trust and rely on his team. Hopefully, during the hours of being blindfolded gave him time to reflect on his behaviour.

Allan was silent as the rope was tied around his waist and then one of his guides walked him to the plank. He got down on his hands and knees and worked his way methodically across to the other side in complete silence. When the planks flexed which was often, he paused then continued. When he reached the other side, Kurt helped him step off the plank. Allan removed his blindfold and blinked for a while allowing his eyes to adjust to the daylight. The video was on as Kurt pulled him aside away from the team. Kurt asked, *'How do you feel? Turnaround slowly and look where you have been'*.

Allan saw two planks tied together with rope and positioned on two carpenter's stools. He was one metre off the ground, and the venue was a well-manicured park. It was not the 50 metres of dense bushland he had visualised. His demeanour changed rapidly from sombre to instant aggression. Allan came within millimetres of Kurt's face and in a low hostile tone, *'I know what you were trying to do you &%#$#$$#$. I get it! You have achieved what you set out to do!'*

Within seconds of his outburst, he ran to the other side of the park. Kurt assumed it was to release his built-up anger. Allan came back minutes later and apologized.

Kurt accepted his apology then said, *'We did not do this to embarrass you. The takeaway is you believed you were 50 metres off the ground as you crossed the ravine. You demonstrated complete trust in your team and did it in a congenial and co-operative manner. It is a credit to you'*. Kurt

The Most Unlikely Salesperson

continued, *'Be honest with me, will this experience impact on how you work with your team from here on?'*

Allan paused to think about the question then in a subdued-vocal tone, *'It has taught me a lesson and I will try and be a better manager'*.

Kurt followed-up with David a week later. He said he noticed a difference in Allan's behaviour and was particularly pleased accidents and complaints had reduced significantly. He mentioned sales and administration were working collaboratively. David and everyone in the office wore a rubber band. Kurt, *'Do you mind my asking, why the rubber bands?'* David, *'When any of us are back into our old habit, we flick the rubber band, giving ourselves a mild sting. This is to remind us of the new behaviour we need to embrace'*. An unusual approach Kurt thought—but it worked!

Kurt followed up six weeks later, David was chuffed with how interdepartmental relationships had improved. They discussed other issues within the company that led to training for management, administration and the sales team.

Allan managed to behave reasonably well for three months, then, and unfortunately, resorted back to his old habits. David had no choice but to terminate his services. Sales continued to go from strength to strength, and several years later the company was sold to a competitor as part of a restructure of the holding company. David resigned but continued to work as a general manager for other companies.

Patrick hired two additional consultants, Steve Donahue and Matt Dillinger, as well as a support person, Margery who was married to Matt. This increased the size of the team to six. He decided to integrate them quickly using experiential learning, but this time water was the medium. Challenges were going to be on the Nymboida River near Coffs Harbour, a coastal town approximately an hour's flight north of Sydney.

Upon arriving at the river, the team were driven by minibus along a narrow-unsealed road heading toward the top of a mountain. It was winter and the temperature was 4° Celsius, a similar scenario to and previously experienced in Bundanoon. The wind chill factor dropping the temperature to below zero. They were taken to a cabin and given a woollen jumper and a wet suit to change into. The jumper felt like wearing a large scouring pad. The wet suit was meant to keep everyone dry and warm. It was difficult to assess what was more uncomfortable, the cold or the constant itching of the wool.

The view outside the cabins was peaceful with tall trees and thick bushland. The mountains engulfed the cabins, and the river was a fast-moving mass of blue water with white crests. The water tumbled over rocks and created small waterfalls while making its way down the mountain.

Ray Jones the chief instructor warned everyone that parts of the Nymboida River were so dangerous, it was safer to get out of the water and walk around the rapids. The waterfalls were rated one to five, level one was a gentle ripple through to level five that could pull a person under the swirling water and drown them.

Going down the Nymboida River

Kurt wondered what challenges to expect and how the new members of the team would react when his thoughts were interrupted by Ray, '*You are in for a fun time*'. Kurt could think of other words, but fun was not one of them.

It was 8:00am as they stood in the shadow of a mountain, a cold breeze was blowing, and the itching of the wool was almost overwhelming. Most don-blue lips, blueish bare feet and physically shook from the cold. The instructors went through their safety talk, then divided everyone, including other people not associated with the company, into three raft teams of six people each.

Kurt's raft captain introduced himself as John. They pushed-off heading towards their first rapid. John said it was a two-rated rapid which felt quite gentle. Within ten minutes the raft speed increased considerably as the water flowed wildly and the splashes of icy cold water hit occupants and pooled inside the raft. Everyone's feet and bodies became colder. The sun was gradually shining through the trees and started to warm their bodies, a welcomed relief.

They began to feel confident passing over two and three rated rapids when John said a five was coming up, so they paddled to the shore. The terrain was flat as they walked alongside the river. After 500 metres John told them to follow a steep path on the left side that led to a ridge about 30 metres above the rapids. Looking down they could see exposed rocks and the water swirling around each one as water passed down to more rocks. John explained, *'The quickest way down is to jump'*.

His instructions were, *'Walk to the edge, hold onto the life jacket with both hands, look for a safe place to land to avoid the rocks, then jump away from the cliff face. Hold your breath and go in feet first to break the water. The velocity of the jump will take you deep into the river. Stay relaxed because the life jacket will take you back to the surface. When you surface, lay on your back and use your legs and feet to push-off from the rocks'*. So much to remember Kurt thought.

He added, *'Or you can keep walking across the ledge and down the other side where we will all meet near the clearing'*.

The choice was up to each individual. Abby and two others did not hesitate and started walking toward the meeting place. Kurt stepped closer to the edge and looked down. He decided to be the first to jump, or he may change his mind. He held onto the life jacket, looked for where the pockets of water were between the rocks and jumped. Whilst the speed of the descent was an uncomfortable feeling hitting the water was sensational. The velocity must have taken him down four or five metres before he stopped for a matter of seconds, then catapulted to the surface. What a feeling! He floated on his back and regularly push away from rocks and boulders. This was relaxing and even surreal. The river flowed fast, so it did not take long to reach the meeting area. He looked back and saw two others in the group had jumped and were close behind.

The three days were filled with exhilarating emotions, overcoming challenges, learning about self and each other. Evenings were relaxed with people openly expressing their thoughts, fears and feelings. If there were any perceived relationship barriers, there were none now. Everyone got on well for months after the experience however, a new problem had surfaced.

Steve and Matt had not sold a single project and Patrick was not prepared to address their lack of performance. Both were close friends of Patrick. He thought introducing new products and services would solve the revenue problem, but these were incompatible with the company's strategic plan. This concerned Kurt, who spoke

> *To succeed in sales, requires commitment, determination, sales and sales strategy skills and a personable demeanour.*

openly about it to Patrick and gave notice to leave. Abby followed shortly after.

Salespeople who consistently do not meet sales targets tend to:
- Talk extensively about past sales in other companies
- What they are going to do
- What they are going to achieve
- Write lengthy sales reports in line with their excuses.

An Australian saying is: These are 'gunners' and 'goffers.' They are gunner do this, gunner do that, goffer this, and goffer that, and achieve nothing. This behaviour will continue for as long as management accept it. Management needed to find a suitable and different role in the organization for these people or terminate their employment. Sales is relatively easy to get into which could be a reason why so many people try sales. To succeed requires commitment, determination, sales and sales strategy skills and a personable demeanour. Not everyone is suited for a sales career, and for those not suited, they need to find a role that complements their personality and skills set.

Lessons learned

- Try the untried. You never know what you will learn from the experience.
- Do not avoid—in fact embrace—opportunities to step out of your comfort zone. The feelings of discomfort may be intense but will not be there for long.
- On the other side of a challenging experience, you are not the same person as you were before—you decided to get out of your comfort zone. You will have grown.
- If there is no real danger but you still feel fear, accept the fear and do it anyway. Overcoming fear can be liberating.
- Give encouragement to others who are in a state of fear, especially if you feel the same. Your empathy, while focussing on the other person, will dramatically reduce your own fears.
- Always stick to your values, even if others do not agree.

Chapter 10
The Australian Training Company

A ustralia at the time presented a major opportunity for a new approach to sales training and development. For decades, the content of sales training was generic and derived from American seminar speakers, books, audio and video product sources. Sales seminars were popular with large venues regularly booked out.

Sales techniques had a heavy emphasis on the multiple ways of overcoming sales objections and closing sales. It was far from being customer centric. An example was where one speaker advocated, '*When a customer says no, I am not interested, you need to say you do not mean N-O. You mean you need to K-N-O-W more*'. The two words no and know, were spelt slowly by the speaker, letter by letter to make a dramatic point.

The seminar speakers were dynamic and charismatic, leaving salespeople feeling exhilarated. The audience could hardly wait to put into action what they had learned.

Those who tried to apply the new skills, gave up in as few as two to three days, when the excitement wore off—as did their motivation. Salespeople reverted to the comfort of their previous selling habits, rejecting what they were taught. When asked why, '*It is not how we sell in my industry. It is high-pressure selling*'.

> *American-style sales techniques had an emphasis on overcoming sales objections and closing sales, and were not customer centric.*

The Australian Training Company was established to provide tailored in-house training in areas of sales, customer service, telephone, sales management, leadership, teamwork, and infield sales coaching. In addition, keynote presentations and structured training were combined to complement client sales conference objectives. The company's bi-line was 'Pioneers in Customized Training'. Course content was based on research, proven methodologies, and sound psychology.

Client projects were expected to be 6 to 12 months. A commitment was made not to work with a client's competitor for a period of two years after the project was completed. This was synergistic with the company's core values. As it turned out clients reciprocated through loyalty and did not use other providers. This commitment became a key point of difference for The Australian Training Company.

The keynote presentations, combined with structured training, worked well for clients. It enabled them to provide training in the one place for their whole sales team.

The Brick Manufacturer

This brick manufacturing company wanted to use their sales conference as an opportunity to launch a new promotion and upskill the customer service team. The offer was: when a new homeowner purchased bricks for their new build, they would receive pavers for their driveway at no charge. The company sought feedback from the customer service team and found they did not like the idea. In fact, they were critical.

The upcoming sales conference was in two weeks. Management had quite a problem to sort out in a short period of time. The Divisional General Manager, Stan Bukowskl considered cancelling the promotion, but decided to ask his Sales Manager, Mark Gelder to find a way forward.

Mark approached Kurt because he had previously completed sales training with Kurt while at another company. Mark, *'Could you do some digging and find the reason for the negative comments?'* He also wanted to know how the promotion could be revitalized for the sales conference.

Kurt interviewed individuals within the customer service team to understand their role and listened to their concerns. The team were defensive, *'Customers are not interested and will not be persuaded by free pavers'*.

Kurt, *'I understand. Do you mind my asking, would you feel comfortable and allow me to listen in when a customer comes into the showroom? It will give me a first-hand experience of what you are telling me'*. No-one objected in the slightest to the observation request.

After listening to four customer visits, a pattern was emerging, and it became obvious why customers were not interested. The customer service team shifted straight into talking about the paver promotion after briefly greeting customers with, *'Hello, good morning or good afternoon'*.

They did not:
- Give their name
- Ask for the customer's name as part of the introduction
- Develop rapport
- Ask questions.

Customers appeared overwhelmed, wary and by the look on their faces rejected the feeling of being 'sold to'.

The promotion had been introduced too early in the sales process. Customers reacted and pushed back with rebuttals, *'That's nice but...'* and, *'We'll think about it'*.

> **The customer service team attracted the rebuttals and were not aware they did.**

The customer service team attracted the rebuttals, were not aware they did, and felt frustrated. Understandably, they reacted critically when management asked about the promotion.

When no customers were in the showroom Kurt asked, *'Why do you think the last couple said they want to think about it?'* Response, *'I have no idea'*.

They could have asked customers, *'Do you have a plan of your new home? What builder will you be using? When do you intend to start building?'*

If the customer service team had used a 'pull' rather than a 'push' approach, interacting with customers by building rapport and asking questions, it would have led to their knowing:
- Personal details about the customer
- When and where the house was going to be built
- The type of brick and colour they want
- The name of the builder
- The plans of the new home.

It would then be appropriate to introduce the paver promotion, *'Your timing to select bricks for your new home is perfect. The reason I say that is we have a promotion until June 30 whereby you can receive pavers for your driveway at no charge. Let me show you the two styles we have available'*. Later injecting and leading toward a sale close, *'Which style do you think would suit the bricks you have chosen?'* If the timeframe of the build is imminent, *'Is it okay if I include the pavers with the bricks you like?'*

Kurt gave Mark a verbal summary and recommended:
- The sales conference proceed
- Demonstrate customer scenarios via live role plays

The Most Unlikely Salesperson

- Role plays presented by Kurt and one of the customer service team on stage
- Kurt to coach them to prepare for the event.

Mark enthusiastically embraced the recommendations and chose Lyall French for the role play. Lyall had been with the company four years and was liked by the team. The coaching covered the basics of how to approach a customer, qualifying questions to ask, handling rebuttals, sales objections and closing.

The difference between a rebuttal and a sales objection.

A rebuttal is attracted early in the sales process and often can be a reaction by a customer based on their past negative purchase experiences. This can be minimized by the way the salesperson approaches and begins the conversation.

Sales objections on the other hand, occur late in the sales process because the salesperson had not applied or poorly applied sales skills. In fact, they have attracted the sales objection.

A rebuttal or sales objection is not an obstacle to a sale when handled correctly. It is an opportunity to get the sales and buying process back on track.

The conference was held on the Central Coast of New South Wales, with 85 employees consisting of managers, salespeople, customer service and agents. Stan welcomed everyone and gave an overview of the conference, then introduced Kurt.

After outlining what they can expect, Kurt paused, '*I would like to ask for a volunteer to join me on stage to do a few role plays*'.

> *Audience body language can sometimes reflect negative attitude, 'You will never convince us this will work!'*

The audience dropped eye contact instantly and only five salespeople raised their hands including Lyall, who Kurt chose. The customer service team who were against the promotion, sat in a cluster with their arms folded and legs crossed at the ankles. Their body language reflected, '*You will never convince us this will work*'.

Kurt was conscious of their body language. He planned to alleviate their concerns when he introduced skills and attitudes, and ways of thinking—making their job easier and more enjoyable.

The conference moved at an energetic pace. Lyall and Kurt switched customer and salesperson roles effortlessly using examples the attendees could relate to. Lyall did an outstanding job applying the skills he and Kurt had practiced days earlier. Most importantly, everyone appeared to enjoy the experience. It was pleasing to see a change in the customer service team as they unfolded their arms, uncrossed their legs, and leaned forward in their chairs taking in what was being demonstrated.

On completion of the role plays, Lyall and Kurt invited the attendees to ask questions to uncover any sales variations from what was demonstrated or any concerns they might have.

Lyall was asked, *'How did you feel applying the skills?'* Response, *'At first, I felt uncomfortable but the more I practiced, the more it made sense. I did try qualifying questions and handling sales objections on real customers during the week, and found it really worked'*. Lyall's validation provided reassurance.

Kurt felt humbled that Lyall and he had turned around a customer service team mindset that could have cost the company a considerable loss of revenue and customers missing out on pavers. As Kurt left the stage, Stan came up to him shook his hand and expressed how pleased he was with the role plays and the attendees' reaction.

Kurt followed up with Mark a week later. The feedback was positive and resulted in sales training for the sales team.

The Electrical Wholesaler

The electrical wholesaler was a large five branch independent company in Sydney, New South Wales (NSW). The Managing Director was Peter Jenkins and the General Manager, Ken Johnson. One of the reasons for winning the business was they felt comfortable and trusted Kurt. He had worked in the industry for one of their suppliers, the electrical switchgear company. Peter was in his mid-fifties, an ex-chartered accountant and Keith, about the same age, had worked in the industry since leaving school.

Kurt started with the infield sales review. The review would disclose if there were any changes in the industry, competitor activity, understand the challenges faced by the sales team, and identify their sales competence level.

The company's major competitors were large national and international businesses that had an extensive network of branches throughout Australia. The bulk of the products sourced in the industry were from a limited number of manufacturers or agents.

The Most Unlikely Salesperson

These competitors dominated the industry and had two distinct advantages:
- Greater purchasing power provided superior supplier trading terms which in turn allowed them to sell products at a lower price point
- An extensive number of branch locations meant customers did not have to travel far for their supplies.

Since leaving the electrical switchgear company, Kurt noted there were several mergers between large competitors. There were more products procured from China. However, time didn't change the branch structure and the way the businesses operated—they were the same. Every outlet had a branch manager, a second in-charge, an external salesperson or two, and an internal team.

The internal team had people in the warehouse, counter sales, phone sales and a delivery driver. Anyone joining the industry started in the warehouse to ensure they became familiar with the extensive product range. If they showed potential, promotion was serving on the sales counter and then phone order sales. Employees were multiskilled and stepped into one or more roles as needed. Once an individual worked in a branch for several years and had a good track record, they were offered an external sales role. Success as an external salesperson provided an opportunity to become a branch manager. Like many industries, people move from company to company to pursue career advancement. The industry remained price sensitive and was highly competitive.

Peter had a salesperson based in each branch. His concern was poor sales, particularly one salesperson, Denis Rachofsky. Peter stated, '*If he does not show marked improvement, I am going to have to let him go*'.

Kurt started the infield sales review with Denis. He soon learned Denis was the youngest in the sales team at age 25. Denis looked anxious and was fidgety. Kurt reassured him, '*Denis, I look forward to our day together. I want to know there is nothing to be concerned about. Please do not change your routine. Do what you normally do. Ignore my presence during a sales call. Could I ask that you see me as your apprentice for the day? I am here to learn from you, the more I learn, the greater value I will be to you when we do the training*'.

'I am here to learn from you, the more I learn, the greater value I will be to you when we do the training'.

Although management provided reassurance as to why their salespeople will be spending a day each with a consultant, and whatever was discussed stays with the consultant, the sales team appeared to be apprehensive and fearful. Some showed their feelings openingly as Denis did, others try to hide it. Kurt was conscious of this, so

The Most Unlikely Salesperson

his aim was to create an environment whereby the salesperson felt comfortable and to be themselves.

Denis nodded in agreement, but it took several sales calls for him to start feeling relaxed. When he did, the conversation flowed effortlessly and centred around his monthly sales target and the concern for not achieving it.

By mid-morning they had met with a number of customers on building sites, when a customer rang Denis and said he needed cable and conduit urgently. Denis made a note of the items and Kurt assumed he would phone the branch and pass the order to an internal team member for processing. This was not the case. Denis reacted by abandoning his sales call plan and immediately returned to the branch, picked and packed the order and delivering it to the customer. This took an hour and a half. Kurt went along with it because he did encourage Denis to do what he normally does, and this was it. Kurt, *'Denis, how often does this happened?'* Response, *'All the time'*.

He discovered these customer phone calls were a regular occurrence for the whole sales team, and they reacted in the same manner. The reaction was an issue in itself, another was branch managers expected their salespeople to return and work in the branch when one of the team members was absent. Going back to the branch to process a customer order or to replace an absent team member was the cultural norm. It appeared any excuse was a valid reason for the salesperson to return to the branch.

No-one ever questioned the cost associated with these behaviours, nor did anyone look for an alternate. Using a courier for deliveries and a labour hire company when team shortages occurred would have been considerably less costly and dramatically increase the number of daily sales calls per salesperson and sales revenues.

Time with Denis was followed by Kurt accompanying the other salespeople on electrical contractor and industrial account sales calls. They were initially reserved as expected, but soon spoke openly about what they liked and disliked about their job, internal team concerns, improvements they thought were needed and competitor activity.

The sales team had not been through sales or customer service skills training. They relied solely on their product knowledge and years of industry experience. A common characteristic of the team was they left school at age 16 and started with the company as a junior employee. Kurt rated four salespeople at Level 2, and one Level 3.

Sales Competence Levels overview

Level 1: Beginner

- Limited sales related product, industry, and client knowledge
- Unaware of the requirements needed to succeed in external sales
- Lack understanding of client purchasing influences and the decision process
- Knowledge of sales and sales strategy is limited, usually what they have read or heard from other salespeople.

Level 2: Novice

- A degree of sales knowledge has been achieved through trial and error
- Lack understand of how skills are applied in a structured sales process
- Unaware as to why sales rebuttals, objections and sales related difficulties reoccur
- Inadequate knowledge of business development, account management, purchase influences and the decision-process.

Level 3: Disciplined

- Knowledgeable from attending sales seminars and sales courses throughout their career
- Knowledge of sales is often out of date
- Good personal relationships skills and know their clients well, but minimal knowledge of the client organization
- Limited sales strategies and tactics.

Level 4: Competent

- Consistent sales performers
- Business development skills
- Knowledge of the sales and buying process, client personal and organization
- Sales strategies and tactic skills but may need assistance or advice from senior management.

Level 5: High-Flyer

- Dramatically outsell peers
- Build rapport effortlessly
- Well informed of client decision processes and influencers that impact the buying process
- Thorough understanding of client personalities and the client organization.

Level 6: Professional[1]

- Ability to objectively critique sales meetings
- Comprehensive information on client personnel involved in the decision process
- Create a strategic sales approach that differs from competitors
- Practical application of the sales and buying process.

---

[1] Detailed description of the Sales Competence Levels is located on page 204.

He then moved onto interviewing the branch managers and the internal team. They were dedicated people who enjoyed working in the industry and like the sales team, had no prior sales and customer service training. To win business the emphasis was on discounting.

A week after completing the infield sales review, Kurt met with Peter and Ken to present his findings and recommendations. Ken was friendly and easy to get along with, whilst Peter was analytical and methodical. He took his time reading the report, questioning the content on one page, then flipped pages to ask how it related to a statement made on a different page. The presentation was expected to take 45 minutes. It took just under an hour and a half.

Sales success was limited because winning business was reliant on discounts not sales skills or sales strategy.

The recommendations covered three main areas:
- **Career paths**: internal personnel are not to be promoted automatically to an external sales role unless they want to and demonstrate the necessary attributes.
  - Suitable induction and sales training needs to be provided.
  - If the person chose to remain in an internal role with the aim of becoming a branch manager avoiding the salesperson role, then that needs to be an acceptable career path.
  - Appropriate management skills training needs to be provided.
- **Personnel back-up**: appoint an internal back-up person for every branch salesperson, preferably someone senior like the second-in-charge of the branch who can delegate tasks. This will allow the salesperson to spend more time in front of customers and potential customers.
  - Change the focus to uncover new account opportunities and grow existing account customers.
- **Skill and development training**: a comprehensive sales and customer service training and development programme.

Peter looked very serious as he read through the last page of the report that outlined the timeframe and the cost of implementation. He looked up and said, '*When can you start?*' They agreed on a date and the following week Kurt started preparing the sales and customer service course content.

Structured classroom-style sales training had to be after business hours. The schedule was four hours from 5-9:00pm in the evening. Training for the branch managers and employees followed. Infield sales coaching for the sales team was one week after completing the basic training.

Business development skills was a top priority. Fortunately, few customers required a phone call to arrange a meeting. This meant salespeople could walk into a customer's building site or premises without prior notice.

Chris Tregear was the first person on the list to be coached. Based on Kurt's infield sales review experience, Chris was not suited for an external sales role. He had a great track record working within the branch taking phone orders, working the sales counter and stock purchasing. Peter rang Kurt several days before he met with Chris and expressed his concerns that he had not created a new customer account in three months. Peter was relieved when Kurt told him they would be concentrating on business development for the first coaching session.

Kurt met Chris at his branch, then drove to Sydney's Kings Cross. They arrived at 8:30 in the morning. Chris became increasingly distressed as they walked toward their first sales call. Numerous attempts to relax him had failed, so Kurt suggested they have coffee. As Chris was about to take his first sip, Kurt offered to do as many sales calls as needed for him to feel comfortable before attempting a new sales call himself. The look on Chris's face was outright relief.

They spoke about sales call protocols because there would be two of them and one customer. They discussed sales call objectives and the sales process. This was in line with what Chris had learned in the classroom. The first call was the Westfield Tower Building. They walked in and saw a security guard behind the desk. Kurt asked for the person responsible for the electrical maintenance of the building. The security guard looked at a list of contacts and said it was Bill Holmes the Electrical Maintenance Engineer. He then asked for their names and the company they represented. Chris and Kurt signed the visitor's book and were given name badges. The security guard phoned Bill and asked Chris and Kurt to stand near a side elevator door. The doors opened and Bill walked out. Kurt introduced Chris and himself and asked if he had an office they could go to? They stepped into the elevator and headed for the basement where building maintenance was located. On their way down Kurt engaged Bill in small talk.

> *To hear the word, 'No' or 'No thanks' is a form of rejection and counterproductive to the sales relationship.*

When they arrived, Bill offered them a cup of tea which they accepted. Kurt had spoken to Chris previously to always accept the offer of a beverage. It is polite and integral to social norms when welcoming a guest. If he did not feel like drinking tea or coffee, then ask for a glass of water. To hear the word, *'No'* or *'No thanks'* is a form of rejection and counterproductive to the relationship.

The conversation flowed as Bill spoke about his family, interests and answered questions about his job, the challenges and the stock he keeps on site. The timing was right to start asking business related questions. Kurt, *'Bill, do you mind telling us who your current electrical wholesaler is?'* It was one of the large national competitors.

> *Asking to be a back-up supplier is a soft approach and one prospects are open to.*

Kurt, *'Would you be open to consider having a back-up supplier?'* Bill responded by nodding his head. Kurt, *'It would give you an opportunity to compare service levels'*. Again, Bill nodded to agree.

Asking to be a back-up supplier is a soft approach and one prospects are open to. It is impossible for a wholesaler to have stock available on every product. The stock product range is in the thousands. Having a back-up supplier makes prudent sense and shows respect for the prospect's current supplier relationship.

Kurt, *'Would you like to know the speciality lines we stock that could be of interest?'* Bill, *'Yes, I would because I am having trouble finding a particular light fitting'*.

Kurt showed Bill the electrical wholesaler's visual aid brochure that outlined the company's history, product categories and let him know the branch was only two suburbs away. This meant he could easily access stock when needed. Chris was prewarned and knew at this point in the sales process Kurt would hand over control over to him. Kurt, *'Bill, I'll ask Chris to take it from here because he is the expert in lighting'*.

Chris witnessed the sales process from the time they walked in the building and spoke to Bill, through to the presentation stage when he took over. What he learned in the classroom Chris witnessed being applied in a real-world sales environment. The outcome of the sales call was Bill opened an account and placed a small order including the light fitting he wanted. This was a new account customer, and one Chris continued to grow the relationship and sales.

They left the building and headed up the street and sat on a bench to discuss the sales call. Kurt noticed a huge smile on Chris's face. Kurt, *'Chris, you look very pleased with yourself'*. His head was down as he nodded and continued to have a smile on his face. It was as if Chris was reflecting on the sales call. Kurt, *'Let's begin by recapping our sales call objective'*.

Sales call objectives are at their most effective when only one to three are set per sales call.

Chris and Kurt had spoken about possible objectives earlier that morning. To begin experiencing the link between setting the objective and the sales outcome, they kept it to one objective, to identify the person with the authority to purchase. In this case, Bill was the person, and the objective was achieved—a new customer account opened and an order were bonuses. Sales call objectives are most effective when set at one to three objectives per sales call.

Kurt used a writing pad to outline the sales process and to reinforce the skills Chris had competently applied. At this point, those Chris did not apply, Kurt left out. As he wrote notes and spoke about the sales process, Chris repeatedly interrupted. Chris, *'Yes but...'* This was followed by telling Kurt what he did wrong.

Being self-critical and interrupting at this stage of the coaching is common for salespeople who are perfectionists and driven to a high standard of sales performance. Chris was too hard on himself by not acknowledging what he did well. This had to change.

Kurt, *'Chris I appreciate where you are coming from, but could I ask that you set those thoughts to one side, just for now?'* He agreed, and Kurt was able to continue with the feedback on what was applied competently. Kurt, *'Do you agree with the summary of the sales call and what you did well?'* Chris, *'Yes'*. Kurt, *'Is there anything you would like to add that you did competently?'* Chris, *'No'*.

Chris paused, *'It makes sense what you just went through'*. Kurt, *'That's great Chris. Now, if you had the opportunity to do the sales call again what would you do differently? I would like you to give a critique on what you did well, and any skill you would like to have applied differently. Start from the time you took over the sales call'*.

The question required Chris to think logically, recall the sales process and how he applied his skills. This was the first time he had experienced sales coaching, and being a perfectionist, his self-critique weighed heavily on what he believed he did poorly or had missed. He soon learned to give Kurt a balanced assessment.

To be meaningful, performance self-evaluations need to be balanced and objective focused.

When he began, he was nervous, but soon sounded confident as he proceeded with his self-critique. The repetition reinforced his learning and had a positive impact. Kurt complemented Chris on his self-critique and recapped what he had stated to again reinforce the learning. Chris expressed concern about his nervousness. Kurt said it was natural and part of our 'fight-flight-freeze' response.

They discussed the side effects of nervousness that can include sweaty palms, jittery-vocal tone and shaking. Kurt suggested not to be concerned and to try some exercises that might help him. For example, slow deep breathing to calm himself, and redirect the focus from himself to what he could do for a prospect. They finished on a positive note and their attention was now firmly on the next sales call and a new set of objectives.

They went into several adjoining buildings, but the maintenance engineers or electricians were not on the premises. Chris received a phone call and had to attend an urgent personal matter. The day together was cut short, and they rescheduled another day the following week.

They met at the western end of Talavera Road, North Ryde, north-west Sydney. The street appeared to be a kilometre long with large commercial office buildings either side. This was an ideal environment for Chris to continue expanding his business development skills.

The Most Unlikely Salesperson

Walking door-to-door was considered old fashioned and would intimidate many salespeople. However, it is the most effective way to increase the number of face-to-face sales calls, and an appropriate strategy to meet trades people. Chris looked anxious and asked Kurt if he would do the first few sales calls. He responded by saying he would do as many sales calls as it took until Chris felt comfortable and had a go himself. Chris appeared relieved.

They walked into the first building and headed to the reception desk. The receptionist wore her name badge making is easy for Kurt to do the introduction. Kurt, *'Good morning, Sue. My name is Kurt Newman and this is Chris Tregear. Could you help us out? Who would be the person responsible for the maintenance of the building?'* Sue responded, *'The building is contracted to a property maintenance company'*.

Kurt noticed a small stack of 'with compliments slips' on the right-hand side of Sue. Kurt, *'Would you mind writing the name of the company on one of the 'with compliment slips' and if possible, the person we would need to contact?'* Sue wrote the information and gave it to him. Kurt, *'Thank you Sue, greatly appreciated, and have a wonderful day'*.

Every building Chris and Kurt walked into had their maintenance contracted to an external company. Leads were growing rapidly. After 1½ hours they decided to have a break at a nearby café. Kurt asked Chris if he would like to do the next sales call, he agreed.

It took several approaches before Chris got into the rhythm and it was gratifying to see his confidence grow. Their time together resulted in 32 names and phone numbers for Chris to follow-up and arrange meetings.

The next month Chris created a company sales record for the greatest number of new customer accounts. He did two years in external sales and then become a branch manager—a role Kurt believed he was better suited to.

During one of the follow-up meetings Peter informed Kurt, a competitor and one of the national wholesalers were cutting costs. Reducing costs was nothing new to the industry, but the way this was done could be to Peter's advantage.

The cost-saving strategy Peter presented had two components:

- The first was to take a company vehicle away from every salesperson and change their role to internal sales. This would be a regressive career step for the salespeople.
- The second was a selected number of salespeople would be promoted to branch manager. Branch managers were expected to take on the additional role of external sales because they had a company vehicle.

The Most Unlikely Salesperson

Kurt expected Peter to be excited about the strategic advantage this created for his business, but he could not see it as yet. Kurt responded to Peter's approach by addressing some of the possible challenges the competitor would have, *'Branch managers are swamped with operations and administration tasks and what I have discovered, they do not like to work external sales. This means there is a high probability their customers will feel neglected due to less or no visits from the branch manager. It will be safe to assume branch managers and salespeople will feel demotivated and some may end up leaving. Employee morale and productivity will be affected. I would suggest your sales team double their efforts and spend more time meeting with prospective customers. This is a great differentiator for your business'.*

Peter had his usual reserved and serious look, then sat back in his chair and smiled. Kurt continued, *'Peter, to widen the differentiation gap, from your customer's perspective, I would recommend you go on joint sales calls with every salesperson in your team'.* Based on his reserved manner, Kurt knew he would feel uncomfortable doing this, but it was the right strategy.

Kurt, *'Your role will be supportive, and it will provide you with the opportunity to understand your key customers' businesses and get to know them personally. Your competitor CEO's and managing directors do not take the time to meet with customers on sales calls. Can you imagine how your customers will feel when they meet you in person?'* Peter listened intently as he absorbed what Kurt said then nodded affirmatively. Kurt, *'Peter, will you do it?'* He reacted with a quick, *'Yes'.*

Kurt worked closely with the sales team for the next six months. The competitors' account management dropped-off significantly, resulting in their customers switching to Peter's company. Within

> *Cost-cutting applied prudently can create greater efficiencies, but this was outright foolish.*

months customers openly stated they did not recall the last time they saw a salesperson from the national wholesaler. When good account management falls away, so do customers.

Cost-cutting applied prudently can create greater efficiencies, but this was outright foolish. Peter's competitor reduced costs quickly by selling-off a company vehicle from every branch. Their management did not think of the ramifications of their decision:

- What effect would the decision have on morale and productivity in each branch?

The Most Unlikely Salesperson

- How many salespeople and branch managers would leave? Competent people tend to be the first to resign.
- Would a drop in account management be anticipated? If so, how many accounts would be affected or lost?
- Would a drop in sales be anticipated? If so by how much?
- Is this a good strategy?

> Too often companies make decisions that result in reduced revenues. There have been numerous cases where management retrenched their salespeople, but keep the same number of personnel in administration, human resources, and operations roles. It does not make sense to keep the same number of support personnel yet retrench those who produce the revenue.

The national wholesaler was eventually sold. Sales growth for Peter's company had always been in the single digits, but by taking advantage of the competitor's cost-cutting decision, revenues increased by 20 percent.

The good news about Denis is he did turnaround his sales career and 18 months later became a branch manager. Kurt did numerous projects for Peter over the next decade.

The Shipping Industry

Kurt was one of two speakers at a breakfast function attended by 30 managers. He met Nick Fisher, the Australian Operations Manager for one of the world's largest container shipping companies.

During the coffee break they spoke and hit it off instantly. There was a feeling of mutual alignment and respect. Kurt discovered Nick had a similar background in the Royal Australian Navy. Nick had been in the British Royal Navy and transferred to the Royal Australian Navy during the latter part of his naval career. He served as a lieutenant on HMAS Otway submarine. He stood 195cm and was married with three children.

Kurt asked if Nick's employer, the shipping container company, did sales training. He replied they recently hired a firm, and the course was on the weekend. Kurt, *'That's okay Nick. Would you mind if I call you next week to ask what you thought of the course?'* Nick, *'That would be fine'*. Kurt, *'If you are perfectly happy with the experience, then keep using their services but if not, let's talk'*. Nick agreed.

126 Chapter 10 The Australian Training Company

Kurt called the following week to ask how the training had turnout. Nick, '*It was disappointing. The trainer did not stay after the session, he just left*'.

The company Nick had used was a mid-sized consulting firm that use sub-contractors, and the person who did the training appeared to lack the care-factor so important in nurturing a client relationship. Listening to Nick, the sales course had not been tailored and was a standard off-the-shelf programme.

Kurt, '*Would you be interested to meet?*' Nick, '*Yes. How about next week*'.

Nick was not responsible for sales, but he was part of the Australian senior management team and aware of current organizational risks and opportunities. Kurt wanted to meet Nick's management colleagues and the chief executive officer to ask how they felt about the recent sales training. If the feeling was the same as Nick, there was the chance of securing a new client.

In a business-to-business setting it is common for multiple people to be involved in the decision process and the selling/buying cycle to be long. This is when strategic sales skills are needed to navigate what is now a complex sale.

> *In a business-to-business setting it is common for multiple people to be involved in the decision process and the selling/buying cycle to be long.*

Challenges during the early stages of a complex sale:

- Your organization is not known by the prospective client
- Your product or service requires a substantial financial outlay
- There has been no allocation of funds or planned budget
- Executive and senior people from different departments are involved in the decision process.

Kurt faced all four challenges with the shipping container company, but the mutual trust and respect he and Nick had developed could shorten the complex sales process. Creating trust means being genuine, be yourself, and there is no difference from cultivating a friendship. Trust can be the difference between a client proceeding with one salesperson's proposal and rejecting another.

Trust can be earned by demonstrating the following traits:

- **Competence**: knowledge, skills, and attributes to stand out from competitors. A comprehensive understanding of a client's business and knowledge of key personnel.
- **Credibility**: honesty and integrity. Stick to what is right for the client and not be swayed by what they want to hear. Base decisions on the client's perspective and not your perspective.
- **Reliability**: consistent actions. Ensuring what you say and do has the client's interest at heart.
- **Personal**: you show your real self, and the client feels comfortable in your presence. Any tension is defused with humour.
- **Selfless**: the focus is on achieving client outcomes and doing what is right, even if it means not securing the sale.
- **Independent Thinker**: you have the strength of character to express your opinion, even if the client is likely to disagree. Ask questions that allow the client to reflect and consider an impending decision.

These traits have been at the centre of how Kurt operates to this today. If you focus exclusively on getting the sale or the commissions, you will not create sustainable long-term relationships. Being motivated by greed will drive you to unacceptable behaviour. You may do well financially in the short term, however you will need to change jobs regularly when colleagues and clients discover who you really are.

Multiple barriers can be experienced when trying to arrange a meeting with the executive level management—the Chief Executive Officer, Chief Financial Officer or Chief Information Officer.

The barriers can be:

- An overly protective assistant who is the blocker preventing the appointment
- Delays because the executive is in meetings, interstate or overseas
- The executive is too busy to answer their phone or respond to emails.

Kurt intended to ask Nick for an introduction and avoid these setbacks. He had to strategically manage the impending complex sale to reduce the time of the selling cycle.

So what is a Complex Sale? It is a sales environment where many people referred to as stakeholders are involved in the decision process. It is not unusual for the selling/buying cycle to take months and sometimes years due to varying factors including but not limited to budgets, external delays and different agendas that motivate stakeholder self-interest. This process can become quite complex hence the term complex sale. Selling skills alone will not suffice. To understand this selling environment, think of a game of baseball. There are four bases and the pitcher. Depending of the role of one or more stakeholders play directly or indirectly in the decision process, they are allocated one or more bases. The pitcher is the metaphor for you the salesperson.

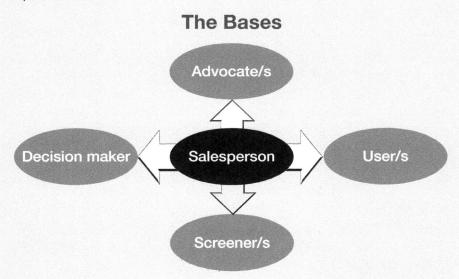

A salesperson's initial connection with a prospective client is usually the Screener. The preferred strategy is to develop an Advocate/s. They have influence and credibility with the stakeholders on the other bases and can identify them for you. This can significantly reduce the time of the selling/buying cycle.

The complex sale

Unless strategically managed, the selling cycle time of a complex sale can become unacceptably longer than the norm—risking the sales opportunity. In fact, progress can stall when the decision maker needs to get others involved in the organization. This can be professional courtesy or when the decision impacts a direct report's area of responsibility. If the decision maker were to proceed without consulting those affected by the decision, there is a high risk of direct or covert push back during the implementation of the product or service.

A logical first step in strategic sales is every stakeholder in the client organization who has influence and involved in the decision process needs to be identified.

A common mistake salespeople make when dealing with stakeholders:

- Not identifying all the stakeholders involved in the decision process
- Not contacting or interviewing every stakeholder
- Choosing a stakeholder based on their title
- Not qualifying stakeholders
- Assuming one stakeholder has the authority to confirm the proposal
- Targeting only the financial decision maker
- Investing time with a stakeholder who has no or limited influence.

As stakeholders are identified they are assigned to one of four bases. Each base has a role criteria, therefore stakeholder titles are irrelevant. If titles were used as the criteria, there is a high risk of failure because stakeholders in different organizations can have the same title, but different levels of authority. Stakeholders who meet the same role criteria share the same base. During tough economic times—perceived or real—stakeholders tend to increase in numbers that can substantially increase the time decisions are made.

Base roles and criteria overview:

- **Financial decision maker:** has the power to give final approval and are responsible for the impact of a decision on the organization. They can redirect internal funds from one allocation to another.
- **Screener**: often more than one stakeholder who share the task of assessing a product or service proposal to ensure it matches the organization's purchase criteria. Screeners can influence the financial decision maker, but they cannot give final approval.
- **Advocate**: has influence and creditability across all stakeholders within the organization. They firmly believe the problem the organization has can be solved by the salesperson's company. The advocate is a stakeholder who may have had previous experience with you, the product, service and the company. They like, trust and believe in you, and will guide you through the buying process.
- **User**: are stakeholders who will be directly involved with the product or service on a day-to-day basis. Their evaluation of a proposal is subjective. They can be a valuable source of information about the specific problem.

Nick was one of the screeners, and Kurt also wanted him to be his advocate. Kurt, *'Nick you are part of a huge organization. Could I ask that you advise and introduce me to the people who would be involved in the decision process?'* Nick, *'The CEO is Henrik Sorensen who I report to, and he would make the decision. Jeremy Stanton is the CFO and Bob Bellinger is the National Sales Manager. I will arrange a meeting'.*

Financial Decision Maker

The stakeholder on this base makes the definitive yes or no decision, even if other stakeholders disagree with the decision. The financial decision maker can be difficult to meet in person and they tend to rely on and are influenced by other stakeholders. Their preference is to review two proposals before making a final decision. When presenting to a board or a management committee it can appear there are multiple financial decision makers.

However, there is always only one, even in business partnerships. The difference can be a partner's job responsibilities or a dominant personality.

The financial decision maker:

– Gives final approval
– Is responsible for the bottom line
– Can redirect funds from one allocated source to another
– Can overrule the recommendations of other stakeholders
– Is responsible for the impact of the decision on the organization
– Needs to be found early in the selling/buying cycle
– Responds to knowing how a product or service will create financial gain or savings for the organization.

Screener

It is not unusual to meet with one or more screeners during the first sales meeting. Screeners prefer non-generic proposals that are aligned with the organization's purchase criteria. They can have an impressive title, well-appointed office and hold a senior position. These representations can create the impression the screener has the authority to make a final decision. To make sure a clear distinction between a screener and a financial decision maker qualifying questions need to asked.

Screeners can:
- Provide details of the organization's problem or goal ambitions
- Recommend a proposal to the financial decision maker
- Block the progress of a sales opportunity
- Give the impression they are the financial decision maker
- Continue to reorder or purchase in a limited capacity after the initial sale.

Screeners become receptive when:
- The advocate has provided relevant information to you prior to the sales meeting
- You have been introduced by the advocate
- The organization's problem or goal ambitions are clearly understood
- Their expectations and measurements of evaluation have been agreed
- You are prepared to negotiate, if necessary.

Advocate

Advocates are able to:
- Outline the full extent of the organization's problems or goal aspirations
- Introduce you to other stakeholders
- Provide background information on every stakeholder
- Advise how to overcome barriers
- Hold additional stakeholder roles.

An advocate is not an advocate unless they are asked and agree to the role.

The ideal advocate:
- Has influence and creditability with other stakeholders
- Sincerely wants to help you
- Relationship is built on mutual trust and respect
- Has experienced the product or service and believes your company can solve the organization's problem or help them achieve their goal aspirations.

Advocates can be found in:
- Prospective client organizations
- Existing client organizations
- Your company
- Third-party organizations.

> When the advocate role for a sales opportunity is one of the first to be confirmed, information and influence begins to expand. This has a direct impact on reducing the time of the selling/buying cycle.
>
> An advocate's motivation is not driven by status, or public recognition but personal conviction, satisfaction, achievement, and goodwill for having introduced you and your company to solve the problem.

Nick had the ability to advise Kurt on any of the above as an advocate. Although Nick had not experienced Kurt's sales training services, he believed he would be able to improve the company's sales performance.

Kurt could have approached an additional advocate from a small list he developed, but the relationship with Nick, his knowledge and influence made it unnecessary. Nick was the perfect advocate.

The list was created by reaching out to clients, past clients and contacts where solid personal and business relationships had been established. An advocate is not an advocate unless they are asked and agree to the role. When Kurt needed an advocate, he contacts them individually and asks them to be his advocate, coach or advisor to describe the role. This is provided they meet the criteria as previously outlined.

User

Stakeholders in this role are numerous and hold a technical, support or front-line position in the organization. Users are a valuable source of information and can provide you with detailed operation or application issues that can significantly add to shaping a proposal.

Never underestimate the users' influence.

User evaluations of a proposal is subjective because they will be directly involved with the product or service. Their feedback is sort after by screeners and the financial decision maker.

Salespeople who minimize the importance of users or try to oversell them risk having their proposal rejected by screeners. Their influence is never to be underestimated.

Interacting with a user:

– Seek their opinion, ask to be shown and actively listen to create mutual respect and emotional buy-in

> - Discuss the product or service in a relaxed manner and not overly formalized. They will be inclined to provide other stakeholders with positive feedback
> - Be informative. Provide examples or case studies showing how the problem or service solved a similar problem. Demonstrate how their job will become easier, less stressful or enjoyable.

Arranging to meet the financial decision maker can be time-consuming especially in large organizations. Video conferencing may shorten the timeframe, however the greatest impact is in-person and particularly important during the first meeting. Video conferencing cannot create the same level of influence because it is two dimensional and many non-verbal cues are missed.

Fortunately for Kurt, Nick offered to arrange a meeting with the CEO Henrik Sorensen, the financial decision maker. The other stakeholders were the CFO Jeremy Stanton, a screener, and the National Sales Manager Bob Bellinger, another screener as well as a user. Nick informed Kurt about the industry, competitors, culture and core issues. The information was vital input to tailor the proposal.

> When a presentation is given to a management team or a board of directors, they want to discuss the proposal after the salesperson has left. 90 percent of major purchase decisions in complex sales are made without the salesperson being present. Therefore, it is crucial for relationships to be developed based on trust and mutual respect, between you and every stakeholder, prior to the formal presentation. This preparation allows you to identify stakeholders who are blatantly or covertly influencing other stakeholders to vote against the proposal.
>
> Once an obstructor has been identified:
>
> - Meet them in person and ask questions in a non-confrontational manner to uncover their concerns
> - Ask a senior screener or advocate to speak to them on your behalf.
>
> If a stakeholder has concealed their intention to vote against the proposal and does so during the management or board meeting, the greatest defender is the advocate. Having developed several advocates per sales opportunity will strengthen your position.

> An advocate can be on their allocated base, a combined advocate/screener, advocate/user and advocate/financial decision maker—the latter being the most powerful for you. Other stakeholders can be on base combinations or three roles.
>
> An advocate may not be able to change a stakeholder's perspective, but they can neutralize the extent of the impact on the acceptance and confirmation of your proposal.

Nick introduced Kurt to Henrik, a slim looking person in his late fifties. He was friendly but had a serious presence. The small talk did not last long before Henrik got down to business. Henrik, *'What do you know about the shipping industry?'* Kurt, *'Nothing, but I learn fast'*.

Henrik smiled then noticed Bob walk passed the office and called him in, *'Have you got some time to educate Kurt on the shipping industry?'* Bob, *'I have an hour'*. Bob and Kurt headed for an available conference room. Bob began explaining, *'There are two size containers, a 20 foot and a 40 foot'*.

This was the beginning of a comprehensive outline adding to the information Nick had already given Kurt. Bob did a great job covering the industry, company and several major competitors. Kurt asked Bob about himself and learned he had been with the company for a relatively short time, however he had years of shipping experience, jogged daily to keep fit and had a relaxed manner.

When the lesson was over Kurt thanked Bob, then headed back to Henrik's office. Kurt walked in unannounced, Henrik said nothing but extended his arm with open palm offering Kurt a chair. His office was impressively large, comfortably positioning his oversized desk, filing cabinets, a three-seater lounge and two sizable armchairs. Everything appeared in new condition and spotlessly clean. Henrik's desk had a laptop and a few pieces of paper on it. That was it. Sitting behind his desk Henrik projected confidence and control.

Kurt, *'Henrik, thank you for the opportunity to learn about your company and the industry'*. Kurt sensed, from the previous meeting with Henrik, he needed to keep interactions concise and business focussed. Asking personal questions or about the previous and unsatisfactory sales course would have been a waste of time and potentially annoyed him.

Henrik, *'Tell me about The Australian Training Company services'*. To answer his question, Kurt provided a helicopter view of the services with the expectation Henrik would zero in on what caught his interest. It worked. He instantly responded to the infield sales review, but his vocal tone

The Most Unlikely Salesperson

sounded somewhat concerned. Henrik, *'If I let you go out with my salespeople, how will they and our customers react to you?'*

The question was asked in the first-person indicating Henrik had emotionally bought into using the service. This more than likely was a subconscious reaction. If the question were framed in the third person 'How do salespeople and customers react to you?' This would have been logical, and one step removed.

Kurt, *'I appreciate your question Henrik. The process would begin by Bob informing the sales team I will be accompanying them on sales calls and explain the reason for it. Shortly after that, I would contact every salesperson to arrange a mutual day and time'*. Kurt continued, *'Prior to the first sales call, I will spend time to get to know every salesperson, explain why I am with them, and suggest they see me as their apprentice, so they know they are in control. My role in front of customers is passive, meaning I do not get involved in the sales process. If a customer asks me a question, I will answer briefly, and then look to the salesperson to take back control. I do not give coaching advice after the sales call, although I do get asked this often by keen salespeople'*.

Henrik leaned forward and nodded as if to reflect on what Kurt had said. A slight pause before Kurt continued, *'Henrik, my core focus is to understand your salespeople's world and identify their level of sales competence. I can only achieve this by creating a safe environment where your salespeople and your customers feel comfortable in'*.

Kurt paused again then asked, *'How do you feel about what I have said?'* By asking a client how they feel, not what they think, the response tends to be the truth. By asking what they think does not necessarily reveal the truth.

Henrik looked deadpan, *'Can you give me a proposal?'* A great question that can lead to concluding the interview, but Kurt did not have enough information. Kurt, *'The short answer is yes, but I need to ask some questions, if that is okay?'* Henrik, *'What did you want to know?'*

> **By asking a client how they feel, not what they think, the response tends to be the truth.**

Kurt asked a series of questions, *'How many salespeople are in each state? What outcomes do you expect? What is your budget? When did you envisage starting?'*

Henrik, *'We have 20 in the national sales team. Most are in Sydney and Melbourne. A report on the sales team. We have spent our training budget, so funds will need to come from another source. Start as soon as possible'*.

His answers were quick and direct. Henrik did not want a report on every salesperson. The plan was to assess the mean sales competence level of eight salespeople ranging from the best to the worst performers. Kurt informed Henrik he did not want management's assessment of the salespeople—allowing him to remain objective. He only wanted their names, mobile numbers and location.

Before Kurt left the meeting, they agreed on a day and time for the presentation of the proposal. Locking this in saves time and provides a timeline for the proposal to be completed. They shook hands and on his way-out Kurt asked, *'By the way Henrik, will anyone else be at our meeting?'* Henrik replied, *'Nick, Jeremy and Bob'*.

The meeting

Kurt arrived at The Shipping Container Company ten minutes before the appointment and approached the reception desk. Kurt, *'Good morning. Kurt Newman from The Australian Training Company for Henrik Sorensen'*.

He handed over one of his business cards. By providing his first and last name, the name of the company, and the first and last name of the person Kurt wants to see—projects confidence. It avoids being asked 'Does he know you?' and 'What is this concerning?'

Within minutes Henrik's secretary, Margaret Stilton came and introduced herself to Kurt. Margaret appeared to be in her late twenties, a professional persona and projected maturity beyond her years. Margaret walked into Henrik's office with Kurt and within seconds of arriving he asked her to notify the managers of the meeting. Kurt greeted Henrik and sat on the lounge chair directly opposite him. He had five copies of the proposal prepared including one for himself.

As they waited for the managers, Kurt took the opportunity to get to know Henrik. Kurt, *'Do you mind if I ask how long you have been with the company?'* Henrik, *'28 years'*.

Being conscious of how task focussed Henrik was, Kurt wanted to see his reaction if he continued to ask questions of a personal nature. Surprisingly, he opened up and told him he was a keen tennis player, liked soccer and enjoyed going to the opera. That was it. He then politely smiled, raised his right hand as if to give a stop signal.

Henrik, *'Show me your proposal'*. At that moment the managers were heard talking as they walked along the corridor. Kurt, *'Okay, but the managers will be here any minute'*. Henrik, *'Do not worry about them'*.

He pointed to the five proposals stacked on the coffee table that was between them. Kurt grabbed a copy and to stall for time, he turned the proposal around so Henrik could easily read it, opened the first page, and using a pen Kurt drew his attention to the first heading. He could feel

The Most Unlikely Salesperson

Henrik's impatience and expected a reaction. Henrik gestured for Kurt to hand over the document.

Kurt had pushed the boundaries far enough and did not want to jeopardize the relationship, so he gave him the proposal document. Henrik scanned through the pages in a matter of seconds, looked at the last page that outlined the fee structure, then closed the document as the managers entered his office. Henrik did not let on what he was thinking. His face was a blank canvas.

The managers sat down, and introductions were made by Henrik as Margaret came in asking if anyone wanted tea or coffee? Beverages were ordered and light-hearted conversations flowed effortless. Margaret returned with a tray of teas, coffees and an assortment of biscuits. Kurt handed every manager a personalized copy of the proposal. Kurt, *'If acceptable to everyone, I will step you through the proposal and answer any questions you might have, but first, let me give you an overview'*.

He had their undivided attention with four pair of eyes waiting for what was next. Every manager's proposal was closed. Kurt stated the objectives of the report. He had memorized and quoted the most critical findings he believed prevented better sales performance. He then outlined the recommendations.

He spoke in an animated-vocal tone to keep their attention. At the conclusion of his overview, he suggested they look through the report and if they had any questions to ask. He remained silent whilst they worked their way through the document. Henrik sat back quietly and looked at Kurt from time to time and did not let on what he was thinking or how he felt.

He had made up his mind, yet seconds before, it was impossible to read what he might do.

Jeremy, *'I think it is expensive'*. Kurt nodded to acknowledge he had heard Jeremy and considered one of two options to respond. One was to ask what he was comparing the fee to, and the other was to break the cost down to the smallest unit being a dollar amount per salesperson per day. Jeremy being the CFO, Kurt chose the second option, and was about to go through the numbers when Henrik interjected. Henrik, *'When can you start?'*

The timing of his question was unexpected, but task focussed financial decision makers process information rapidly and follow through quickly. Henrik had made up his mind, yet seconds before, it was impossible to read what he might do. The managers appeared comfortable with Henrik's decision.

The Most Unlikely Salesperson

Kurt had pre-planned several available dates to start the project and offered these to Henrik, who chose the first one. He thanked Henrik and said he looked forward to working with him and his team. The managers stood up and started to leave, and Kurt packed his things preparing to follow. Henrik, *'Kurt, I would like you to stay and meet the New South Wales Sales Manager Ross Hanlon. He will select the salespeople for the infield sales review'*. Kurt met Ross whose workstation was only metres from Henrik's office.

Ross was in his mid-forties and had been in sales and the shipping industry for his entire career. On a personal level, Kurt discovered they were fairly close neighbours only living a suburb apart. Ross was married and had two schnauzer dogs. He organized salespeople in Sydney and Melbourne. He asked them to arrange account management and business development sales meetings. This was so Kurt could assess sales competencies in both sales environments.

On completion of the infield sales review, a common cultural thread was every salesperson projected confidence, were intelligent, friendly and career-driven, particularly those who were under 30 years of age. The mean sales competence level[1] was three. The business operated in an extremely competitive market. Competitors regularly undercut rates as a way of gaining new customers.

Kurt contacted Margaret and arranged a meeting with Henrik to present the findings and recommendations. Knowing how he preferred to operate, Kurt began by providing a brief verbal overview and then handed him the report. He remained silent while Henrik scanned through the report. Henrik looked up leaving the fee structure page open, *'When can you start?'*

The infield sales review was the beginning of a five-year working relationship with Henrik and his Australian based organization. During this time, Kurt did projects in sales, customer service, operations, administration, and team building in the Blue Mountains of NSW.

Henrik was an astute individual and an experienced successful executive, but he was impatient and tended to be non-verbal—a common trait of highly task focussed individuals.

The following are two examples of how Henrik modified his behaviour to improve his connection with employees:

Example 1: Henrik was well respected. However, during the training sessions with the operations and administration teams, Kurt was told by

---

1   A detailed description of the Sales Competence Levels is located on page 204.

Chapter 10 The Australian Training Company **139**

the junior employees they feared Henrik. Kurt thought Henrik would want to know, so he broached the subject.

Kurt, '*Henrik are you aware some of your employees, particularly female staff are afraid of you?*' He appeared shocked but did not say anything.

Kurt, '*Would you mind if I suggest you acknowledge the operations and administration teams as you walk past them? Stopping to ask how their weekend was or how their job is going?*' Again, no comment but an accepted non-verbal nod.

Six weeks later during one of the training sessions Kurt overheard several individuals glowingly comment on how Henrik had changed. It validated the behaviour changes Henrik had made, and the positive effect he was having on his people.

Kurt let Henrik know anticipating a comment, but he drew a smile. A typical Henrik response.

Example 2: Henrik called Kurt to say he had a problem with the marketing manager. He asked what was the problem?

Henrik, '*He lacks confidence and stutters whenever he presents information. I want you to talk to him*'. Kurt, '*What is the name of your marketing manager?*' Henrik, '*Brian Jamison*' Kurt, '*I would like to meet Brian, talk to him, and then get back to you. If that is okay?*'

Henrik agreed and hung up. Kurt contacted Brian who did not say much and sounded relieved when Kurt suggested they meet over a coffee. Kurt's first impression of Brian was a warm harmonious person. He was in his late twenties and had a marketing degree.

After sitting down Brian candidly stated, '*I become incredibly nervous around Henrik and lose my concentration. I presented a marketing report last week, Henrik listened briefly then opened his laptop and started responding to emails whilst I spoke. It put me off*'.

At the core of the problem were two different working styles. Henrik was task focussed. He only wanted to know the key points of a report and then move on to what he had to do next. Brian, on the other hand, thought he did the right thing by going into the greatest of detail.

Not to defend Henrik's behaviour, but he would have thought the work in front of him was more important than listening to information of minor interest.

Kurt, '*I totally understand how you must have felt. I will speak to Henrik. However, can I suggest whenever this happens, stop talking until you regain Henrik's full attention. The silence will interrupt what he is doing*'.

The Most Unlikely Salesperson

Brian, '*I will find it difficult but will give it a go*'. Kurt, '*Give it a go, and when you do let me know. If I do not hear from you in a couple of weeks, I will call you to see how you are getting on. Is that okay?*' Brian, '*Yes*'.

Kurt met with Henrik the next day and spoke frankly about the impact he was having on Brian. Kurt then added, '*Please slow down and do one thing at a time. Close your laptop and give Brian your full attention*'. He responded as expected with a smile and a nod.

Kurt followed up three weeks later with Brian, then Henrik. Although their relationship was a work in progress both felt it had improved significantly to the point Brian stopped stuttering.

At the end of Henrik's term in Australia he was transferred to manage another country. Henrik eventually retired to South America to enjoy his two passions: playing tennis and watching soccer.

Nick was promoted, then transferred overseas. After several years, he left the company to take on a global CEO role. He has, and continues, to work at this executive level of management. To this day Kurt and Nick keep in close contact.

The Major Business Chamber

The Chamber had a membership of 3000 businesses. Daniel Tomson was the Chief Executive Officer. Kurt met Daniel at a network function and after sharing similar points-of-view on a range of topics, Daniel spoke about the problems he was having with the Chamber's operations team. Kurt offered possible reasons for the problems but suggested he would be able to provide specific recommendations if he was able to carry out a review. Daniel agreed.

Later that week Kurt provided a proposal which was immediately confirmed due to the urgency to resolve—so Kurt thought. However, it was not. Just prior to starting the project, one of the managers told him Daniel had two other proposals on his desk. Daniel knew the content of the two proposals, so made a quick mental comparison and decided on The Australian Training Company. Clients see greater value in starting with the review process. The review process provided meaningful information and a solution to decision makers to solve the real problem.

The project involved analysing the organization's current structure, the strategic plan, interview individuals within the operations team and course-training contractors. Kurt asked his wife June and friend Steve Donaldson to be part of the review team.

Chapter 10 The Australian Training Company **141**

The Most Unlikely Salesperson

June had co-established The Australian Training Company about a decade earlier and knew the business well. She projected an innate ability to make people feel comfortable in her presence. Therefore, her soft skills would be of great value in the interview process. She also has extensive corporate experience and a strong sales background, so when the opportunity arose to be involved in the review, she jumped at it. Steve Donaldson was a trained psychologist and had experience in process improvement projects. Steve's greatest asset was his understanding of human behaviour.

The team worked well together and completed the review within the designated timeframe. Kurt met Daniel and presented the findings and recommendations. One of the recommendations was to reduce the management reporting tiers from seven to three, and the strategic objectives from the existing 21 down to five. Although the changes were considerable, Daniel accepted the recommendations and asked to start the implementation immediately. The project was booked for the following week.

Around the time of the project's completion, Daniel gave notice to the board of directors he was resigning. He accepted a CEO role for a member-based organization in Canberra, in the Australian Capital Territory. Although his leaving would be a loss for the organization, it was a perfect career move for him. He was in his late forties, intelligent, politically astute, and well connected.

As part of the handover process, Daniel gave Kurt's contact details and the review report to the new CEO, Maureen O'Halloran. After numerous phone calls and email attempts to contact Maureen, it was obvious she did not want to speak to Kurt.

Seeking a way forward, Kurt decided to do a background check on the new CEO and discovered Maureen had a Master of Business Administration Degree, spent her working life in the public service and this was her first CEO appointment. Upon commencement, Maureen reinstated the seven management tiers and increased the bureaucracy dramatically. The new CEO created an arm's-length-approach to members by establishing layers of people between herself and the membership. She relied on newsletters,

Not knowing how to turn the situation around, the board of directors were looking for answers.

media releases, her management team, and employees to communicate with members and the business world. Two years later Kurt was informed by a consultant, Mike Brown that Maureen returned to a public service role.

Mike introduced Kurt to Clyde Lowe who had close connections with the board of the Chamber. The board were concerned the current membership was less than 800 and the organization continued to haemorrhage members. The board did not know how to turn the situation around and were looking for answers.

Kurt, '*Why are companies not renewing their membership?*' Clyde, '*I do not know, but urgent action is being taken to trim the organization*'.

It was not difficult to figure out what had happened. The layers of management and additional staff increased fixed overhead costs significantly. Also, the bureaucracy created a disconnect between members and the organization. Members no longer felt part of the Chamber, so they questioned the value of membership and did not renew. Employees were retrenched. The rapid slide in membership and revenue needed to be addressed.

Clyde, '*There is an opportunity for the three of us. There is an interest at board level to provide tailored training and development programmes for the membership*'. Clyde added, '*They are offering the use of a vacant floor in York Street, rent free for six months*'.

Something did not feel right. In hindsight Kurt should have listened to his intuition and rejected the offer to work with Clyde and Mike. However, the opportunity to be involved with the member companies outweighed the ill-at-ease feelings he had. The uncomfortable feelings remained constant, but Kurt keep focussing on the impact he could have on the member's businesses.

Mike and Clyde were about to register a new company and offered June and Kurt a shareholding. The company was to be contracted to the Business Chamber. Kurt politely declined and suggested The Australian Training Company contracted to the new entity instead. They accepted and as fortune would have it, a written contract or Memorandum of Understanding was never forthcoming. This gave June and Kurt the freedom to terminate the verbal agreement at short notice if anything improper were to happen.

The new company kicked off with a team of seven located on Level 4, 93 York Street Sydney. Kurt interviewed a cross section of stakeholders within the Business Chamber and identified 23 courses the organisation needed. His role according to the agreement was to research, design, write and facilitate these courses. Mike and Clyde were to grow the business.

Fortunately for Kurt, a third of these courses were on file or at various stages of development within The Australian Training Company. It was only four months later, the full set of courses including visual aids were completed. No sales were forthcoming from Mike or Clyde, so Kurt began arranging appointments and attending functions. He managed to secure

The Most Unlikely Salesperson

a project for a large retail furniture store that also manufactured its own furniture.

The furniture business was located in Canberra. Kurt took one of the employees with him, Benjamin Jenkins a bright young person in his early twenties who recently completed a communications degree. They stayed in Canberra for the duration of the infield sales review and interviewed every employee, jointly wrote the report and on the fifth day they were scheduled to present the findings and recommendations to the board of directors.

Kurt did the presentation whilst Benjamin sat at the back of the room. The board consisted of eight people including the owners Dennis and Judy Lynn. Dennis was the CEO and Judy held the Chair role. A copy of the report was given to every board member. Kurt outlined the scope and the objectives, then proceeded to expand on the key findings.

Half-way through Dennis leapt out of his chair, picked up the report, and slammed it on the table. Dennis, *'This is absolute rubbish!'* and followed with quite a few expletives. Kurt stood at the opposite end of the long table and listened. When Dennis finally finished what he felt he had to say, Kurt was about to respond when Judy interrupted. Judy, *'Shut up Dennis and sit down. You know Kurt is right but, you are upset that he told you what you know is true'*. Dennis sat down paused for 30 seconds and apologized for his behaviour. Judy, *'We are all sorry Kurt, please continue'*.

After the presentation, Dennis asked Kurt and Benjamin to join Judy and himself for dinner at a local restaurant. Dennis must have felt uncomfortable because the evening started with another apology before moving onto light-hearted conversation and questions about the recommendations in the report. The evening ended on a high note.

Another four months passed. Kurt was concerned there was no business development or accountability from Mike and Clyde. He decided to confront them. They had a list of excuses and nothing that indicated a sales opportunity could be moved closer to conclusion.

Kurt spoke to June about the situation and they both agreed if they stayed it would be a waste of time. The next morning Clyde walked into Kurt's office appearing incredibly upbeat. He showed him a higher purchase contract for computers valued at $20,000. Clyde and Mike had already signed the document and assumed Kurt would. This was a 'line in the sand moment' Kurt was not going to cross.

Kurt, *'I am glad you came in today Clyde because I want to talk to Mike and yourself. Would you like to have coffee downstairs?'* They sat in a nearby café. Kurt, *'Let me begin by saying I will not be signing the contract. You stated and gave an assurance of a revenue forecast based on the relationships you have with the Business Chamber, but six months later the result is nil'.* There was no reaction, so he continued. Kurt, *'The rent-free period will end this month, so overheads will increase dramatically. It is plainly clear both of you like spending time in the office instead of doing what you agreed to do, and that is business development'.* A slight pause for effect. Kurt, *'June and I are leaving within the hour'.*

They were not expecting this, and both had a stunned look on their face. Kurt stood up, shook their hands and wished them well. He returned to the office and told June about the meeting. They packed their belongings, farewelled employees and headed for home to work out what would be next.

They lived in Belrose, a northern beaches Sydney Suburb, about a ten-minute drive from the seaside suburb Dee Why. There was a four-bedroom house converted into a medical centre. The doctors had moved out, and it was up for lease. Parking was four cars in the front, two at the rear, the house was a street away from a shopping centre, and a ten-minute walk in the opposite direction to the beach. Kurt signed a three-year tenancy agreement, purchased office furniture and large palms for the front of the car park. June hired a young office administrator Kylie Engler, and Robyn Smith joined part-time to work with Kurt. This was the beginning of a new era for The Australian Sales Training Company.

Lessons learned

- Create a 'pull though' approach to sales. This allows the client to feel in control. A 'push approach' or high-pressure selling may result in a sale, but it will not sustain a relationship built on trust or repeat business.
- Continuous learning and skills development can change your life.
- Commitment and determination provides the fuel to persist despite the 'nay-sayers'. These are people who say it has never been done, and it cannot be done.

  The greater the obstacle, the greater the sense of achievement. The outcome often grossly exceeds the original objective.
- There is nothing to fear about business development except acting on a false belief. This lowers self-worth and immobilizes productivity. Meeting a client for the first time is exciting and over time friendships develop.
- Once the hood of low self-worth has been lifted a whole new world of possibility is realized.
- 'The game of baseball' is a metaphor for strategic selling. Identify the stakeholders. Start with finding and developing an advocate relationship. This will make the process of achieving the sales result easier, interesting and enjoyable.
- When confronted by an aggressive client, remain calm, listen, let them say what they feel they need to say. It shows respect. Do not interrupt because it will inflame the situation.

  With no negative energy left, the client is ready to hear a response. Speak in a normal tone of voice and slightly slower speech rate. This can have a reassuring emotional effect and influence the receptivity of the client in a positive way.
- Before presenting to a board or management team, take control from the onset by suggesting how you will proceed and ask for their agreement. You will gain their undivided attention, respect and confidence.

Chapter 11
Office Products and the Office Academy

Kurt joined the local gym and enrolled in a group fitness class. After the warm-up stretches, the instructor paired similar physical-size participants for a circuit exercise session. Kurt was matched with Phil Saddleton. It did not take long before an akin friendship started to develop amongst the running and lifting of weights.

Kurt, *'What do you do for a living?'* Phil, *'I am a sales manager, and what do you do?'* Kurt, *'I am a sales coach'*. The questions and interaction flowed effortlessly. It felt as if they had always known each other.

Phil worked for a small Sydney City office supply outlet that was part of a national co-operative consisting of 140 stores. Phil launched straight into business related questions, *'How would you improve sales?'* Kurt responded, *'I would need to understand what you are currently doing before I can make any recommendations. We could schedule a day, where I accompany you on sales calls'*.

Phil had not been involved in sales training before, so he looked forward to the opportunity and enthusiastically agreed. Kurt outlined the process of the infield sales review.

Welcoming body language, eye contact and vocal tone is crucial for an easily connect with people.

Phil's business development skills were to walk into a prospective client, ask for the person responsible for ordering stationary and then strike up a conversation. It was direct, it worked and suited the business and industry. Phil had a natural affinity for sales, although he was not conscious of it. He projected warmth through his body language, eye contact and vocal tone that allowed him to easily connect with people. His demeanour did not waver even when confronted by an aggressive person. Phil built relationships with empathy and confidence.

Kurt observed an adequate number of sales calls to give Phil his feedback, so he suggested they take a coffee break. Kurt, *'I have never come across*

The Most Unlikely Salesperson

a salesperson who is as naturally gifted as you are in applying soft skills. A great example is the last sales call where Jennifer Rodgers, the Administration Manager, gave you a rebuttal by stating she was happy with her current supplier. However, the respectful way you spoke to her Jennifer felt so comfortable she opened an account and gave you a stock order'.

The look of surprise on Phil's face revealed he was not consciously aware of the positive influence he was having on prospective clients and clients. Kurt outlined what Phil was doing so he had a clearer understanding of why he was able to develop the client relationships and achieve the sales results. He then outlined the recommended sales process and subsequent sales skills that needed to be developed.

The objective for Phil was to reach a level of sales competence giving him the ability to self-evaluate his own sales calls and that of his sales team. Phil accepted the verbal recommendations and said he will get the managing director's authorisation.

Phil, *'Hi Kurt, I have the MD's okay to proceed. Would you mind if we included my three salespeople?'* Kurt agreed. After completing the structured sales training, Phil worked at the city-based outlet for another two months. He was then transferred to head office as the National Sales Manager of the co-operative group.

Phil rang Kurt to say he wanted to catch up. They met at a café near the beach in Dee Why. The career advancement and responsibilities were significant from managing a local sales team of three to 140 nationally. Whilst Phil sounded passionately excited, there was a sombre moment when he expressed concern. He was unsure how to handle the role. Kurt listened intently and then came up with a suggestion.

Kurt, *'Why not start a sales academy'.* He continued, *'The organization would have a proven sales methodology, one that would create common language and skills throughout the national sales team. Having 140 salespeople, the sales academy would have scale and be cost effective'.*

The sales academy caught Phil's interest. Phil eagerly responded, *'I will need to get one of the directors to sign off on it'.* Kurt, *'I understand. This being new, let me outline what it will look like, so you have enough information for director approval. The first step is the infield sales review'.*

Phil had experienced a mini version of the review—limited to identifying sales competence. The scope for the sales academy would include significantly more objectives and cater for a large diverse team.

Kurt, *'The infield sales review will uncover blocks preventing better sales performance, including evaluating the sales team's competence. Warehousing, stock control, processes, distribution issues, and major competitor sales strategies will also be identified. A formal report will be written, summarizing the findings and recommendations. Part of the recommendations will be used as input to design a tailored sales training programme for the sales academy'*. Phil rang three hours later with confirmation to proceed.

The agreement for the sales academy covered six areas:

1. The sales academy would be known as The Office Academy and owned by the Office Products Organization.
2. The research, course design, implementation and updates would be the responsibility of The Australian Training Company.
3. Every salesperson would be required to meet a minimum sales competence standard. Meeting the standard would result in a competence rating, details outlined in participants' manuals.
4. Classroom structured training provided for 8-15 participants per day.
5. The sales recruitment and selection process to be linked to The Office Academy. Successful final interview applicants would be required to complete The Office Academy's sales course before employment was confirmed. Should they not meet the required sales competence criteria, they would be deemed unsuccessful. The condition of employment would be stated at the first interview.
6. On completion of the structured classroom training, every salesperson would be coached by the national sales manager. The time frame was half to one day implemented in their sales territories.

Phil wanted to know how to coach salespeople, so Kurt offered to work with him to develop the skills. He showed Phil the six Sales Competence Levels. These consist of attributes, knowledge and skills associated with each of the levels. Kurt, *'I would like to suggest Sales Competence Levels become an integral part of The Office Academy'*. Phil, *'Let's do it!'*

The Sales Competence Levels:

- Level 1: Beginner
- Level 2: Novice
- Level 3: Disciplined
- Level 4: Competent
- Level 5: High-Flyer
- Level 6: Professional.

The sales competence levels are outlined in Chapter 14[1]. The mean sales competence level across industries is Level 3: Disciplined.

Phil and Kurt agreed on the following:

- Level 3 would be the minimum standard for the organization's sales team. To gain a sales competence advantage, Level 4 needed to be achieved. Few were expected to reach Level 6

---

1   A detailed description of the Sales Competence Levels is located on page 204.

The Most Unlikely Salesperson

- On graduation of the structured sales training, a salesperson would be rated Level 1. Their correct sales competence level would be ratified during the first infield sales coaching session. This was to ensure skills developed in a classroom setting were applied in a business-to-business selling environment.

Kurt began by phoning individual salespeople to arrange a time and place to meet. Phil had already selected and contacted salespeople for the review and let them know to expect a call from Kurt and clarified why.

When salespeople are not notified by management about the phone call, reactions can be anger, anxiety and fearful thoughts they might lose their jobs. This can take time to work through before a salesperson is ready to have a conversation about the review.

The first salesperson Kurt contacted was Eugene Stockton who liked the idea of meeting earlier for a coffee. They met at 8:15am the next morning at a café in Parramatta, Western Sydney. Eugene ordered two coffees, and they spoke about rugby league because it was one of Eugene's passions.

After exchanging opinions about their favourite rugby league team, Kurt bridged into the day's format. He explained what always happens on accompanied sales calls—Kurt being the apprentice. Kurt, *'Eugene, today I am your apprentice. I am here to learn from you, what you do and why you do it. If you have any concerns or frustrations about your job, the organization or competitors, please feel free to express these because anything you say will be held in the strictest of confidence'*. He paused to wait for a response and to answer any questions, but Eugene simply nodded to show he understood.

Kurt, *'I will be spending time with a number of salespeople to identify how the sales team sell and uncover any issues preventing better sales performance'*. Eugene, *'What do you mean by issues preventing better sales performance?'* Kurt, *'For example regular stock outages and slow deliveries that result in orders being cancelled'*. Again, he nodded.

They left the café and headed to the first sales call. As the day progressed, between sales calls and regular breaks Eugene spoke candidly about what he liked and disliked about his job, what he believed needed to be done to improve how his branch operated and how to counteract competitor discounting of products.

The day was almost over with one last task to do. Kurt, *'Eugene, I prepared a questionnaire and will be asking every salesperson the same questions. It is to identify common problems that need to be addressed. Do you mind if I ask you the questions and write your responses?'* Eugene, *'That's fine. What do you want to know'*.

He did not hesitate to answer and when he thought it was appropriate, he expanded in great detail. On completion of the questionnaire, it was time to finish for the day. Kurt, *'Thank you for answering the questions. I really appreciate your frankness. I want you to know it has been a most enjoyable day and to reaffirm, what you have told me will remain confidential'.* Eugene, *'Thanks Kurt. I had a great time and amazed at how quickly the day went'.*

The infield sales review uncovered interesting facts and observations. 60 percentage of the sales team worked for the organization for more than five years, eight percent worked in the industry their entire careers. Every salesperson felt nervous to begin with, but as soon as they realized Kurt was not a threat to their employment they did not hold back.

Meeting every salesperson well before the first sales calls established rapport that was returned by their honesty and willingness to be an active part of the process. When concerns perceived or real were addressed, they relaxed, ask questions and conversations flowed freely. As trust grew, their true self emerged and they opened up about difficult co-workers, stock issues, warehousing, clients, competitors and ineffective procedures. When similar information was expressed by a number of salespeople, a trend developed that led to uncovering the real problems.

Kurt followed the same process over a two-week period with a cross section of salespeople Phil had selected for the review. The mean sales competence level was identified and issues affecting sales and profitability.

The following is not a comprehensive list of the findings, but a summary of the sales and sales related issues:

- No sales targets
- No accountability. Salespeople left largely to their own means
- Below average sales competence. Mean Level 2
- The mean daily sales call could not be accurately calculated. The definition of a sales call varied from branch to branch. Best estimate four sales calls per day
- Salespeople worked in the branch. There was no-one to delegate tasks. It was believed only they can do what needs to be done
- The branch managers summoned salespeople to the branch whenever a shortage of staff occurred. This was a comparative disadvantage for the business, as the overhead cost of a salesperson was greater than a warehouse or administration employee
- Average number of new accounts per month was two
- No account management plans were established. Salespeople over-serviced or underserviced accounts based on their subjective

The Most Unlikely Salesperson

feelings and not the current level of sales or potential sales. Underserviced accounts showed poor sales results

- Poor sales territory and time management skills. Selling time was lost due to driving from one extreme area of the sales territory to the other
- Passive and no proactive business development. New accounts were opened when a prospective client walked into a branch and decided to open an account, or a current client gave a referral
- Professional development was restricted to product and industry knowledge
- The dominant sales culture was reactive and internally focussed
- Consistent stock outages, inadequate stock levels on key product lines and obsolete stock on branch warehouse shelves
- Large numbers of client back orders, cancelled orders and account closures existed. Clients were not given a delivery date for their back order or offered an alternate brand
- Salespeople were selling on price, creating low profit margins.

The infield sales review findings and recommendations were accepted. Implementation consisted of the following:

- Design a three-day tailored sales training programme. The sales process to become an integral part of the Office Academy and to be incorporated in the organization's customer relationship management software
- Appoint a senior person within each branch responsible for carrying out tasks on behalf of the salesperson
- Salespeople were barred from their branch and only allowed to attend weekly sales meetings
- Sales territories to be sub-divided into four areas, each area representing a week. Salespeople to work area one then area two and so on until the cycle starts again. The objectives were to increase the number of sales calls and sales per day, reduce travel time and costs
- Mornings were to be dedicated to business development and afternoons account management
- Regular infield sales coaching provided to lift sales competence
- Select a national labour hire company to use when there were staff shortages
- Review current warehouse and stock control processes by a specialist consultant.

These changes were welcomed by the career minded salespeople, but there were those who objected to the new measure of accountability, so they resigned.

Phil achieved Level 6 Sales Competence, scoring 96 percent in the theory exam and the practical involved Kurt accompanying him on sales calls. During the post sales calls evaluation, Phil had to provide an objective analysis. His evaluations were precise, and he easily met the required standard.

Phil Saddleton receiving the Level 6 Sales Competence Award from Kurt Newman

The Office Academy was to become a profit centre for the organization. To generate seed funding, Phil approached suppliers and convinced them to become sponsors. He created three categories: gold, silver, and bronze. Each category with a range of benefits and financial commitment. Gold sponsorship for example, offered direct access to the sales team and invitations to the Office Academy's Quarterly Sales Events. Suppliers could present their products and offer sales incentives. For the sales team, the events offered networking, sales training, and recognition for achieving a higher-level of sales competence. To be financially viable, The Office Academy required six gold sponsors. 16 applications were received in addition to silver and bronze. The opportunity to increase sales and build a closer working relationship with the Office Products Company resonated with suppliers.

The three-day sales training programme was regularly reviewed and was eventually reduced to two long intensive days. The Office Academy increased its range of services to include Strategic Business Planning for the co-operative's branch network owners and managers, Telephone Customer Service Skills, Professional Tele-Sales, Business Technology Selling Strategies, and Effective Telephone Skills. Suppliers were invited to send their salespeople to any course of their choosing.

The Office Academy had a profound effect on the business' culture and produced incredible sales results. Phil designed a range of annual awards to recognize outstanding sales achievers. These included:

- Salesperson of the Year and Runner Up Salesperson of the Year.

The Office Academy medal and brochure

The first year this was won by Michael Fuz and Tim De Oliveria, respectively. They were 22 and 19 years of age. The award was based on the highest all-round score for sales. Michael and Tim surpassed 145 salespeople to win these awards. It validated their hard work, good attitude and the conscious application of knowledge and skills to achieve the results. Other award categories were Number of New Accounts, Profit Margin, Most Improved Salesperson, and Category Expansion

- Michael also won the Highest Profit Margin Award beating his sales peers by seven percent. An incredible effort considering the fierce competitive nature of the stationery and office supply industry. He went on to reach Level 6 Sales Competence, and after further training became a sales coach for the organization. The following year Tim De Oliveria won the Salesperson of The Year Award
- The Category Expansion Award was for new product categories sold per sales call. For example, a full range of ink cartridges. Mike Pilkington from Toowoomba, Queensland won this award by selling a new product category every 2.1 sales calls over the 12 month period. A remarkable achievement
- The award for opening the greatest number new accounts in a month was an amazing 43 and won by Clair Wilson from Cairns, Queensland.

The sales team's expectation of sales lifted dramatically. The mean for opening a new account per month increased from 2 to 15. Anything less was frowned upon by fellow salespeople. The criteria for a new account was defined as a confirmed order with a minimum value of $50. Daily sales drives were initiated spontaneously, resulting in 16 salespeople creating 58 new accounts.

Three salespeople attained Level 6 Sales Competence: Phil, Michael, and Eddy Abo Faour, an ex-butcher who changed careers to sell stationery and office supplies. The three became sales coaches for the organization.

The Office Academy encouraged joint sales calls with supplier salespeople. This was to secure more sales at larger dollar values. The sales team's competence and confidence had grown to such an extent they found themselves analysing supplier salespeople.

This is a comment from Michael about the supplier salespeople, *'Within minutes of meeting a client, the supplier rep spoke about the product and how good their company was... They did not try to get to know the prospect and identify the real problem, or what the prospect was trying to achieve...They did not build any rapport. They asked very few questions and assumed the prospect wanted a particular product'*.

Feedback was given to relevant supplier management and urged to send their salespeople to The Office Academy. Larger supplier companies were repeatedly offered tailored content to meet specific sales needs. However, only one in-house course was confirmed, and two salespeople sent to The Office Academy's Sales Programme. Suppliers were reluctant because of possible repercussions from other stationery and office supply clients that were competitors to the Office Products Company.

There was a new and noticeable respect given by older experienced salespeople to the next generation, like Michael. Michael no longer heard, 'When I was your age...' Wining Salesperson of The Year, the Highest Profit Margin Award, achieving Level 6 Sales Competence and then becoming a sales coach validated his credibility. Older salespeople rated at a lower sales competence realized they could learn from Michael, despite his newness to the industry and his young age. Michael told Kurt they were keen to know what he did and how he did it. Michael's response, *'I worked hard and applied everything I learned in The Office Academy'*.

Phil become one of the most skilled salespeople and sales coaches Kurt had worked with. His people skills, willingness to learn and his ambition drove his success. He left The Office Products Company to pursue a national sales and marketing position with Campbells Wholesale where he established another sales academy. He named it Campbells Sales Academy. It had a similar financial structure to The Office Academy. Three courses were developed including Sales, Tele-Sales, and Sales Management. Phil was in the role for several years before leaving to become the CEO of Australia's largest shop fitting business.

The Most Unlikely Salesperson

Lessons learned

- Friendships through mutual interest can unexpectedly lead to finding a new client.
- Reach out to people in a manner that makes them feel comfortable. It is a sales skill that can be refined in your personal life.
- When people are treated with respect and honesty, they generally reciprocate in-kind.
- By relaxing, it is amazing the number of ideas and inspirations that surface.
- Winning sales awards is not limited to highly experienced salespeople. Young dedicated and committed salespeople can also win awards for high performance.

Chapter 12
Warringah Chamber of Commerce

June and Kurt were settling into their Dee Why offices and becoming familiar with the area. After several weeks a local businesswoman, Penny Glenn came into the office. Penny introduced herself as representing the Dee Why Chamber of Commerce. Penny expressed interest in knowing about The Australian Training Company and asked about June and Kurt's background. They politely answered and when Penny asked them to join, they did not hesitate and signed up. Being new to the area, they thought it was an opportunity to network and meet other businesspeople.

Penny then stated, '*The annual general meeting is in two weeks. You should both be on the committee, and Kurt you should stand for President*'. Kurt tried to get out of it, '*I appreciate you suggesting this, but I know nothing about Chambers of Commerce, and have no experience in formal meeting procedures*'.

Penny was quick to reply, '*You know about business and would make a great contribution to the Chamber. You can always learn procedures*'. Kurt gave it a second shot, '*I am somewhat of an autocrat, so things would have to be done my way*'. Penny was not going to be put off, '*The meeting is at the Dee Why RSL Club and starts at 6:30pm. Register your nominations for the two roles*'. Penny presumptively said she looked forward to seeing them at the meeting and left.

Kurt felt certain June would be voted onto the committee due to her strong sales background. He thought there would be no chance of winning the President's role. He did not know anyone and had no previous experience with Chambers of Commerce. They both agreed to attend and register their nominations.

They arrived at the club and were directed to the first floor where the Dee Why Chamber had booked the smaller auditorium. Members greeted everyone as they arrived and name tags were handed out prior to entering

The Most Unlikely Salesperson

the room. Tables were set with a white cloth for the formal dinner. Proceedings started minutes before the main meal was served.

Tony Sarani, the presiding President began by welcoming everyone and then thanked the committee for their effort over the previous 12 months. The proceedings highlighted the Chamber's achievements, and shortly after the current committee were stood down. The first role for re-election was the President. Three people including the current President, a past committee member and Kurt had nominated. They were required to individually stand, introduce themselves and provide an overview of their background.

Kurt was shocked, he had won by a clear majority. The shock was followed by disbelief, how did this happen? What now? He had no idea. June was elected to the committee to manage events. Kurt walked to the podium to give his acceptance speech totally unprepared. He thanked the members and said he looked forward to getting to know and working with the committee.

The committee consisted of 13 members, too many for such a small organization. In the short term, Kurt let that slide, so he could concentrate on how the committee was structured and functioned. There were only three newly elected committee members, June and Kurt were two of them. The balance was a carry-over from the previous year's committee. Being volunteers and employed during the day, meetings and functions were held before or after business hours.

Once Kurt had reviewed past committee records, the member list and the accounts of the Dee Why Chamber of Commerce he was appalled at the state the organization.

Major issues that required addressing were:

- 11 committee members had no specific role or accountability
- Committee members attended meetings spasmodically, and gave no prior indication of their attendance or impending absence
- Few member records were kept and those found lacked the minimum required information
- Financial records were inadequate
- The committee took no responsibility and blamed each other for failed tasks
- A limited number of industries represented the membership. The great majority were retailers
- Friction between the Chamber and the Mayor of the Warringah Shire Council meant there was no relationship between the Chamber and the local council.

Kurt began by meeting individual committee members to canvass the idea of having five members become portfolio holders with defined objectives, roles and responsibilities. The balance of eight members would be in a support role to those responsible for the portfolio. Where possible, similar professional backgrounds or interests would be matched. Several portfolio holders would have two support people. The idea was unanimously endorsed at the next committee meeting.

The objective overtime was to reduce the committee from 13 to five portfolio holders and three support people who could switch from one role to another as and when required. The interim structure of five portfolio holders and eight support people, Kurt believed was not sustainable, and in time those who were non-committed would resign. To create role clarity, Kurt implemented an accountability statement. Every committee member was required to complete the two-page document.

The document was like a job description but outcomes, not task orientated. Major headings were: job purpose; accountabilities; key performance indicators; objectives; and action plan. Once satisfactorily completed, the portfolio holder and Kurt signed and dated the document.

The portfolios were assigned:
- President: Kurt Newman
- Treasurer: Rob Pellegrini, a chartered accountant
- Membership: Carey Plant, a print business owner
- Media: Scott Nilsson, a sales manager from the local newspaper
- Events: June Newman.

Portfolio holders were responsible for the outcomes of the tasks delegated to their supporter.

The natural process of selection did not take long. It began when five committee members did not complete their accountability statement despite multiple extended deadlines given. Kurt rang them individually, and after listening to their excuses he responded. Kurt, *'I understand and appreciate you letting me know why you have not had the time to complete the accountability statement. Could I suggest you resign from the committee, but remain an active member?'*

No-one refused the suggestion and there were no hurt feelings. It was as if they expected it and pleased to be offered the opportunity to leave the committee. Kurt thanked them for their past contribution and looked forward to seeing them at future functions. The organization now had the right number of people on the committee, and the smaller team felt energized and dedicated.

The Chamber had no business plan. The process of developing a business plan was expected to reinforce the relationships within the new team. Sorting the administration problems were well underway with a number of committee members actively working on it. The process also included implementing software to manage accounts and membership records. Three major objectives for the next 12 months became integral to the business plan:

- Double the membership
- Change the name of the organization to embrace a wider geographic area of businesses
- Develop local, state and federal government relationships.

Double the membership

This would require substantial resources in terms of time and to a lesser extent money. There were many an opportunity to expand membership into trades, home based business, contractors, small to medium commercial and industrial businesses. A larger and diverse, yet inclusive, membership would be more relevant and better value to all members.

Change the name of the organization

The current organization's name implied the Chamber was for Dee Why businesses only. A regional name would attract a wider range of potential members. To double the membership meant a change of name was necessary. After some discussion, the committee decided on the Warringah Chamber of Commerce and Industry Ltd.

The proposed name change had to go to an Extraordinary General Meeting (EGM) of members and required a 75 percent majority vote. June hired a room at a local function centre easily accessed by all members. Kurt addressed the meeting and read the motion followed by a clarification for the name change from Dee Why Chamber of Commerce to the Warringah Chamber of Commerce and Industry Ltd. There was robust discussion and debate before the motion went to a vote. Every member voted in favour of the motion, except one retailer. The name change was passed.

Develop local, state and federal government relationships

Members told Kurt they were frustrated whenever they had a business problem that one or another of the three levels of government could solve were not solved—in fact members felt stone-walled. The Chamber's aim was to establish the government relationships and represent the businesses of the region. The Chamber would have influence and authority and gain the attention of the appropriate government official to act on the member's concern. This in itself, would be an incentive for a business to join the Chamber.

The Dee Why Chamber of Commerce had a poor relationship with Mayor of the Warringah Shire Council. There had been long term personal tensions between the past President and the Mayor that either party was not prepared to resolve.

News release

Another issue preventing better connections was no committee member had ever contacted politicians on both major parties, state and federal levels. These relationships needed to be initiated and developed.

Scott was responsible for media. Kurt approached him with the task of establishing the relationships. Kurt, *'To implement our third objective would you approach the Mayor, state and federal politicians to let them know about the Chamber and what we are aiming to achieve? Perhaps invite them to be one of our guest speakers?'* Scott's usual friendly manner changed rapidly to discomfort. Scott, *'I am not capable'*.

Kurt tried repeatedly to encourage and convince Scott to take on the task, but nothing was going to change his mind, so Kurt said he would do it. Scott's face instantly shifted to relief.

John Pecora was the Mayor. Kurt phoned him. Kurt, *'Good morning, John. My name is Kurt Newman the President of the Warringah Chamber of Commerce. I would welcome an opportunity to meet you, perhaps over*

The Most Unlikely Salesperson

a coffee, to let you know the changes that have happened to the Dee Why Chamber of Commerce. I would also like to discuss ideas on how the Chamber could work closely with the Council'.

John's reaction was instant, *'Okay, when did you want to meet?'* His vocal tone sounded as if he welcomed the phone call. Kurt, *'How would Friday 10:00am at the Sandbar Café on Dee Why Beach sound?'* John replied, *'That's fine, I'll see you there'.*

John had an introverted personality, but as he relaxed, he became quite animated and engaging. He said it was his second term as Mayor, gave an outline of the core issues he faced and what he wanted to achieve. John also spoke openly about his family and professional background. It became apparent they both wanted a closer working relationship between the Chamber and the Council for the good of the business and wider community.

To move the relationship forward, Kurt asked John if he would like to be the Chamber's next business breakfast speaker. He accepted without hesitation.

The next day Kurt contacted the State and Federal Labour Party Offices and left multiple messages. There was no response, so he assumed there was no interest. He then phoned the State Liberal Member Brad Hazzard, the Federal Member for Mackellar, Bronwyn Bishop, and the Federal Member for Warringah, Tony Abbott.

They all became involved with the Chamber to varying degrees. Brad would attend functions unannounced, Bronwyn was by far the greatest supporter addressing members on numerous occasions, explaining relevant government changes impacting on business including the goods and services tax (GST) that was about to be introduced. Tony Abbott who would eventually become the Prime Minister of Australia, never attended a Chamber function, but Kurt kept in touch with periodic phone calls, Chamber newsletters, media releases and occasionally they met at functions.

As the committee settled in, several members did not take their role seriously and Chamber tasks were not implemented. They saw Chamber duties secondary to their full-time paid role. To help the committee, Kurt showed how he schedules Chamber duties and business responsibilities based on a priority system, so both are accomplished. He highlighted the importance of their role to the local business community and to their credit they incorporated the priority system. The change in attitude created a closer working relationship within the committee and impacted the Chamber's performance.

In keeping with the Warringah Chamber of Commerce's values, all the accounts were independently audited.

June presented a 12 month schedule of breakfast and evening business network events and put forward a recommendation for the Chamber to host a Spring Ball. The profit would go to a local charity, yet to be chosen. June's plan was universally accepted.

The date for the Spring Ball was on a Friday, leaving only eight weeks for June and her supporter Sue Henning to organise. The occasion became one of the largest, most prestigious fund-raising events on Sydney's Northern Beaches. It was held in The Grand Hall of the International College of Tourism and Hotel Management in Manly, New South Wales. The Grand Hall was part of the St Patrick's Seminary, a 60 square feet six-level heritage listed building constructed in 1889.

June and Kurt considered a range of charities but decided to look for a smaller charity that needed financial support. By sheer coincidence as they approached the local shopping centre near Belrose, several people were handing out leaflets. They would normally have kept walking because the handouts were of no interest and a common occurrence. On this day, they stopped when approached by a person who introduced himself as Bill Fleming.

Warringah Chamber of Commerce continues to grow

Bill said he was one of the parents raising money for the Allambie Special School that wanted to purchase a minibus to transport the children. Bill walked them over to meet his son Brian who was eight years of age and in a wheelchair. Bill spoke about the physical and mental difficulties children like his son face daily, many not living past the age of ten. Some of the children's ability to communicate was limited to using a utensil in their mouth and tapping on a computer keyboard.

June and Kurt knew this was the charity. They spoke to Bill about the Chamber and the upcoming Spring Ball. He joyfully invited them to visit the

The Most Unlikely Salesperson

school which they did the following day, meeting and interacting with the children. They also met Sheila Lockyer the Principal, teachers and volunteers. The volunteers were mostly parents of the children.

On their way home, Kurt rang individual committee members asking for their approval for the Spring Ball profits to be donated to The Allambie Special School. It was a unanimous 'Yes' vote.

300 tickets were sold at $95 each. At the time, this was a premium price for an event. Local businesses generously donated products and services that were auctioned during the evening. This generated additional funds.

June approached Stan Zemanek, a high-profile night-time broadcaster on radio station 2UE to promote the Spring Ball. June found him to be a generous and kind-hearted person. Stan's announcement on his show was delivered with great passion and empathy. Sadly in 2007, Stan passed of a brain tumour.

Kurt phoned Sheila Lockyer, *'Good morning, Sheila, it's Kurt Newman. I would like to arrange a mutual time to give you a cheque for $10,000 which is the money raised from the Spring Ball'*. Sheila sounded surprised, *'Thank you. I spoke with the children, and they want to put on a show. It is their way of saying thank you?'*

Kurt was deeply touched the children felt this way and instantly accepted. The show and cheque presentation were scheduled for 10:00am in the morning the following Wednesday. The Chamber Committee were invited as well as the local media, parents, teachers, teacher's aides, local council representatives and several state and federal politicians.

The presentation of the cheque

The school's assembly room was so tightly packed with people, many had to stand and watch these beautiful children perform from the hallway. Everyone in the audience felt the love and courage of the children as they put on their show in a fun and happy manner despite any physical or mental condition that may have prevented them from doing so. There was not a dry eye in the assembly room as the audience admired these brave beautiful children.

The Most Unlikely Salesperson

After the show, the formal presentation of the cheque took place, followed by a guided tour of the premises and to meet the children. During the tour, Kurt was regularly approached by parents expressing their feelings of gratitude for what the Warringah Chamber of Commerce had done for the school and for their children. There were hugs and tears of joy. It was an emotional and gratifying day.

Within 18 months, membership of the Chamber grew three-fold. There were bi-monthly newsletters and articles *Chamber Chatters* in the local newspaper, Chamber events and word-of-mouth attracted new members from suburbs throughout Warringah and a diversity of businesses and industries. New members grew rapidly and included trades, home-based small businesses, through to large corporations.

June and Kurt completed a three-year commitment to the Chamber and resigned several months after the Spring Ball. Increasing business commitments also contributed to their decision to resign. By coincidence, the three-year lease on the Dee Why building had ended, Kylie was about to marry and move out of the area, and Robyn decided to retire with her husband. The timing was perfect for a change. June and Kurt decided to convert an area of their home into an office and manage the business from there.

Lessons learned

- Unity can be created in a shared vision.
- Additional competencies can be developed and used in multiple areas of your life.
- Don't let a lack of knowledge or skills prevent you from participating, others are willing to pass on their expertise.
- If your knowledge and skills can add value, then pass these onto others.
- There are a variety of people, backgrounds and professions to meet and get to know.

The Most Unlikely Salesperson

Chapter 13
Sales Role: Luxury Cars

After completing a number of projects and in the short term with no new and confirmed business expected, an opportunity arose to change direction. For years Kurt wanted to experience what it would be like to sell luxury cars. He decided to speak to June about his intentions.

There were several downsides to this new pursuit, including having to work every weekend and take time out of the training and development business. This not only would be a change in work-life approach, it also impacted on their family and their social life. He spoke openly about why he wanted to sell cars and the affect it would have on them personally and professionally. June did not hesitate and gave Kurt her support.

Kurt bought Saturday's *Sydney Morning Herald* Newspaper and scanned through the sales job vacancy advertisements. A Lexus Dealership advertised for a salesperson. Kurt rang the contact listed Jeffrey Farrier, the Sales Manager. After a brief conversation, Jeffrey asked him to come in for an interview. He thought this was easier than expected. Perhaps he did not want to grill a potential salesperson with many questions over the phone? Fortunately for Kurt, he was familiar with the brand because at the time he was leasing a Lexus car.

The interview was scheduled for 9:30am the next day. Kurt walked into the dealership showroom when he was approached by a neatly dressed bald man about 160cm tall. Kurt told him why he was there, and the person introduced himself. It was Jeffrey. They walked to his office and sat down.

Jeffrey immediately began the interview by telling Kurt about the dealership and the cars. He also shared information about himself and this was his first job as a sales manager. He continued talking in a speech-rate that projected high energy and enthusiasm. Not the best interviewing style because he did not ask Kurt any questions. It was as if he was trying to sell him on the job and the dealership.

There was a slight pause as if Jeffrey was thinking what else to say, when Kurt asked him several personal questions to which he openly responded. He learned Jeffrey had sold cars for many years both in Australia and the

United States, was married with two children, recently built a house in south-west Sydney and he had a huge billiard table.

The interview felt like it was almost over when Jeffrey asked his first question, *'What car do you drive?'* Kurt, *'A Lexus LS400'*. Jeffrey's eyebrows lifted and looked surprised, *'Can I see it?'* Kurt, *'Sure, it is around the back in your customer car park'*.

As they walked through the dealership to the car park, Kurt casually asked Jeffrey more questions. Kurt, *'How long have you been in the job? What attracted you to selling cars? What do you enjoy most about working here?'* Jeffrey answered promptly and in detail.

Kurt was about to ask other questions when they arrived at his car, so he stopped and waited in silence. Jeffrey casually glanced at the vehicle as if he had confirmation. Jeffrey turned and asked, *'Can you start next Monday?'* Kurt, *'Absolutely'*. He was surprised to be offered the role after only one interview. They shook hands.

In time, Kurt would appreciate working with Jeffrey. He was kind and caring, a team player, and had a gift for calculating percentages quicker than a calculator.

Kurt arrived at 8:30am the following Monday morning. Jeffrey introduced him to the other salesperson Len Rodgers, the administration team, finance team, workshop manager, general manager, and the dealer principal. There were three sales offices just off centre, facing the main entrance. Kurt was given the middle office between Jeffrey and Len. Showroom vehicles were between the main entrance and the sales offices. The cars were displayed in a ribbed fashion facing each other about three metres apart. This allowed customers to comfortably view each vehicle as they walked up the centre aisle.

The department's ambience reflected the brand's prestigious image. Sales offices were fitted with high quality furniture including executive style chairs. The restrooms were comparable to a five-star hotel.

After Jeffrey's introductions, Kurt was left to his own accord. There were no customers in the showroom, so he took the opportunity to learn about the different models. He sat in each car to familiarize himself with the dashboard layout.

He then read several vehicle brochures and paused. Not being technically inclined, he did not understand the meaning of kilowatt power, in terms of how that power felt underfoot. The respective numbers of two most popular models were 114 and 166, quite a gap, consequently Kurt headed to see Tony the Service Manager. Kurt, *'Tony, when would be a convenient time to ask you a few questions about the IS200 and GS300?'* Tony, *'Give me two minutes and I will be with you'*.

The Most Unlikely Salesperson

When he returned, Kurt was pleasantly surprised how helpful and technically competent Tony was. He showed him the two brochures highlighting the engine capacities. Kurt, *'I have no idea what these numbers mean in practical terms'*. Tom, *'Why not take each car for a test drive?'* On reflection, an obvious thing to do.

He borrowed a demonstrator IS200 vehicle that had the 114KW engine and drove it onto the expressway. Kurt pressed hard on the accelerator pedal and thought the car needed time to process the information before moving. In his opinion, the car needed considerably more power. On return to the dealership, he grabbed the keys to the GS300. This had the 166KW engine. The sedan was larger and felt heavier but a different driving experience entirely. Its greater kilowatt capacity propelled the vehicle forward at an exciting pace. He now understood the meaning of the kilowatt numbers.

The majority of potential customers worked Monday to Friday. If they wanted to see and test drive a vehicle it was left to the weekend. As Kurt had intended, he volunteered to work every weekend to maximize the number of face-to-face connections. He balanced the weekend work by taking time off during the week.

When a company hires a new salesperson, a common concern is the ramp-up time. This is the amount of time the salesperson takes to become fully productive. Ramp-up time can include, but is not limited to the induction, product and service training, sales training, and coaching.

The longer the ramp-up time, the greater the cost to the company, and for the salesperson a loss of additional income such as bonuses if that is part of the remuneration package. There is also the possibility of losing self-confidence and motivation. Reducing the ramp-up timeframe is critical for these reasons.

Ramp-up time can be divided into two functions:

- **Passive** is reading relevant product and service brochures, reports, scanning the internet for information and approaching people within the company who may have answers to your questions.
- **Active** is connecting face-to-face with potential customers/clients, initiate phone calls, emails and video conferencing.

During the early stages, it is natural to feel overwhelmed at the amount of information to be absorbed from becoming familiar with the industry if new to it, competitors, company processes and procedures, software and products and services.

> To succeed from the beginning, take the initiative and do not rely solely on the company to provide the next step. Ask questions, move the process along by doing what needs to be done. Accept that mistakes could be made, and any feedback is an opportunity to progress. This is not a honeymoon period and to think it is, can backfire creating increased pressure down the line.
>
> By giving the ramp-up time its full attention for both passive and active functions, can result in new ideas and innovative ways to sell the products or services the company had not previously considered.

Although Kurt was new to the automotive industry, he quickly identified what he needed to know to accelerate his ramp-up time. These were:

- How to proactively sell luxury cars regardless of working in a retail sales environment. Salespeople in the dealership did not initiate business development, relying on media advertising to attract customers to the showroom.
- How to create a relaxed customer atmosphere within minutes a customer enters the showroom. Kurt sensed customer initial reactions were defensive or reserved. According to an article he read listing the top ten most trusted professions, at the very bottom were politicians, followed by real-estate salespeople and then car salespeople. This clarified why the general public did not trust car salespeople.
- How to create a memorable customer experience when delivering their new vehicle? This was an exciting time for them, but what could he do to make the experience a special occasion?

Retail car sales to an outsider may appear easy—sit around and wait for customers to come in the showroom. Non-sales activities needed to be fulfilled during quieter periods, but Kurt wanted to minimize these and spend more time with customers or working on business development.

Non-sales tasks whilst relaxing, do not produce sales revenues and from his perspective were counter-productive, particularly in retail sales. Why? Because feeling relaxed then having to quickly increase energy and concentration when a customer came into the showroom was something he did not enjoy. Kurt's aim was to connect with more potential customers, more often and set a target of six to eight face-to-face customer interactions per day. He felt this was a fair and an achievable number.

Being proactive meant taking vehicles to places where potential customers might be. Kurt did not have an answer as to how, until he noticed an advertisement for an upcoming agricultural event in Bowral, a regional town 1½ hours south-west of Sydney. He wondered if it was feasible to be an exhibitor, he contacted the organisers and was told the cost of hiring a medium size marque. Fortunately, there was a space available. Bowral was close enough to drive a demonstrator vehicle to the event saving the cost of hiring a platform truck.

He put the idea to the dealer principal, and he suggested to take two vehicles, a four-wheel drive LX470 and a large luxury sedan LS430. Len the other salesperson was rostered off on the two scheduled days of the event. Kurt's asked June to drive the sedan and work with Kurt.

When June and Kurt arrived at the event, they were surprised at the superbly presented marque the organisers had set up. It had a thick layer of hay strewn on the ground, the smell of the fresh hay created an ambiance of warmth and felt welcoming.

Exhibiting at the Bowral Show

It was a busy two days with large numbers of local and regional families and farmers attending. Exhibitors displayed a wide range of products from farm supplies, sheep rugs, bedding through to wine. No one represented a car dealership—June and Kurt had it to themselves. The event created interest in the Lexus Brand and resulted in two potential buyers. Both were farmers. Unfortunately for one of the farmers, finance for the LS430 sedan was rejected. Disappointing for both the farmer and Kurt.

A week after the event the second farmer came to the dealership, referred to the four-wheel drive he saw and bought it. The profit from the sale paid for the agricultural event and from a marketing perspective gave the dealership exposure to an area that had not been previously serviced.

The idea fuelled confidence to try similar events in shopping centres. This was nothing new and had been done by various dealerships. After only two such events, Kurt recommended discontinuing with the activity

The Most Unlikely Salesperson

because the time and cost was not worth the effort. The problem was most people thought the vehicle was on display for a raffle ticket promotion.

He had to find another way. The dealership invested in a range of media advertising to generate customers and there were always walk-ins, but Kurt was focussed on trying a different approach. Drawing on his business development experience—in particular asking for referrals—he decided to implement the same system. Why not ask customers who had just bought a vehicle? He always believed, like to attract like, people gravitate to people who have similar values, backgrounds and interests. So, when a customer proudly shows their new car to family and friends, there would be a good chance they might also like the brand and the vehicle, therefore opening additional sales opportunities.

> *The combination of the commitment and perhaps feeling rewarded creates the right environment to ask for referrals.*

Asking for referrals was easy, but as Kurt looked around, no one was doing it. For other industries, this was not unusual. Asking for referrals was not the 'norm' for car sales. Generally, salespeople do not ask for referrals because:

- They do not feel comfortable asking
- They do not know how to ask
- It is not measured by the company, so it does not get done
- It is not part of their sales process.

For Kurt, the plan to implement 'asking for referrals' was:

- Timing of the referral request
- Requesting the referral
- Ask qualifying questions and contact details
- Thank and let them know what he will do.

1. **Timing**

Ask customers for referrals after completing the delivery and handover of their vehicle.

The timing and how the customer feels need to be in harmony to maximize the opportunity to receive quality referrals. The customer has made a huge commitment via a loan or outright purchase and is now in an excited frame of mind taking delivery of their new vehicle. The combination of the commitment and perhaps feeling rewarded creates the right environment to ask for referrals. The customer would want family, friends, and work colleagues to have a similar experience.

Kurt knew of salespeople who never asked for referrals or go to the other extreme and ask just about everyone with whom they encounter. Asking everyone is not strategic and grossly dilutes the value of the referral.

The following example scenario was by Robert, a salesperson who did not have a strategic approach. Patrick the client, did not buy the product from Robert, but this did not stop Robert from asking. Robert, *'Do you know anyone who would be interested in…?'* Patrick, *'You can speak to Mary, a work associate'*. Robert asked for her phone and email address and thanked Patrick.

Robert then rang Mary, *'Good morning, Mary. My name is Robert. Your colleague Patrick gave me you name because he thought you might be interested in…?'* Robert spoke for a while and finally secured the appointment with Mary.

During the early stages of the sales process Mary became curious. Mary, *'Did Patrick go ahead and place an order?'* Robert, *'No'*. This was when the ambience of the meeting changed. When Mary realized Patrick did not buy the product, Mary disengaged?

Remember like-to-attract-like. As it turned out, Mary was disappointed Patrick gave Robert her name just to get rid of him she thought. Mary told Robert outright, *'I am not interested'*.

What if the potential customer genuinely cannot afford the product or service, but wants to give you a referral? This is a personal choice. Kurt has never accepted this type of referral. He would always thank them and politely refuse the offer. Practical experience dictates, the chance of this type of referral converting to a customer is highly unlikely. Therefore, it is a waste of time, time that could have been spent on other productive sales opportunities.

2. Ask for the referral

You may have their timing right, but can end up with few, poor-quality or no referrals. This usually happens when the question asked is too broad. Robert, *'Do you know anyone who would be interested in....?'* Typical response, *'I cannot think of anyone at present, but when I do, I will let you know'*.

Although the intention may be sincere, the follow-through rarely happens. The broad question needs to be reworded so the customer can think of specific organizations, individuals, or groups of people. Example: *'Lyn, would you mind if I asked you a question? Do you know of any family members or friends who might be interested in buying a new car?'*

Asking about family members or friends will help Lyn focus on the people in her personal life. If the conversation leading up to the purchase was work related, then the natural flow would be to ask for a referral in their workplace. Example: *'Lyn, you mentioned you work as a senior partner in a law firm. Is there anyone in your office looking to buy a new car?'*

3. Ask qualifying questions and for contact details

Qualifying questions provide answers about the referee's wants or needs, likes, and dislikes in relation to the product or service. Example: *'What vehicle is your brother Jason currently driving? What type of vehicle is he interested in? Why does he prefer that brand? What has he done so far to find a new vehicle? Would you know if he is interested in new or pre-owned?'*

Whether a substantial or limited amount of information is given by the customer, ask for their permission to refer to the conversation. It is not only courteous and respectful, but there could be parts of the conversation the customer may want you to keep to yourself. Example: *'Thank you for letting me know Jason's interest in purchasing a new four-wheel drive. Is it all right with you if I refer to our conversation? What is his mobile number? Is there any day better than others to contact him?'*

The information can help you transition from the introduction to the reason for the call effortless. Example: *'Good morning, Jason, my name is Kurt Newman. Lyn your sister recently bought a car from me and asked I give you a call. Have I caught you at a convenient time?'*

If the time is not convenient, '*I appreciate you telling me. When would be a time that suits you?*' If the time is convenient, '*Lyn mentioned, you have a four wheel-drive that recently had its 10th birthday and thought you might be interested in test driving a new one*'.

4. **Ask the customer to make the introduction by phone, email or in person**

It is ideal when the customer has a strong bond and intimate knowledge of the person or persons they are referring. Example, '*Lyn, I will diarize to contact Jason on Tuesday next week. Could I ask you for a favour? Would you let him know I will be calling him, so he expects my call?*'

5. **Thank and let them know what you will do**

This shows gratitude and lets the customer know what to expect. Example, '*Thank you Lyn for Jason's details. He sounds like an incredible brother. After I have spoken to him, I will call and let you know the outcome, if that is okay with you?*'

By giving the customer feedback about the referral provides an opportunity to reconnect and strengthen the relationship. Not every referral will convert to a sale, and whatever the outcome the customer needs to feel appreciated for having introduced you. Example, '*Good morning, Lyn. It's Kurt Newman. Have I caught you at a convenient time? The reason for the call is, I have spoken with Jason who told me he was taking delivery of his new four-wheel drive later that day. Although the timing was out, I want to thank you again for having referred me to Jason*'.

When a relationship has been built on trust between the customer and the referred person, you automatically become part of relationship. This substantially increases the likelihood of a sale. A customer who was referred will tend to refer others, who in turn become customers. The cycle continues because the customer assumes this is the way you do business. Whilst referrals can be given without you asking, it is always prudent to be prepared to ask. Research has shown 11 percent of salespeople ask for referrals, yet 91 percent of customers would be prepared to refer the salesperson to others. This highlights the fact salespeople are not aware or not skilled in this type of business development.

Any sales strategy needs to produce results. In Kurt's case, two of his most productive customer referrals generated $365,000 and $280,000 respectively in vehicle sales.

The opportunity arose was when a married couple came into the showroom and casually glanced at different vehicles on display. As Kurt approached, they stopped at a GS300. Kurt, *'Good morning, my name is Kurt Newman'*. The husband, *'I am Richard, and this is my wife Danielle'*. They shook hands.

Kurt, *'Is there anything in particular you are looking for or are you browsing?'* Richard, *'Just Browsing'*. Kurt, *'That's fine. I will be in the middle office, and if you need any assistance let me know. By the way, would you like a coffee?'* Richard replied, *'Yes'*. His vocal tone sounded like he had been wanting a coffee for hours. It created smiles all round and Danielle nodded affirmatively.

Kurt headed off to get the coffees and when he returned, Danielle was sitting in the GS300 with Richard standing near the driver's side leaning in and speaking to her. Kurt, *'It is a beautiful car. Would you like to have the coffees in my office, and we can chat'*.

The car was for Danielle and her questions demonstrated she was well informed about the brand and model. It appeared Danielle had made up her mind, the GS300 was going to be the car. Richard asked if the dealership had the same model in silver, but pre-owned and let Kurt know their budget range. This was below the new vehicle price. He checked stock and fortunately there was a pre-owned silver GS300 in stock and within their budget.

Then came an expression of interest, often known as a buying signal, but in this instance a last hurdle to overcome. Danielle, *'Would a wheelchair fit in the boot? A close friend of mine is a paraplegic, and the boot would need to be large enough for her wheelchair'*.

Kurt had no idea and as for the size vehicle, the boot was reasonable but not large. Kurt, *'I do not know, but do you mind if I ask where you live?'* Danielle frowned at the unusual question, but answered, nevertheless. The suburb was 20 minutes from the dealership.

Kurt, *'Will you both be home this evening around 6:00-6:30pm?'* Richard and Danielle in harmony, *'Yes'*. Kurt, *'What I'd like to suggest, if it is okay with you, is to come over this evening with the vehicle, and if you could arrange to get your friend's wheelchair, let us see if it fits?'* They smiled and agreed.

He arrived at their home and the wheelchair was near the garage. Kurt opened the boot as Richard walked toward him with Danielle close behind. They greeted, then Richard placed the wheelchair in the boot. It was a tight fit but comfortable. They invited Kurt into their home for coffee. Danielle

The Most Unlikely Salesperson

told Kurt about her two adult daughters and their ten-year-old grandson whom she adored. Kurt was given a tour of their home including the downstairs four-car garage where Richard proudly exhibited his imported 1969 Mustang. Richard had fully restored the vehicle and was a Ford Mustang enthusiastic.

They walked back upstairs and sat at the dining room table, where Danielle had prepared brewed coffee accompanied by a chocolate cake sliced into wedges. Halfway through drinking the coffee, Danielle agreed to purchase the vehicle. The transaction was concluded.

Richard came into the showroom a week later and said his eldest daughter needed a new car. He bought an IS200 sedan. Within weeks, his other daughter and her husband came in and said Richard told them to see Kurt. They bought the same model sedan. Several months later, Richard referred one of his neighbours who bought an LS430. Richard also bought himself a new four-wheel drive. To this day, June and Kurt keep in touch and have attended many of their family functions.

Kurt introduced himself to a married couple, Christen and Anne Sorensen. Kurt, *'Is there anything in particular you are looking for or are you browsing?'* Christen replied with a smile. He appeared slightly reserved as he stood in front of an LS430 and asked several questions.

Kurt answered their questions as well as suggested Christen and Anne sit in the car, which they did. They spoke in a Danish accent that reminded Kurt of Henrik from The Shipping Container Company. He decided to ask a personal question hoping it may help them feel relaxed. Kurt, *'Christen, Anne, do you mind if I ask, are you Danish? Christen, 'We are from Copenhagen but have lived in Australia for over 20 years'.* Kurt jokingly, *'We were almost neighbours at one time, I was born in Austria'.* Both countries have similar cultures and are in the heart of Europe— Kurt thought it might open the conversation. The response was a smile and a nod. Well, that clearly did not work!

He had to find another way to connect. Kurt suggested they take the car for a test drive, which they agreed to do. He sat in the back seat and casually asked questions switching from Christen to Anne and back again. The conversation gradually expanded, and the atmosphere lightened as they shared more details about themselves as they got to know each other. Christen said they were looking for a family car and a four-wheel drive for his work. Kurt, *'If you do not mind my asking, what do you do for a living?'* Christen, *'I am a builder'.* His response was direct and short. Anne changed the subject by telling Kurt they live on a rural property north-west of Sydney and have two teenage daughters.

176 Chapter 13 Sales Role: Luxury Cars

The Most Unlikely Salesperson

On their return to the dealership Kurt was about to ask how they felt about the LS430 in hope of closing the sale, when Anne jumped in, 'We want to buy the car we drove'.

It is a good reflection of the relationship when a customer feels so comfortable, they decide to go ahead and buy without the salesperson asking. Kurt responded to Anne's request, 'Thank you, Anne. We will do the paperwork shortly if that is okay with you?' Anne, 'Yes, of course'. Kurt turned to Christen, 'Now let me show you the four-wheel drive that may interest you'.

Christen sat in the driver's seat whilst Kurt gave him an overview of the dashboard layout and then suggested Christen test drive the vehicle. He politely declined and appeared content to remain seated casually looking around at the interior. Kurt was quiet, allowing Christen to be with his thoughts. It was only a matter of minutes and there was a change in demeanour. He appeared to have made up his mind. Christen said, 'I will arrange my own finance and will be back in two days'. Kurt, 'That's great. Let us do the paperwork and we will put the two vehicles aside for Anne and yourself'.

Kurt had the following day off, assuming it would be a day or two before finance was approved. There was plenty of time. Unbeknown to Kurt, Christen walked into the dealership the next morning and paid for both vehicles.

Len, Kurt's colleague, did the paperwork for Christen and took credit for the two sales. Kurt tried to reason with him but made no progress. Reluctantly, he spoke to the dealer principal outlining what had happened. He acknowledged the sales were rightfully Kurt's. What prevented correcting the situation was the documentation had been processed in Len's name. Although Kurt felt frustrated and appalled at Len's unscrupulous behaviour, there was nothing he could do.

Kurt went back to Len, closed his office door, expressed his disdain, and told him he would continue to look after Christen and Anne by delivering the vehicles. Len did not respond. Kurt phoned Christen and Anne to thank them for their purchase. He then arranged a mutually convenient day and time to go through the functions of each vehicle and hand over the keys.

The saying 'what goes around comes around' was pertinent. Len's behaviour was about to be reconciled. The dealer principal must have reflected on the situation and spoke to Len, then walked into Kurt's office and told him Len's next two sales will be credited to him. Kurt thanked the dealer principal for the decision.

Chapter 13 Sales Role: Luxury Cars **177**

The Most Unlikely Salesperson

Kurt delivered the two cars and showed Anne the functions of the LS430 and Christen the LX470. He was about to leave when Christen invited Kurt into their home for coffee accompanied by cake, Anne had baked earlier that day. Their two daughters joined them briefly, grabbed a slice of cake and headed for the backyard. Christen and Anne were relaxed and spoke freely about their background, family life, the construction business and the local Danish Community. Christen invited Kurt to join him later that evening at the Danish Club. At the Club, Christen introduced Kurt to his friends, and in a semi-serious tone instructed them to buy their next car from Kurt—a lovely gesture.

Len behaved increasingly erratic. This was amplified when the dealership hired another salesperson, Ronda Bennett. He appeared to propel himself out of his office as if he were leaving a burning building whenever a customer came into the showroom. The customer's first reaction was shock. They were in the showroom for less than a minute and there was Len standing next to them. In the main, customers were polite, but their body language told a different story. Their discomfort and defensiveness were shown by automatically stepping back several paces to create distance between themselves and Len. Unfortunately, he never picked up on the customers non-verbal cues nor the fact his actions contributed to his lack of sales. After six weeks of unacceptable sales results, Len decided to resign and joined a non-prestige car dealership.

Sales and profit margins were good, but Kurt continued to focus on taking the customer experience to a level that defied the general public's perception of car salespeople. What worked well when a customer walked in the showroom was:
- Greeting the customer with a friendly smile
- Introducing himself in a relaxed manner
- Asking an alternate question, 'Is there anything in particular you are looking for or are you browsing?' If they said, 'Just browsing' he would give them the physical and emotional space to browse. Kurt would then offer a connection, 'That's fine. I will be in the middle office, and if you need any assistance let me know. By the way, would you like a coffee?'
- If the timing wasn't appropriate to offer a coffee, Kurt would leave and go to his office appearing to be busy and from time to time casually glance over to see what vehicle the customer showed interest in.

Every time Kurt left a customer on their own, respect was given, and it was typically reciprocated. When a salesperson approached the customer, their response was, '*We are dealing with Kurt, or I am dealing with that bloke in the middle office*'. When out-of-hearing range, he noticed they would point to his office letting the salesperson know they were dealing with him.

When customers were ready, they either signalled by waving to get his attention or they walked into his office. Kurt noticed their demeanour changed from when they first walked into the showroom reserved or defensive, to being open and friendly. This provided the opportunity to get to know them and develop the relationship. Interestingly, Kurt was never asked by other salespeople why or what he did that created the environment for customers to want to deal with and ask for him.

Every salesperson was expected to complete a sales training course organized by the dealership's head office. The course was part of the brand's commitment to its dealer network and was mandatory for salespeople to attend. A contract consultant Sue Bosworth was the facilitator and part of her introduction was to proudly announce her recent purchase of a new BMW—a very strange statement. Certainly not a good first impression when trying to establish credibility on how to sell a competitor's brand.

> *Sales colleagues never asked why or what Kurt did that encouraged customers to ask for him and to only deal with him.*

The greatest value of the course was meeting and getting to know the salespeople from other dealerships. Also, it was during the role play sessions, Kurt saw first-hand how his colleagues sell. Although his colleagues up-sold and embellished their abilities during the morning tea break, the role plays showed how skilled or not skilled they really were. This was the catalyst to re-evaluate what he did. The aim was to create differentiation from a customer's point of view. Changes he planned were minor.

Three areas came to his attention:
- Continue with what he did when a customer came into the showroom
- Spend more time getting to know customers on a personal, and if appropriate business level
- Create a vehicle handover process the customers would always remember.

Kurt spoke to June about the handover and asked her to purchase a large basket and fill it with quality product jams, cheeses, biscuits, wine,

The Most Unlikely Salesperson

and anything she thought a customer would like. They decided on a budget of $150. The basket contents were substantial. June finished the basket with ribbons and cellophane wrapping—all adding to the stunning presentation.

Kurt did not tell the dealer principal he was going to give his customers a personal thank-you gift. The reason behind this decision was no expenses would be billed to the dealership, therefore no obligation to let the principal know.

The basket would be given to customers regardless of the vehicle's value or profit generated. The plan was to place the basket in the boot of the car prior to delivery.

Kurt always started the handover process by opening the bonnet to show the covered engine look clean and neat. From there, he walked the customer to the driver's door and asked them to sit in the driver's seat. He then took them through the dashboard functions. From there, influencing the customer to move to the rear of the car and open the boot.

Customer's emotionally charged reactions were unexpected. It ranged from a firm-extensive handshake and multiple-verbal thank you, to tears and hugs. Several female customers screamed loudly with excitement. The delivery and handover took on a whole new meaning for customers.

The first opportunity to implement 'spending more time getting to know customers' turned out to be quite a challenge. The customer was looking at an LS430 sedan then sat in it.

Kurt did his usual approach, *'Good morning, my name is Kurt Newman. Is there anything in particular you are looking for, or are you browsing?'* There was a long period of silence as he waited for a response. The customer continued to look around inside the cabin of the vehicle as if he was engrossed taking it all in.

Kurt waited, then asked, *'And your name is?'* An impatient vocal response, 'John'. It appeared as if he was angry and wanted to be left alone. John's abruptness was not taken personally, and he was about to leave and give John some space. Kurt, *'I will be in the middle office, and if you need any assistance let me know'*.

John then declared, *'I hate buying cars'*. Kurt nodded to let him know he heard him. Kurt added, *'I can appreciate how you are feeling and will make the process as easy as I can'*. John did not change his angry disposition and sounded reluctant to answer any questions as he remained in the car scanning the interior and feeling the leather seats.

Kurt had dealt with customers and clients like John before. They can become quite irritated and aggressive if they feel the salesperson is:

– Wasting their time asking personal questions

The Most Unlikely Salesperson

- Excessive using small talk
- Talking too much or too slowly
- Not getting down to business.

This customer behaviour can be off-putting for salespeople who do not know how to handle this interaction. However, this type of customer personality will make a quick decision provided the salesperson:

- Is direct, honest and logical
- Is concise and quotes relevant facts to back up any statements
- Is quick to reach the bottom-line
- Looks after the details
- Offers an alternate choice allowing the customer to make the decision.

John eventually stepped out of the vehicle and walked around it. Kurt remained stationary and took an impersonal approach to connect with John. John opened one of the rear doors, left it open and began to leave the showroom. John as he left said, '*I will be back*'.

Kurt thought of several options to keep John in the dealership. He knew it would have been futile, so he responded in an uplifting expectant-vocal tone, '*That will be great John. I look forward to seeing you on your return*'. There was a risk John would not return. Kurt watched him leave to see where he would go. John was approached by a woman as soon as he was outside the building and they both headed toward the BMW Dealership.

John returned 30 minutes later, with the same woman and said, '*This is Jennifer, my wife*'. He continued, '*I am also looking for a car for Jennifer and have a BMW 735 and 323 to trade*'.

To suggest the right vehicle, Kurt turned to Jennifer to ask questions, but John answered every time. It was an awkward situation. He thought Jennifer would have pulled John aside and told him to let her speak, but she remained silent. Kurt noticed Jennifer looking at a GS300. With a stretched arm and open palm, Kurt signalled offering Jennifer to take a closer look. She sat in the car with a huge smile on her face—that spoke volumes. Whenever Kurt tried to connect and involve Jennifer, John took over. The atmosphere felt heavy and overly serious.

Jennifer was visibly becoming uncomfortable as John's vocal-tone was increasingly impatient. Kurt decided it was time to close the sale. As far as he was concerned the LS430 and the GS300 are the two sedans John was interest in for himself and Jennifer. To leave it any longer would have stalled the momentum of the sales and buying process.

Kurt, '*Do you mind if I ask the sales manager and the dealer principal to get involved? I want to make sure we are able to give you the best deal on these two cars*'. There was no hesitation as John instantly agreed.

Chapter 13 Sales Role: Luxury Cars **181**

The Most Unlikely Salesperson

Kurt left John and Jennifer in the showroom to get Jeffrey and the dealer principal. He gave them a brief overview and, on their return, Kurt did the introductions. John tried numerous negotiation tactics including low balling, which is offering a ridiculously low figure, speaking in an intimidating vocal-tone and remaining silent for a long period of time when a counteroffer was made. John's attempts were respected but resulted in no gain. After considerable theatre, John bought both vehicles. Within minutes he transferred $265,000.

To help Kurt with the delivery, Ronda drove one of the vehicles. John and Jennifer lived in a modern large two-story home with an eight-car garage beneath. John was a different person from the one Kurt met days earlier. John was friendly, upbeat and spoke about his career and financial investments. He was a doctor, owned several medical centres and was an entrepreneur.

After the handover, he gave Kurt a five dollar note, and said the BMW 735 was low on petrol, but it would get him back to the dealership. Looking at the petrol gauge and the distance he had to travel it was going to be a careful journey. Rhonda drove the other trade-in vehicle back to the dealership.

The people who came into the showroom made the job interesting, challenging and an absolute joy to deal with through to confrontational. Kurt did not take difficult behaviour personally, particularly when a customer negotiated in an adversarial manner. By understanding their buying process and expectations made it easier to find a way forward.

Some of the most memorable experiences at the dealership were:

- A customer wanted to buy a car for his daughter's 18th birthday. His name was Anh, originally from Vietnam. He projected warmth and gentleness. His face lit up whenever Kurt asked questions about his daughter, Bian. Anh decided on a white IS200 sedan and did not require finance. A bank cheque was going to be the method of payment, however Anh returned an hour later with $66,000 in a plastic bag.

  When Kurt delivered the vehicle to Anh's home, he introduced his family, then proudly took him on a guided tour of his property. He wanted Kurt to stay for lunch, but he had to be back for a meeting, so they compromized agreeing on a cup of tea.

- There was a period when successive sales were to doctors. One of the most pleasurable was a Dr Alan Montague. He emailed his interest in an ES300 a mid-size sedan and sent the same email to numerous dealerships. Kurt phoned him as soon as he received it and asked preliminary questions, *'When did you want the vehicle? What exterior colour would you like? Will the vehicle be leased?'*

Dr Montague answered each question in a monotone, sounding somewhat disinterested but with a slight infliction in his voice stated, *'I really like the two-tone grey'*. Kurt responded, *'We have a two-tone dark grey and silver ES300 in stock. Would you like to see it?'* Dr Montague sounding several octaves higher, *'Yes!'*.

They arranged to meet that evening at his home in Wahroonga, on Sydney's lower north shore. Dr Montague introduced himself as Alan. Looking at Alan as he drove the car, he knew he was about to be its owner. Kurt had the documentation with him assuming Alan would buy the vehicle, which he did. Two days later he returned to do the handover.

Halfway through explaining the dashboard layout, Alan's mobile rang. It was a salesperson from another dealership following up on his email. He told the salesperson, *'I have just taken delivery'* and hung up.

- A customer who was an accountant for a not-for-profit organization, well dressed, in his late 40s wanted to trade his 18 month old black GS300. The car had an immaculate clean white interior. His name was Bruce Dixson. Bruce told Kurt the car reminded him of a recent failed relationship. As he spoke, the emotional pain was reflected on his face. The car was in as new condition.

  Bruce paid $106,000 and leased it over a five-year period. Kurt advised him not to sell because the financial loss would be considerable. Bruce said he did not care. Kurt did what he could to minimize the loss, but it was still a substantial amount. Ironically, he bought the same model and the same colour configuration.

- A young Chinese Australian Jim Wong, mid-30s wanted to compare the LS430 sedan to the S-Class Mercedes Benz on behalf of his parents. He said they owned several businesses and did not have the time, consequently the task was delegated to him.

  Jim wanted a loan of the vehicle for 24 hours for his parents to test drive. Before agreeing, Kurt asked him a series of questions to understand Jim's parents likes and dislikes. He wanted to ensure the LS430 was the right car for them. Jim described in detail how he and his parents looked on the internet and decided it was between the two brands and the specific models. Kurt asked for his driver's licence, took a photocopy, Jim signed the documentation then Kurt handed him the keys.

  The vehicle was on loan several times over a two-week period. Kurt and Jim communicated regularly. This was the turning point and the differentiator because it built trust and respect. Jim recommended the LS430 to his parents who went ahead with the purchase.

– A middle-aged customer, Dorothy Carmichael drove from the Blue Mountains to trade her 15 year old, rust ridden vehicle for an IS200 sedan. Her old vehicle was in such appalling state its financial value was negligible. To minimize any embarrassment she may have felt, Kurt did not tell her how little the car was worth. Instead, he discounted the cost of the new car and added the amount to her trade-in. When he presented the figures letting her know what he had done, Dorothy had a huge smile and almost levitated out of the chair with excitement. She instantly agreed to proceed and stated how much she appreciated Kurt's honesty.

> *Kurt's primary focus was to do whatever he could to create an enjoyable and memorable experience for the customer.*

The gross profit for this sale turned out to be four times higher than the dealership's average for this model. There is always the need to make a profit. However, Kurt's primary focus was to do whatever he could to create an enjoyable and memorable experience for the customer. He never knew the profit per vehicle sold unless Jeffrey told him, or he read it on the end-of-month commission statement. Margins, however, were always good.

Prior to the public release of a new model, dealer principals and sales staff were required to attend a training session and learn about the vehicle and comparisons with equivalent competitor models. This was facilitated at the brand's head office.

Jeffrey and Kurt shared one of the test drive vehicles with another dealership principal who spoke passionately about selling value. His main points were:

– The new functions of the car compared to its competitors
– The lower recommended retail selling price giving the model a cost advantage
– No discounting.

Two days after the training, a customer who would not give his name phoned to negotiate the cost of the new model. He had not driven, nor seen the vehicle, except for what he saw in a brochure. Kurt suggested he come into the dealership. The person interrupted Kurt before he finished the sentence and blurted out the net figure he was quoted. It was a substantial discount off the retail price. Kurt asked who gave him the quote. It was the same dealer principal who said he was not going to discount.

The customer outright asked if Kurt could do better? He was not going to participate in discounting particularly on a brand-new model. Kurt politely declined and wound up the phone call.

The question that came to mind was why did the dealer principal discount, and discount so generously? Less customer resistance? Low self-worth? Perhaps he did not believe the vehicle was worth the asking price? Poor sales and negotiation skills? Kurt mentioned the phone call to Jeffrey who had been in the industry for well over a decade. Jeffrey shook his head in frustration, '*They say they will not discount and end up being the first to do so*'.

Kurt was conservative when it came to discounting because he believed the focus was on creating value and an experience the customer will always remember. This differs from transactional selling that has no emotional connection between the salesperson and the customer. From the customer's perspective, it is all about achieving the lowest cost. If there was a clear indication a customer only wanted to discuss discounts and a mutual fair outcome was not possible, Kurt let them walk out the door or conclude the phone call.

A lose/win outcome cannot be sustained where the salesperson loses and the customer wins. These types of customers are disloyal and will go from one supplier to another to gain a lower cost.

Several customers Kurt let go, because a fair win/win outcome was not possible, contacted him after they bought a car from another dealership. He thanked them for letting him know and genuinely wished them well. One dealership traded and sold a $67,000 vehicle grossing $500. That is a clear lose/win. Not all business is good business.

The Most Unlikely Salesperson

The downside of discounting, but is not limited to:

- Creating a new lower cost norm, resulting in no credibility of the asking price and ignored by the salesperson and the customer
- Cheapening the brand's value
- No respect for the salesperson
- A demonstration of poor sales and negotiation skills.

So what can be done? Instead of discounting offer something in lieu that aligns with the customer's values—preferably of higher value to the customer and a low cost to the business. A customer's peace of mind is an example of value. The offer could be free servicing and longer vehicle warranties, both in recent years becoming popular. A price hypersensitive customer solely motivated by cost tend to take up more of your time compared to other customers and are difficult to deal with.

For most customers price is important, but other important purchase criteria can be:

- How they feel during the buying process
- The personalized attention they receive
- The relationship developed with you
- Post-sale customer attention and benefits
- A sense of well-being
- Guarantees or warranties.

Selling value is not restricted to the product or service. It can be you, the backup team, the organization's culture, how they feel every time they use the product or service. It is a matter of identifying what a customer values the most and where possible provide it in unexpected quality, quantity and personal experience.

Kurt had been in the job for five months. It was early December, and the festive season was well underway with people busily preparing for Christmas. Customers who purchased their cars from Kurt returned to give him thank you cards, gifts and verbally expressing how they felt about the customer relationships developed. It was a humbling experience and totally unexpected. By mid-December, Kurt's desk was crammed with customer gifts. No two gifts were the same, ranging from a bottle of Chivas Regal Scotch, a company T-shirt through to a home-made Christmas Cake. When a prospective customer walked into the dealership they were automatically drawn to the volume of cards and gifts in Kurt's centre office.

The adjoining offices had six to eight cards stuck on the wall. It was quite a startling contrast and customer first impression. His desk was becoming so crowded there was little room to work, so he decided he would take the items home that evening.

The dealer principal came into his office looking annoyed and ordered everything be cleared and he would be telling the others to take down their cards. Kurt was about to tell him he intended to do so, but instead asked what motivated him to want the items removed. There was no reply. He turned and headed for the next office.

Kurt left the dealership just shy of 12 months. The trigger was when the dealer principal told him to stop giving gift baskets to customers. Kurt did not understand why, after all, the baskets were no cost to the dealership and more importantly, it was his way of saying thank you to customers. The surprise and joy were shared special moments.

Kurt soon learned the reason for the decision. The dealer principal called a meeting of the sales team to show a range of standard customer gifts. It was a structured system whereby a specific gift was to be given based on the model a customer purchased. It started with a mug that had the brand's logo on the side. This was for the purchase of an IS200 sedan. At the time, the entry level model was around $65,000. In Kurt's opinion, this was an extremely low value gift. He could not believe what he saw as the full range was rolled out. It went against his core values and there was no way he was going to be part of it. The dealer principal must have noticed the look on Kurt's face, so he added the system had to be adhered to. This meant a higher value gift could not be given in place of a lower value gift, it had to be in line with the model purchased.

> To gain a competitive edge, organizations like to strive and encourage their employees to be innovative and take calculated risks. It begins with one employee, grows from there and should be nurtured by management. Culturally this creates ownership of the idea, personal responsibility, accountability and motivation.

The combination of systemizing customer gifts and the low value of each gift item were unacceptable to Kurt. This was micromanaging and controlling every aspect of the sales process—taking away a salesperson's freedom to be creative and initiative. He had two cars to deliver, and asked June to make-up the last two baskets. After the customer handovers he gave notice to leave.

The Most Unlikely Salesperson

His strategy spending additional time getting to know customers personally and professionally when appropriate, and the gift baskets made a huge difference to the relationships he developed with customers. From a business perspective, it contributed to selling more vehicles at consistently higher profit margins than his colleagues.

Lessons learned

- Be adventurous, experience selling products or services in a different industry, even if for a brief period of time. What you learn, accomplish and appreciate will be invaluable.
- Look for ways to be innovative, creating a difference and value to the customer.
- When the customer enters the store, acknowledge them. Provide the option to browse, giving them physical, mental and emotional space. Always be ready to respond.
- Spend time getting to know customers individually.
- Quality referrals are generated by customers who have just purchased. The referral dramatically reduces the selling cycle.
- Be quick to respond to customer enquiries and close the sale—or a competitor will.
- Customer decisions can be irrational. When this happens, do the 'right thing' by them, and advise accordingly. When they realize you genuinely have their best interest at heart their attitude and how they feel about you will take on a whole new meaning.
- In sales, it is not always possible to meet the decision maker. Ask questions to develop a relationship with the person sent in their place—questions about the decision maker's buying criteria. The more information you uncover, the greater the opportunity to differentiate yourself and the product or service from competitors.
- Empathize and see the purchase from the customer's perspective. When they feel you truly understand, the buying process and experience becomes relaxed and enjoyable.

  Sales and profitability will follow naturally, so do not become obsessed with numbers. Focussing on numbers in whatever measurement may generate more income in the short term, but it will not create long-term loyal customer relationships. These relationships often grow into friendships, referrals, repeat business, reduced selling cycles and greater profitability.
- When an organization's culture changes and is counter to your own core values, it is time to leave and find an organization where your values are aligned.

Chapter 14
Sales Consultants

The Australia Training Company had been operating for ten years, created a solid track record, loyal clients, and repeat business. The range of services as outlined in Chapter 10 were extensive and the easiest thing to do would have been to continue. Having left the Lexus dealership gave Kurt time to reflect on what he really wanted to do.

It did not take long before the phone rang. It was Peter Jenkins from the Electrical Wholesale Company. In a semi joking-vocal tone, Peter said, *'You will only remember one of the sales reps'*. Four had left, and the new salespeople were struggling to meet sales targets. Addressing this problem was Peter's greatest concern. As a result, he bypassed asking for a proposal and confirmed the infield sales review over the phone.

Kurt's passion and his greatest sense of satisfaction was working with companies to improve sales performance, train and coach salespeople. He intuitively felt he needed to change the business and specialize. Peter's phone call sealed the decision. It would mean disruption reorganising the business in the short term, but it felt right. His lifetime goal is for salespeople to reach a level of sales competence to analyse their skills and strategies in the same manner other professionals are able to in their field of expertise. So where to start?

A priority to-do list was developed and written on a whiteboard. The first on the agenda was a name change to reflect what the business does. Sales Consultants was chosen.

A new strategic plan was developed, logo, by-line, stationary, website, review and update of all sales, and sales strategy content.

What continued as normal business practice were:

- Research into global trends in sales
- Marketing new services using sales education content for social and other media
- Keep in regular contact with clients and prospective clients
- Initiate face to face meetings.

The scope of the infield sales review was expanded from sales operations to include company operations that could impede sales and profit performance either directly or indirectly.

Indicators were, but not limited to:

- Ineffective and costly internal processes
- Dysfunction between departments
- Poor attitude
- Incompetence
- Lack of strategic direction.

Depending on the industry and size of the company, these could be marketing, technology, human resources, administration, logistics, customer service and management. This new approach was holistic and expected to be of greater value to a client.

Identifying operational problems impacting sales were within Kurt's skills set, but to develop and implement an effective solution would require someone with specific expertise.

The ideal personal and professional attributes he was looking for were:

- Achieve measurable outcomes across industries, preferably globally
- Ability to handle pressure in a calm manner
- Capable of working with shop-floor to senior management
- Skilled in all aspects of process improvement
- Develop innovative client solutions
- Travel interstate and internationally
- Work long hours in a team environment.

This was quite a list, possibly unrealistic, but a start never-the-less.

Kurt interviewed a number of potential applicants but found they did not have the standard of operational skills and attributes he was looking for. To compromize was not an acceptable option, so the expanded version of the infield sales review was on hold. Until the right person was found, he took the opportunity to practice asking questions about company functions he normally did not get involved in. Peter Jenkins was the first client, and he was surprisingly responsive.

Kurt asked questions about processes within and across the branch network, supplier agreements and discounts, employee turnover, morale within the branches and stock control. Peter did not hold back. His answers were quick and direct. The administration and operational functions overall worked well.

Two areas were identified that needed to be addressed:

- Junior level employee turnover
- Supplier discounts and trading terms.

After spending time with the sales team, Kurt presented the report recommending a tailored and structured sales training and coaching programme. To reduce the turnover of junior employees, he recommended Peter advertise for young people who are interested in a well-defined career path. This would attract a different calibre of applicant from the those only interested in a job. Kurt was aware several of Peter's competitors were receiving greater discounts and better trading terms from suppliers. Kurt provided the competitor discount details to Peter.

The report recommendations were accepted and confirmed for implementation. The sales team embraced the programme as it progressed. Their dedication and commitment were gratifying, particularly as they often felt out of their comfort zone. This did not deter them.

During one of the post-coaching reporting sessions Peter stated, *'Sales have increased'*. Kurt, *'That's great. By how much?'* Peter did not answer, just smiled and looked down at his desk. He tended to keep details to himself, so it was not a surprising response. However, several months later Kurt learned the figure was 20 percent.

Management Consulting Firm Contract

Since completing the major Business Chamber project, Steve Donaldson and Kurt kept in touch and over the years become close friends. On one of their coffee catch-ups, Steve told him he was employed by a management consulting firm, PSL Schnyder. His main role was human resources, finding and inducting consultants to work as sub-contractors. A sales conference was planned for the following month and Steve had a proposal from a facilitator but offered the opportunity to Kurt. Steve, *'Would you be interested?'* Kurt replied, *'Absolutely'*.

He then asked a series of questions, *'What field of consulting does the firm operate, single or multi-industry? Is there a conference theme? Content? What are the expected outcomes? How many people would be attending? The date and timeframe of the conference and who is the decision maker?'*

Steve did not have an answer to every question, but stated the firm provided process improvement services and clients were in both the Australian and international mining sectors. The managing director wanted expansion into other industries, and this was the reason for sales training to be part of the conference. The structure and course content were up to Kurt to recommend, 12 participants, two-day conference, a date confirmed,

The Most Unlikely Salesperson

the venue was the Novotel North Beach Wollongong, and the decision maker was Peter Ditmar, the Managing Director.

Kurt emailed the proposal and several days later rang Steve to followed up. Steve, *'The managing director prefers the other facilitator's proposal because he had written a book'*.

Kurt had not published any books at the time, so could not compete on that criteria. However, when he asked Steve if the facilitator could tailor sales training to meet PSL Schnyder's specific objectives, the answer was no. The facilitator only taught what he had written in his book. Kurt won the business after Steve spoke to Peter Ditmar outlining the difference between the two facilitators.

Kurt arrived at the conference at 7:30am to prepare for the 8:30am start. The allocated room was huge, it could easily seat 50 people. The tables and chairs had already been placed in a horse-shoe shape in the lower half of the room, and a whiteboard and screen for the LCD projector were well placed. Tea, coffee and biscuits were set up immediately outside the entrance where the team started to congregate at 8:00am. Peter Ditmar arrived literally one minute before the first session began. He had a serious and unfriendly manner that did not change throughout the conference.

During the morning session, Kurt approached Peter. Kurt, *'Do you mind my asking for your opinion?'* Peter, *'No'*. Spoken in a short uninterested-vocal tone. Kurt, *'Based on your experience how are you finding the sessions so far?'* Peter, *'Okay. It won't take long before I know what you do and then move on'*. Kurt nodded his head to acknowledge what he had heard.

Peter may have had a rough start to the day and simply reacted to the question or this was his natural personality. Either way, Kurt was not going to continue to engage in conversation. Peter's attitude was reflected in his body language that showed he was preoccupied, and whatever it was, he felt angry. The segway to leave Peter worked perfectly. Kurt, *'I appreciate you being so up front. I had better see these guys who have been waiting to speak to me'*. There was no comment from Peter.

During every session throughout the conference, Kurt made sure he regularly made eye contact with Peter and directed his questions to different consultants or left the question open for anyone to answer.

The Chief Operating Officer, Rob Goulding listened intently. He then unwittingly became an advocate by repeating what Kurt said and gave examples to reinforce what he believed the consultants should or should not be doing. Unfortunately, Rob's language was profane, coupled with aggression and amplified expletives whenever he wanted to make a key point. Kurt tried diplomatically to circumvent Rob's comments, but to no

The Most Unlikely Salesperson

avail. He sounded aggressive and dictatorial, not to mention unprofessional. To reduce Rob's input, Kurt acknowledged his contribution and redirected the question to one of the consultants. This worked reasonably well but a dramatic approach was required to create an effective learning environment. Kurt divided the group into three smaller teams of four and introduced role plays. This learning structure minimized Rob's involvement and increased the overall participation of the team.

The consultants were technically and operationally competent but lacked sales and strategy skills. Their motivation to learn, however, was apparent and extended to conversations throughout the morning and afternoon tea breaks.

During one of the breaks, Kurt approached a group of five consultants asking about Rob's language. Julian, one of the consultants shared, *'He always speaks like that, even in mixed company'*. Others nodded in agreement.

Day two, the learning environment was changed again by:
– Dividing the consultants into small breakaway groups to solve sales problems, applying what they had learned
– Role plays consisted of three per team and rotated between salesperson, client and adjudicator roles giving everyone the chance to play a different role
– Individual account management strategy activities.

Rob was unable to be as verbose and appeared to settle down. Consultants' confidence grew as did their skills development.

At the conclusion of the conference, Kurt asked participants to give him their honest feedback. He handed out a four-page course evaluation questionnaire containing a choice of statements to rate by circling the statement applicable to them and room for comments.

There were four sections:
– Part 1: Content
– Part 11: Personal
– Part 111: Facilitator
– Part IV: General.

Once completed, he gave participants his business card stating they can contact him anytime in the future for advice on sales or sales strategy, with no time limit to the offer. The questionnaire and offer were always made after completing a structured sales training programme. To know there is an 'outsider' if needed, who has their best interest at heart can be reassuring.

The Most Unlikely Salesperson

Kurt contacted Peter seven days after the conference to arrange a follow-up meeting with Steve, Rob and himself. The aim of the meeting was to:
– Ask for their feedback
– Deliver a summary of the course evaluation questionnaires
– Provide a critique of every consultant
– Discuss recommendations.

Peter said Steve was out on a client's site and not expected back until the following week but wanted to go ahead and book a time.

Kurt arrived at the PSL Schnyder office later the same week, and one of the administrative staff showed him to Peter's office. It appeared he and Rob had just finished a meeting. During the conference, Kurt evaluated their behaviour to be task orientated, so he needed to get down to business in an assertive but non-rushed manner.

There was a slight pause after the greeting, creating an opening to take control of the meeting. Kurt, *'Do you mind if I give you an overview of what I have planned for our meeting?'* He looked at Peter and Rob as he asked the question. Rob smiled whilst Peter nodded affirmatively in response. He outlined the four aims. Kurt, *'Are you okay if we proceed in this way?'* They both non-verbally agreed.

Kurt asked numerous questions, *'How did you find the structure, content and pace? My facilitation style? Was there any stand-out consultant or one you might be concerned about? Has anything happened that has surprised you since the training?'*

The feedback was positive and enthusiastic from Rob. Peter had the same persona as he did at the conference. Kurt assumed it was his natural self—an air of reserved superiority with anger just under the surface. He noticed a respectful personal chemistry between them, with Rob being the dominant personality. Rob often answered questions on Peter's behalf, and he appeared not to mind. They had a long working relationship, so they appeared to understand each other well. Rob looked ten years younger than Peter. Rob was personable, enthusiastic, and had a high level of energy. He originally qualified as a schoolteacher, and early in his career had various sales roles. His core responsibility at the firm was to manage the team of operations consultants. His language was just as colourful as Kurt had heard at the conference.

Kurt handed both their copy of the aggregated course evaluation questionnaire and gave his feedback on individual consultants. He answered their questions and gave several recommendations to continue the consultants' development. The meeting was constructive, and Rob reaffirmed on their behalf they were happy with the outcomes. Kurt was about to suggest several recommendations when Rob interrupted. Rob,

Chapter 14 Sales Consultants **195**

'Would you facilitate a one-day sales training session?' Kurt, *'Sure'*. Rob, *'It is in two weeks at the Travel Lodge Hotel in Sydney'*.

Although the timeframe was tight, with a few changes it could be done. Salespeople who react and agree immediately can appear overly keen, perhaps desperate for the business. This sends the wrong signal to the client. To avoid this, the salesperson pauses for a moment, asks if they can check their diary or schedule, then confirm their availability. This was Kurt's approach and followed through with a confirmation email and his invoice.

The one-day session was on sales strategies. The course preparation required the consultants to select five current sales opportunities they were experiencing difficulties with. During each session, consultants were divided into groups of two, so they could discuss their sales situation and the action they will take based on what they had learned. This resulted in practical and interactive learning. Kurt walked from group to group and assisted where needed. Looking around the room, it was pleasing to see the level of concentration and the many 'light bulb moments' when they discovered why a sales opportunity was blocked.

During the morning session, Peter became quite vocal and animated, a side of his personality Kurt had not seen. Peter disagreed with the sales strategy structure and process being presented and clearly expressed his thoughts. The exchange between Peter and Kurt became intense. Consultants sat quietly and looked on. Kurt was not going to back down. Peter unknowingly was arguing for sales strategies that were grossly outdated. Once Kurt explained the difference between the two concepts Peter finally conceded. He went quiet with a smirk on his face. It was as if this was a test to evaluate Kurt's depth of knowledge and if he had the courage to stand up to him. Whether this was true or not he was not going to compromize by agreeing to statements that he knew were incorrect.

Rob sat next to Peter during the session and witnessed the interaction first-hand. At the morning tea break, Rob approached Kurt and said he enjoyed what he described as the 'stoush'. Rob added, *'If you are concerned how Peter might be feeling, do not be. Everything is fine'*. Kurt assumed Rob had spoken to Peter.

He called Rob a week later to arrange a follow-up meeting. His personal assistant Sarah told Kurt he had to meet Hamish McLachlan the General Manager. Hamish was in his mid-60s and dressed immaculately. He did not appear interested in the course feedback, so Kurt kept it brief. He soon understood why Rob wanted Kurt to meet Hamish. It was an offer to join the company. Hamish began by reaffirming the company's need to diversify and asked Kurt if he would be interested in a business development role. The target market was utilities particularly major gas and electricity companies. Kurt knew nothing about the utilities industry and had limited

The Most Unlikely Salesperson

knowledge of the firm's process improvement services but continued to listen.

The role was a contract for 12 months and the package included:

- A monthly retainer
- Bonus payment per sale
- Office space
- Expense account
- Access to secretarial services.

The appeal was the challenge of the role, regular monthly revenue and bonus payments. This did have to be weighed against being tired to the one client for 12 months. He decided whatever happens the learning experience would be worth it, but his value was greater than the retainer offered, so Kurt negotiated an increase and Hamish agreed. Both signed the firm's contract agreement and shook hands.

Kurt's plan was to identify the major operators in the utility industry, list the names and contact details of the engineers he needed to connect with. Most organizations were in the Sydney and Melbourne Central Business District, therefore it would be relatively easy to cluster meetings and save travel time.

Day one 8:00am was to attend the Monday morning sales meeting. Hamish did the introductions then handed out the agenda. Several consultants were interstate on client sites and joined via phone hook-up. The procedure was straightforward. Individuals were required to summarize their previous week's activities and results, then provide a forecast for the week ahead.

After the meeting, Hamish showed Kurt his office. It was one of eight, situated next to the board room and opposite the firm's Executive Assistant, Claire Bloomfield. A tall slim person in her early 50s and spoke in a refined English accent and manner. Claire had the additional role of being Kurt's secretarial support. He soon learned she had a wealth of knowledge, experience and a great sense of humour.

The firm was divided into three departments:

- **Operations** was led by Rob who had four senior consultants. They were responsible for implementing process improvement projects and managing young inexperienced consultants. The young consultants were contractors who remained on client sites and rarely came into the office.
- **Administration** included human resources and was a team of four. This department was managed by Steve.

- **The business development team** was the smallest team, consisting of Ben Jones and Kurt. Ben was a well-spoken Englishman, an ex-civil engineer who started a month before Kurt did. His allocated industry was finance and manufacturing. Peter Ditmar and Hamish worked in sales part-time managing existing accounts.

The role of business development at a macro level was to find the client, build the relationship, introduce one of the senior operations consultants and close the sale. Sounded simple, however the challenge was no-one knew the right timing of the introduction—the result was lost sales. To introduce a technical person made sense because both Kurt and Ben did not have process improvement skills.

To minimize losing sales and to create consistency across both operations and business development, Kurt outlined a sales and buying process flow chart. It showed the point in time when the introduction to a client needed to be. Kurt approached Rob with a rough hand drawn flow chart and stepped him through it. Rob was eager to support the concept, *'Let's do it'*. Business development and operations now had the opportunity to work cohesively and create greater understanding.

From a strategic perspective, the client would meet another person from the same firm and importantly, being technical they would have similar attributes. The operations consultant who attended the sales meeting would be the same person to head the client project. This made it vital to choose the consultant who had the specific skills set, and personality the client felt most comfortable with.

The Sales Process and the Client Buying Cycle

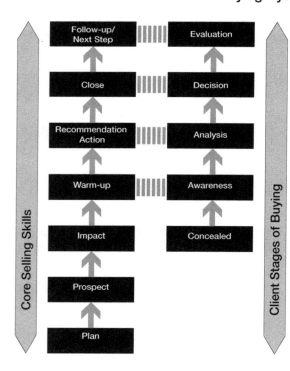

Every senior consultant's technical competence was impressive, but the majority lacked people and sales skills. During a sales meeting they believed they were demonstrating their technical ability and impressing a client by answering any question in the most micro-of-detail. To Kurt, it sounded like it would never end. The question that came to mind was why would a client need the firm's services when they were given the 'what and how' to solve the problem? The answer is, they do not.

In several sales meetings, it went on for so long the client's eyes glossed over as they lost concentration. Kurt politely interjected to lighten the intensity and regain the client's attention.

During the post-sales call review, Kurt realized consultants genuinely believed they were doing the right thing. He used a metaphor, so they understood what they needed to do. Kurt, '*You are providing the menu and recipe but, you only need to pass on the menu*'.

> *Why would a client need the firm's services when given the 'what and how' to solve the problem? The answer is, they do not.*

To minimize the overload of information from reoccurring and to reinforce new habits, Kurt and the operations consultants did numerous role plays. Prior to a client meeting, they set and agreed to concentrate on one to a maximum three sales call objectives. The objectives focused on what they wanted to achieve from the different roles they played. Being technically minded, this made perfect sense to them.

In time, Kurt knew the skills and attributes of everyone in the senior operations team. There were two outstanding individuals, David Tarento was the ex-State Manager of the large window manufacturing company and was hired as the Operations Manager. Both he and Paul Beaumont were highly skilled in operations management and logistics. They also had an acute knowledge of production improvement methodologies. When either David or Paul worked with Kurt, the sales and buying process was implemented as planned and the client became actively engaged.

After working with David and Paul for a month, Rob called Kurt into his office and in his usual colourful language questioned why he was not working with the other two consultants. Kurt explained, '*The problem is I have lost sales opportunities because they are unable to adapt to the sales and buying process. They ask few questions and spend most of the time telling the client in great detail what they would do, rather than focusing on the expected outcomes*'. Rob was adamant, '*I do not want you working with David or Paul*'.

Based on his vocal tone, this was not negotiable. It was tempting for Kurt to ask why but if he did, the conversation would quickly escalate to abuse. Rob had a short fuse. What did not make sense was Kurt did not report to him. There was no expected change in the other consultants' attitude, so going on client sales meetings would be a waste of time. Kurt nodded to acknowledged he heard Rob and walked out of his office. He decided to ignore the directive.

The role was interesting with regular travel to Melbourne and New Zealand. Although Kurt was hired as a contractor, the engagement was turning into an employee/employer relationship. He was regularly called into administration and client problem solving meetings that had nothing to do with him.

Peter was quiet and moody, but what became a concern were his unpredictable tirades. Kurt experienced one of his rants during a meeting when he verbally attacked him. He guessed it must be his turn because everyone else at one time was exposed to it. Kurt remained seated, kept continuous eye contact with Peter and listened until he stopped shouting. If Kurt had interrupted, it would be emotional fuel adding to his anger and prolonging the situation. He had the answers to Peter's accusations, but to create a circuit breaker between the outburst and the replying, he told Peter he would get back to him. The next morning Kurt approached Peter who was in the boardroom, Kurt entered and closed the door.

Kurt, 'Let me begin by saying I did not appreciate the way you spoke to me yesterday'. Peter, no response. Kurt, 'Regarding your statements, let us go through each one and I will give you an explanation'. Kurt proceeded to tell him what he did and why and was prepared for round two. Peter said nothing, so Kurt stood up and left. It was not in Peter's nature to apologize.

After the experiences with Rob and Peter and witnessing their aggressive behaviour with others, Kurt decided it was time to leave. He did not want to work in such an environment. Peter was interstate, so he saw Rob and handed his notice of termination as per the contract and a separate sheet that summarized sales activities that required following though. Rob's face changed to a white shade. This must have caught him off guard. He accepted the notification, but was temporarily lost for words, but then spoke. Rob said, 'Okay. I would like you to change the notice of termination date to be in three weeks' time, so it is beyond the contract agreement. I do not care what you do, you do not have to come into the office'. Kurt was going to ask why, but it did not matter, so they shook hands and parted company.

Steve, Paul and David left within a month. Steve went onto a senior consulting role for a large international company. Paul continued to work as a self-employed consultant in the areas of strategy and process improvement. David accepted an operations role on the Central Coast New South Wales.

Moving forward

After having sold luxury cars and completed the business development contract, Kurt decided not to work exclusively for one client. He enjoyed the responsibility and diversity of working on multiple sales improvement projects in different industries. The next step was to contact clients, get an update on what was happening in their businesses and review Sales Consultant's past services that may need to be updated or possibly dropped.

Kurt began by systematically phoning existing clients, explained why he had not been in contact and asked if he could catch up with them over a coffee. They agreed which gave him the opportunity to reconnect on a personal level, ask about their business environment, current issues, and goals they wanted to achieve.

What was pleasantly surprising every meeting felt as if there was no 12 month time gap. The conversations flowed easily—from where they left off. Only one client hired a consultant during Kurt's absence. Peter Jenkins at the Electrical Wholesale Company. Peter, *'It was time we heard someone else's voice. We have used your services for 10 years and I thought it was time for a change'*. He paused for some time, looked at Kurt intently, then a slight grin turned rapidly into a huge smile. Whatever he was thinking must have amused him. Peter, *'The branch managers and sales reps prefer to listen to you. They quoted what you had taught them years ago. Your training has had a great impact'*. This was reassuring to know. The meeting resulted in a sales training project.

Kurt then spoke with consultants he had worked with, and competitors he knew asking for their opinion on the business-to-business sales environment. The consistent feedback was it had become harder and more competitive. Greater effort and energy were required to achieve the same outcome. The competition in their view had not only intensified between organizations, but also between individuals. Salespeople were now required to develop a higher standard of sales competence and when starting a new job, a shorter ramp-up time.

The conversations resulted in better understanding the industry. In summary:

– Less salespeople
– Higher standard of sales competence required
– Ability to produce great sales results consistently
– Greater remuneration
– Increase use of technology, such as video conferencing.

Video conferencing has been around for years and continues to gather momentum. One prediction is 80 percent of business-to-business sales will be virtual within two to three years of introduction. The attraction of video conferencing has always been:

- **Lower costs**: salespeople can work from home, save on airfares, accommodation, client entertainment and vehicle maintenance
- **Productivity increase**: less non-selling time for example travel, that can be redirected to increase the number of client connections.

Video conferencing has its place in sales however, there are limitations that need to be understood. It is 2-dimensional, attracting challenges not encountered when meeting with a client in-person which is 3-dimensional.

Common challenges:

- **Eye contact**: A screen hinders the ability to connect at a level considered essential to develop a relationship built on trust.
- **Body language**: This cannot be accurately assessed due to screen size limitations often only showing the upper top quarter of a client. A salesperson is unable to gesture freely which can automatically impact on vocal tone and influence.
- **Passive engagement**: Watching a computer monitor subconsciously can feel like watching television that can lead to the client not actively listening and less engaged.
- **Technical issues**: Ranging from screen and vocal lag, webcam, headset, and monitor issues through to being disconnected. Any one or multiple issues can break the salesperson and client interaction. The emotional connection prior to the separation can be difficult to re-establish.
- **Distractions**: These can be wide ranging and unexpected from dogs barking, people walking past in the background, traffic noise to the sound of doors opening and closing.
- **Behaviours**: The salesperson's unconscious behaviours can send the wrong signals and be off putting for the client. These can be looking down, fidgeting, low energy appearing as tiredness, poor body posture, speaking rapidly and at a high pitch voice or monotone.

Video conferencing is a sales tool just like the mobile phone, CRM software, email, social media and other technologies.

> With the competitive environment growing, it is vital for a salesperson to use the most effective tool for any given sales situation. If the objective is to develop a relationship built on trust whether one-on-one, a board presentation or a major negotiation in-person is the best option. This will give the salesperson greater verbal and non-verbal information and emotional connectivity.
>
> Meeting with a client in-person can create a differentiated experience for them, compared to a salesperson who uses video conferencing.

Kurt planned to embrace technologies that add value and made his job easier, but was determined to foster in-person client meetings wherever possible. The next step was to review and update current services. The current services were:

- The infield sales review
- Group structured classroom training
- Infield Sales Coaching
- Sales Competence Levels.

The review of these services resulted in:

1. **The infield sales review**

   As previously mentioned, a more holistic approach was needed to uncover functions within a client's organization that may directly or indirectly impact on sales and profitability. Organizations that simply blame salespeople for poor results miss the chance to uncover deeper underlying problems.

   Paul Beaumont had the skills and experience to play an integral role within the review process and implement systems, processes and transfer skills in areas of operations, distribution and administration. Kurt asked Paul if he would join him to fulfil this role. There was no hesitation in his agreeing. Paul wrote the agreement and within days both signed it. The agreement still exists to this day.

2. **Group structured classroom training**

   After considering various options, Kurt decided to continue using the competence-based format. The content was updated, and new modules added.

3. Infield Sales Coaching

To work with salespeople in 'live' sales situations, seeing how they apply the knowledge and skills learned in the structured classroom training. All together a powerful way to develop and improve sales competence. There were no changes required.

4. Sales Competence Levels

Sales competence levels for complex sales were subjected to the review process and updated. The levels consist of attributes, knowledge and skills as follows:

Level 1: The Beginner

The salesperson is usually promoted to external sales from an internal customer service or sales support position. In large organizations, the previous role could have been operations or administration, and a move into sales is part of the person's career development. The aim for the salesperson is to be in a management position within three years.

Attributes can range from nervous excitement, eagerness and high expectations to outright fear, anxiety and self-doubt.

Knowledge

- Product, industry and client knowledge is often acquired from the previous role
- Unaware of the requirements needed to succeed in external sales
- No understanding of client purchasing influences and the decision process
- Knowledge of sales and sales strategy is limited to what they read in books, looked up on the internet or heard from other salespeople.

Skills

- Capable of continuing to develop relationships with existing clients
- Poor business development skills
- Lack ability to structure a sales process
- Lack ability to create the right selling environment
- Lack ability to apply warm-up skills
- Few questions asked during a new sales call
- Present products or services shortly after the introduction
- Lack ability to deal with rebuttals and sales objections
- Passive when concluding the sales call
- Do not ask for referrals.

Level 2: The Novice

The salesperson can be in a sales role for six months to possibly years. Initial excitement and enthusiasm for sales is given way to a subdued approach to sales.

Attributes: Consciously aware, they lack sales competence and will either continue in this manner or become increasingly dissatisfied and frustrated. When in the latter, they tend to become overwhelmed by sales related problems resulting in outbursts of anger to sales support and management. Frustration is a common bi-product for a lack of sales competence.

Knowledge

- A degree of sales knowledge has been achieved through trial and error
- They do not understand how skills are applied in a structured sales process
- Unaware as to why sales rebuttals, objections and sales related difficulties reoccur
- Inadequate knowledge of business development, account management, purchase influences and the decision process.

Skills

- Lack business development, account management, sales strategy, and sales tactics ability
- Poor time management
- Do not set sales call objectives
- Passive in creating the right selling environment
- Good rapport building skills with existing clients
- Predominately ask personal questions with existing clients
- Listening skills linked to the level of confidence
- Poor rebuttal and sales objection skills
- Passive concluding the sales call
- Use one sales style
- Do not ask for referrals
- Customer relationship management records not up to date.

Level 3: The Disciplined

It is common for a salesperson to remain at this level for their sales career. They develop long term loyal client relationships and are not strategic in their sales approach.

Attributes

- Prefer to follow a daily sales territory schedule and resist any disruption to it
- Tend to look at the disadvantages of change
- Do not like sales training because they believe they know everything about sales
- Appear outwardly confident because of years in sales
- They feel most comfortable dealing with supervisory to middle management and avoid senior client management.

Knowledge

- Gained by having attended sales seminars and sales courses throughout their career
- Their knowledge of sales is often out of date
- Good personal relationships and know their clients well, but minimal information known about the client organization
- Limited sales strategies and tactics.

Skills

- Are capable of, but avoid business development
- Unstructured and subjective sales call objectives
- Sales process applied by 'gut feel'
- Experienced at rapport building
- Ask mainly personal and too few organizational questions
- Active listening skills
- Inconsistent client qualification
- Use one sales style
- Focus on a few key influencers in the decision process
- React to rebuttals and sales objections with a generic answer
- Competent at closing the sale
- Asking for referrals is inconsistent
- Over service clients they feel comfortable with, and under service or avoid difficult clients
- Customer relationship management records not up to date.

Level 4: The Competent

Level 4 are consistent sales performers who frequently sell to large client organizations in a national or state account management role. Strategic and tactical approach to sales and will undertake business development if required.

Attributes

- Can become complacent dealing with a small number of large client organizations
- Inclined to limit the circle of influence by only contacting the same individuals
- Few probing questions asked resulting in negligible or loss of new business
- Can feel intimidated if required to call on executive client management.

Knowledge

- The sales and buying process
- Client personal and organizational knowledge
- Selling strategies and tactics but may need assistance or advice from senior management.

Skills

- Competent business development
- Create account plans and set sales call objectives
- Consistently create the right selling environment
- Excellent rapport building skills
- Qualify and re-qualify when required
- Fair style-shifting skills
- Handle sales objections
- Close sales consistently
- Conscientious customer relationship management records and maintenance.

Level 5: The High-flyer

Large or very small sales teams have one salesperson at this level. They fit the public's perception of a typical salesperson, and are flamboyant, self-indulgent, motivated by money and status. They are best suited for business development.

Attributes

- Dramatically outsell peers
- A sales and not a business approach
- Sell at low profit margins
- Charismatic personality and comfortable building new client relationships
- Sell intuitively so they cannot accurately analyze how and why they sell
- Inability to transfer skills
- Resist change
- Ignore junior client influencers
- A 'salesy' manner, tending to be pushy, so they have difficulty in establishing credibility with senior client management.

Knowledge

- Well informed of client decision processes and influencers that impact the buying process
- Thorough understanding of client personalities and the client organization.

Skills

- Capable business development and sales territory management
- Limited business acumen
- Initiate and create the right selling environment
- Build rapport effortlessly with the decision maker
- Active listener
- Qualify and re-qualifying when required
- Fixed sales style
- Handle sales objections
- Skilled at generating referrals
- Assumptive at closing the sale
- Customer relationship management records not up to date
- Skilled at sales tactics but lack strategic skills.

Level 6: The Professional

Few salespeople reach this level of sales competence. Level 6 salespeople set the standard for sales performance and have a strategic business approach. They:
- Sell at higher profit margins
- Are proactive learners
- Pursue ways to grow personally and professionally
- Tend to move into a sales coaching role full or part-time
- Have an ability to transfer knowledge and skills
- Can become a role model for other salespeople.

Attributes
- Conservative, seek realistic but challenging opportunities
- Methodical, embrace structure, process, and stick with what works
- Independent, dislike rules, regulations and red tape
- Non-reflective, do not agonize over setbacks
- Set short term goals for up to 12 months
- Productive
- Action orientated to achieve tangible results
- Practical
- Learn and refine new skills to achieve better outcomes
- Socialize with a diverse number of people to identify business opportunities.

Knowledge
- Uncover and maintain intelligence on competitors' activities, products and services
- Comprehensive information on client personnel involved in the decision process
- Create a strategic sales approach that differs from competitors.

Skill
- Practical application of the sales and buying process
- Ability to effectively manage a sales meeting and video conferencing
- Objectively critique sales meetings
- Ability to isolate skills and strategies that need to be improved
- Shorter sales cycle compared to the company's average salesperson
- Skilled business-related discussions with senior client management

The Most Unlikely Salesperson

- Skilled dealing with client purchasing groups and boards of directors
- Coach and transfer sales and strategy skills.

Sales and Managing Salespeople

Not all salespeople are suited to the profession, and it is not their fault. There are various reasons why they ended up in sales, but typically:

- The individual has an extroverted friendly personality, and management assume they would be good at sales
- The individual is promoted from sales support, operations or administration. This is part of their career development.

If a psychometric or an objective assessment had been conducted when considering the internal candidate, they would realize the individual would be unsuitable for a sales role.

People who should be in a different role, but are in sales fail can feel so devastated by their failure, they believe there is no option but to resign. Management often try and convince them to stay by offering another role—usually it is all too late. The individual feels leaving is the only way. To avoid this from happening, a trial period should be set up and mutually agreed. Part of the agreement to state that if the individual decides external sales is not for them, they can return to their previous role.

A sales team can be divided into performance categories: typically top, mid and poor. Sales growth opportunities and finding the next top performer occurs when sales management regularly coach the mid-tier one-on-one. This does not mean to neglect other performance categories.

There can be a number of top sales performers, but only one super star performer. These amazing salespeople consistently outperform the mid-tier by four times the revenue. Like a super star, they can be difficult to manage requiring constant attention. However, there are others who just get on with the job.

Sales managers who regularly coach their salespeople, develop their individual sales competence, automatically create a bond of trust and loyalty. The increase in sales is the bi-product of the commitment.

There are sales managers who avoid sales coaching, providing the excuse their administration workload prevents them from doing so.

The Most Unlikely Salesperson

Others spend considerable time coaching mid and poor performers and not the top sales performers. The reasons:

- Falsely assume top sales performers do not need coaching
- Lack coaching skills
- Lack self-confidence
- Have no or limited sales background or feel intimidated.

Sales managers can unknowingly believe the greatest opportunity to improve sales is to work with the poor sales performers. At first glance it makes sense, but after spending an inordinate amount of time and energy, the sales dial will scarcely move, if at all. There is also the inherent risk of losing salespeople from other sales performance categories because an insufficient amount of time has been spent with them. If salespeople feel neglected, they usually are.

Sales managers who spend too much time coaching poor sales performers can find their frustration building to the point they take control of the client sales meeting. Although tempting to rescue the salesperson and save the sale, the sales manager needs to let them fail. You read correctly, let them fail. For the salesperson, it will be embarrassing, emotionally painful but a learning experience they will never forget.

Sales managers who take control of the sale do so because:

- Their ego
- Fear of losing the sale
- A false belief they are showing the salesperson what to do.

Regarding the latter, unless it was a sales coaching objective the sales manager will in effect communicate, *'Whenever you get into an awkward sales situation, I will step in'*. This is counterproductive, and signals to the salesperson whenever they get into an uncomfortable sales situation, wait for the sales manager to rescue them. Admittedly, it can be costly to lose a sale, but the cost of not learning and developing competence is far greater.

The emotional pain associated with losing the sale and the lessons learned will be etched in the salesperson's memory. The same mistake will not be duplicated. To quote Benjamin Franklin, *'Those things that hurt, instruct'*. If a poor sales performer does not improve after being given numerous coaching sessions, it is time to discuss transferring them to another role or alternate career.

The Most Unlikely Salesperson

Top Sales Performers and the Infield Sales Review
- Top sales performers produce incredible sales results
- Are independent thinkers
- Highly driven
- Attended many sales training courses and sales seminars.

When management ask them to participate in the infield sales review their common reaction is, '*I do not want to waste my time*'. They do not want to have their daily plan disrupted, which is fair enough. After all, what is in it for them?

To gain their cooperation and respect, Kurt offers to solve a sales or sales strategy problem that has stumped them for some time. Kurt, '*Let me ask you, is there a difficult sales situation or client, one you have tried to win business, but nothing has worked?*' There is silence for a short time then, '*Yes*'.

Kurt follows through with probing questions about the sales environment, what they did or did not do that created the no-sale outcome. Once understood, '*Thank you for letting me know. If I give you some ideas, options perhaps on how to successfully turn this around, could I ask for your support throughout the project?*'

The reaction is usually a cautious, '*With respect I doubt you have the answer*'. Kurt, '*I appreciate where you are coming from. Bear with me while I show you what you might consider doing*'.

He places his words carefully to keep the top salesperson open minded to what he is about to propose. A pad and pen as a visual aid outlining diagrams, flow charts or key words are used to communicate clear understanding, then he hands over the sheet of paper. Kurt, '*Could I ask you for a favour? Let me know how this works for you?*'

Fortunately, the ideas or options always work and credit to the top salespeople who diligently apply what they were coached to do. Once the infield sales review is completed the top sales performer's energy, active involvement and insights during the structured classroom training has a domino effect on the whole sales team. It is normal for salespeople to feel resistance when the classroom training starts, but thanks to the top salesperson it quickly disappears. This means everyone's sales development begins sooner.

A common trait with top and solid mid-level sales performers is they always look for ways to improve. They hunger for the minor adjustments, and the refinements that take a skill or strategy from good to an elite standard. At times, this can mean going back to basics resulting in better sales execution. Salespeople who experience infield sales coaching—with its one-on-one attention and regular feedback—are motivated to achieve higher levels of sales competence.

Sales coaching can be an amazing platform for salespeople to rapidly grow in competence. However, salespeople will not be successful when they:
- Do not have the personal characteristics for sales
- Are incompatible with the industry, product or service
- Have unresolved conflict between them and the sales manager
- Are incompetent or inexperienced sales manager
- Are ineffective sales coaching structure and implementation
- Have a negative fixed attitude.

The transition from a range of training and development services to specializing in sales performance improvement went smoother than anticipated. This was due to the planning and the energy that went into achieving what needed to be done. Sales Consultants services attracted new clients internationally. Projects required Kurt to work in Singapore, China, Hong Kong, Norway, Japan, South America and The Middle East. The latter were back-to-back projects in Oman, Dhabi and Abu Dhabi. When CEO's and senior managers leave one company and joined another, they contacted Kurt for his assessment of the sales team. Sales in Australia also continue to grow.

The Most Unlikely Salesperson

Lessons learned

- Research competitors from time to time and make changes to continuously differentiate.
- When you are totally committed and passionate about achieving client outcomes, they will always remember you. They may try a competitor for a brief period, but will come back to you.
- Developing trusting relationships within a client organization can lead to giving information normally kept internally. The greater insight this provides you, places you in a unique position to be of unmatched value to your client when compared to your competitors.
- Never back down from a bully whether a co-worker or client. Do not react but respond in time and timing that suits you. Your demeanour should remain calm and controlled.
- Do not accept a first offer salary or remuneration package. Negotiate the number you know is your true value.
- The sales profession continues to change. Notice what everyone else is doing and do not follow the crowd. If you do, you will be undifferentiated and compared to competitors.
- Push yourself regularly to higher standards of knowledge. Read books, go to seminars that provide validated information, and network with successful salespeople.
- Develop your skills. Hire a sales coach with a proven track record and develop attributes—understand what top salespeople do.

Chapter 15
Southern Highlands Chamber of Commerce and Industry Ltd

Following many years in Sydney, June and Kurt decided to move to a country region—preferably within 2 hours of Sydney. After considering a number of locations, it was the Southern Highlands that captured their hearts. The region is 1½ hours south-west of Sydney and for the most part a comfortable highway drive. Technology in its various forms makes it possible to manage a business in a rural setting and commute to the city as and when needed to see clients and business contacts.

Being new to the area, the couple wanted to reach out and be active members of the community. There was an impressive array of not-for-profit organizations to choose from, but their interest was the local Bowral Chamber of Commerce (BCC). Being familiar with business Chambers and the value these organizations can provide, made it an easy decision.

They attended their first function and met the President, Greg Halsey. Kurt asked for an application form and Sales Consultants became BCC's newest member. During a networking evening, Marlene Henderson one of the members, informed them there were four other town Chambers in the district. Kurt, *'Why isn't there one large Chamber to represent the whole region?'* Marlene, *'I do not know'*. This presented a puzzle, Kurt had to find out why.

June and Kurt attended functions over a three-month period and noticed the atmosphere was consistently lacklustre. Membership was shrinking. No action was taken to create greater value for members. To continue in the current manner, it was only a matter of time before the organization became irrelevant or possibly even closed.

Where to start? Kurt instinctively thought about sales. Before approaching a new client, he prepared by gathering information from various sources

The Most Unlikely Salesperson

including, but not limited to, the website, social media, and other contacts within the organization. The knowledge he aimed to acquire was the personal and professional background of the individual, the organization, the industry, questions to ask, and how to tailor the approach. To skip the preparation makes obtaining the initial appointment difficult and there would be a high chance of outright failure and rebuttal.

The BCC clients were its members, and to speak to them was the logical starting point to turn the organization around. But first, Kurt had to uncover information about every member and their business. The ultimate goal was for members to meet potential customers or clients through BCC resulting in increased sales revenues.

For Kurt, this felt like starting a new job—except this one paid no income. The impending workload was considerable, and in addition to managing Sales Consultants. He started with a member's list and began scanning individual websites, as well as LinkedIn and *Few local businesses had professional websites and social media profiles* Facebook Profiles. Kurt was surprised at the number of businesses that only had a local online listing. Few had a website and a professional profile. Perhaps they believed everyone knew them locally, so it was unnecessary to use social media or there was no interest to attract business from outside the district?

Kurt gathered as much information as he could and then began phoning. Kurt, *'Good morning. This is Kurt Newman. I am a member of the Bowral Chamber of Commerce. The reason for the call is I am contacting members to ask for their feedback, so changes can be made in-line with member core needs. Would you like to meet with me, perhaps over a coffee?'*

This mainly went well with appointments locked in, but a number were so angry their typical statements were, *'I am no longer a member. I am not interested. You are wasting your time'*. They cut the phone call short by hanging up after letting-off steam. For Kurt, it reminded him of phone prospecting he did decades ago.

Of those who did not renew their membership, only two did not want to discuss why and refused the offer to meet. The others accepted the invitation, but only after expressing how they felt about the BCC. Kurt wanted to understand:

- Members and lapsed members point of view
- The business challenges they face
- What they wanted to achieve
- Learn about the BCC and its history

The Most Unlikely Salesperson

– Uncover any blocks preventing or grossly diminishing membership growth.

Kurt met with fellow members, lapsed members and Presidents from other Chambers at a local café in Bowral. Others preferred to meet at their business premises and gave Kurt a guided tour.

The fact-finding phase uncovered:

1. No vision, defined purpose or strategic plan existed for the Chamber.
2. The town-centric model created division, dysfunction, limited member numbers and unsatisfactory member value. Functions had as few as nine members attending.
3. Each town Chamber was too small to provide influence and credibility to represent member concerns to the local council, state or federal government representatives.
4. The organization was registered as an association. The committee had three roles defined by name only: President, Treasurer and Events. The remaining six had no title, responsibilities or accountabilities. This resulted in discord, duplication of work and member disagreements. The vast majority did nothing but attend monthly meetings.
5. Communication was poor and morale low.
6. The administration of BCC had no systems or processes in place. One of the numerous problems was financial members could not be identified from lapsed members.
7. A common response from lapsed members was the Chamber was going nowhere and functions were a waste of time.
8. One of the four Chamber Presidents, a retired CEO Morgan Smyth-Jones flatly refused the concept of one Chamber to represent the region. Morgan, '*We tried this in 2008 and it failed*'.

   He was well connected and gave his time to a range of committees. The structure he developed in 2008 was an overarching Chamber to represent the town Chambers. A committee was formed consisting of each town Chamber President and Morgan was the chair.

   The structure turned out to be a band aid solution. It did not solve the real problem or the town-centric mindset that divided the region.
9. The other three Presidents were open to further discussion about forming one Chamber.

Gathering the information took months as Kurt split his time between BCC and Sales Consultants. When the findings were completed, he approached Greg who told him he was resigning and moving out of the

The Most Unlikely Salesperson

district. The Annual General Meeting (AGM) was in two weeks, and although a tight timeframe, it was the opportunity to implement change.

The strategy was for June to stand for the President position until the BCC was de-registered. It was expected to be only a matter of months. June agreed. This gave Kurt the time to do the work required to form the new Chamber. The AGM resulted in a unanimous 'Yes' vote for June.

June as President the Bowral Chamber of Commerce

During the fact-finding phase Kurt was encouraged by the number of like-minded people who shared the vision of a united Chamber representing all businesses in the Southern Highlands. However, the previous failed attempt lingered, and others wanted the status quo.

Rumours and untruths surfaced by those wanting to divide the small start-up stakeholder group. The situation was comparable to a complex sale where the self-interest of a few try to prevent progress.

Kurt addressed the criticisms by meeting individuals and small groups explaining why there was a need for one large Chamber and the benefits to business and the wider community. This generally went well as business owners and managers began to understand the value for their business. However, there were those who were relentless and continued to undermine the efforts of the stakeholder group.

Kurt expected a number of stakeholders to opt out—and they did. It was the realisation of the time, commitment and mindset required to make the new Chamber a reality, and not the naysayers that triggered their decision. Their leaving only strengthened the resolve of those who remained.

The to-do list for the new Chamber structure:

- Meet the three Chamber Presidents, and other interested parties to seek their input and discuss the vision. Invite them to form a larger stakeholder group
- Schedule regular workshops with the stakeholder group to agree on the Chamber name, the suitable not-for-profit structure, culture, and a strategic plan
- Sell the vision and value of a substantial large Chamber to the membership of the town-based Chambers. In summary the benefits were:
  - Greater networking and business opportunities
  - Business education
  - Access to the resources of the New South Wales (NSW) Business Chamber
  - Influence and representation at all levels of government
- Set a date and venue for an official public launch
- June and the BCC Committee to step down from their position, and de-register BCC and two town Chambers. This would then be the critical point of the change process.
- Hire three adjoining rooms at the Gibraltar Hotel, Bowral, to conduct the three general meetings simultaneously
- Hire the auditorium for the expected post-celebration of the new Chamber and members
- Approach and invite local radio and print media to the new Chamber launch.

The tangible outcomes for the structure:

- The stakeholder group of 15 participants reduced to become a core team of eight
- The chosen name for the new entity was the Southern Highlands Chamber of Commerce and Industry Ltd (SHCCI). The Legal Department

The Most Unlikely Salesperson

of the NSW Business Chamber recommended a limited by guarantee public company structure. This was accepted by the stakeholder group

- Three town Chambers in total were dissolved simultaneously resulting in a foundation membership of 100 businesses. The fourth Chamber, the overarching entity had no members. The Businesswomen's Network joined immediately as an affiliate member adding an additional 85 businesses
- The stakeholder group became board members of SHCCI after being informed of their legal responsibilities. Unbeknown to Kurt the board met prior to the inaugural meeting and decided he was going to be the Chair.
- The board roles were Chair, Deputy Chair, Finance, Membership, Internal Communication, External Communication and Events.
- June Newman became the Events Director.
- Every board member had defined portfolio roles with subset objectives and accountabilities. Where possible board members were given a portfolio role comparable to their professional skills
- The auditorium of the Gibraltar Hotel, Bowral, was the venue for the public 9th December 2013 launch.
- The launch guest speaker Katrina Hodgkinson was the Federal Vice President of the National Party of Australia. In excess of 300 people attended including the media, businesspeople, the Mayor and local Councillors.

The launch created excitement and anticipation as it introduced a new era for the region's businesses. It confirmed what a small group of like-minded people who shared a common vision and purpose can achieve. The dedication, commitment, finding ways to overcome hurdles and to finally achieve what others had failed to, was a moment to reflect on with gratitude.

The moment was short lived as the impending next phase was looming— to unify and grow businesses throughout the region.

The board consisted of eight members and fortunately for SHCCI, everyone had a different professional background and experience. Kurt facilitated board workshops including a brainstorming session to develop the organization's strategic plan.

news

SOUTHERNHIGHLANDNEWS.COM.AU

Businesses united across the shire

By Claire Fenwicke

BY now, many businesses have heard of the Southern Highlands Chamber of Commerce and Industry (SHCCI).

But for those unsure, what exactly is it and why should businesses join?

SHCCI chairman Kurt Newman moved down to the Southern Highlands four years ago, and was approached to join the Bowral Chamber.

He wondered why each town had their own chamber, and began approaching chambers with the idea to amalgamate.

"We tried in 2008 without success, so then we had to try option B," Mr Newman said.

"We spent the next six months in meetings, and on December 9, 2013, we finally registered the SHCCI."

Mr Newman said the public, not-for-profit company had the aim of "uniting the business community".

"Businesses don't have to share the nuts and bolts details of their company, but it's about being open-minded working with each other.

"I've discovered a lot of calls go on between members after meeting each other.

"I think it's more productive and enjoyable to share problems and ideas to help each other."

Mr Newman said there was no one reason why a business or individual should join.

"I ask people 'what challenges do you face as a business? What problems?'," he said.

"If we can provide a service, then I'll tell them why they should join."

There are two membership options with the SHCCI: full and affiliate.

Membership benefits include: networking opportunities, new customer referrals, access to NSW Business Chamber's Local Chamber Alliance Porgram, seminars, training, and support.

"We have connections to the NSW Business Chamber, which in turn is connected to the Australian Business Chamber," Mr Newman said.

"We can go to a local, state and even federal level about a major issues."

In the end, Mr Newman said the SHCCI was about linking "with other like-minded entities".

"We help complementary and supplementary services work together, such as accountants with book keepers," he said.

"It's about working together, even if you're competitors, you've probably had the same problems and can help each other."

People have joined the SHCCI for many reasons, such as chances to network, to share discussions with like-minded people, education opportunities and seminars, and people who are new to business to learn about legislation.

"There are around 4000 registered businesses in the Southern Highlands," Mr Newman said.

"200 business members are registered with us, but my personal goal would be to see that come to 600 so we can represent a reasonable chunk of all businesses"

"I want to make people think more regionally than town-centric."

For more information, visit http://shchamber.com.au/

Business unites across the shire

The Strategic Plan was developed:

Vision: To provide business-focussed leadership and a level of products and services that are recognized as best practice.

Purpose: Promote regional economic growth that represent the voice of business, enabling members to grow their businesses and help them succeed.

Bi-line: Passionately committed to economic growth.

Values
- Passionately committed to our purpose
- Action with integrity
- Actively listen to our members
- Encourage business innovation
- Promote economic growth.

The values to align with the beliefs, attitudes, and behaviours of the organization.

The board also signed-off on four objectives:
1. Actively participate and influence economic development of the Southern Highlands
2. Build a strong and representative membership base
3. Be a powerful and effective advocate for business in the Southern Highlands
4. Provide value added member services.

Every objective was divided into an action plan that included objectives, strategies and timelines. Board members completed their accountability statement to ensure every board member's contribution would achieve the organisations overall objectives. Although everyone were volunteers, the ethos of the regular reviews were treated as remunerated roles. Kurt supported every board member where he could, but in the end, it was their responsibility to do what they had committed to.

There was a period board member turnover was regular. Kurt listened to their excuses and after three in succession, he in private suggested they did not have the time to devote to the role and encouraged them to step down. He then proactively looked for a replacement, letting them know what was involved—focussing on the workload in addition to their full-time employment.

Kurt Newman
Southern Highlands Chamber of Commerce & Industry

One who was a stand-out performer was Peter Blain the Membership Director. He set time aside every week to prospect for new members, actively contributed at board meetings and he projected a professional persona.

The subsequent workload was huge, so the board decided to meet at fortnightly intervals—that often became weekly as SHCCI membership and other commitments grew. SHCCI had no paid employees or contractors. The individual board members did the work.

> *In 2015, less than two years after SHCCI was established, the organization broke the NSW Business Chamber's 190 year record by becoming the youngest Chamber to win the Regional Finalist and the Local Chamber of Commerce Award. SHCCI was the best of 270 local Chambers.*

The Most Unlikely Salesperson

Membership numbers grew to 502 businesses. This included affiliate Business Chambers within and outside the region and associations. Primary reasons for businesses joining were:

- The collaborative relationship. Members could attend the other Chamber and affiliate networking functions
- Representation was made on behalf of their members at local, state, and federal governments. The large membership, rapid growth and influence SHCCI generated made contacting politicians and senior management at every level of government possible.

The following initiatives were achieved and implemented:

- Developed a strategic alliance with *Destination Southern Highlands* the official peak tourism body for the Southern Highlands. SHCCI became involved in the 'Live Local, Buy Local' campaign
- Signed a Memorandum of Understanding (MoU) with Workplace Learning not-for-profit organization that assists high school students with practical workplace experience. SHCCI matched member businesses to students' interests to provide the learning opportunities
- Short-term business courses were offered to members through the South-East Region Business Enterprise Centre and a Customer Care Programme designed by Illawarra TAFENSW
- Held bi-monthly meetings with the General Manager of the Local Council to discuss business activity, concerns, opportunities and give feedback
- Relationships developed with local print and radio media that provided a platform to regularly communicate to the wider community
- Attended The Illawarra Regional Advisory Council (IRAC) monthly committee meetings. This was to understand regional issues, develop relationships and to be a voice on the committee. IRAC comprized of 14 representative Chambers
- Walked door-to-door to meet potential new business members
- Sponsored and presented at the Southern Highlands Business Awards
- Provided emotional support, resources, coaching and mentoring services to members
- Initiated the Economic Summit for the region
- Participated on the Economic Development and Tourism Committee.

One of the town Chambers—the only one remaining in the town-centric model—refused to de-register and join SHCCI. The President's decision was motivated by ego and self-interest. The town Chamber did however, become an affiliate member. A number of their members learned of the decision and joined SHCCI direct.

The Most Unlikely Salesperson

SHCCI's revenues were limited to annual membership fees and income from monthly functions. To keep pace with the growth, additional funds were needed. Platinum, Gold and Silver Sponsorship packages were developed to assist funding. These were valued at $10,000, $5,000 and $2,500 respectively. Each offered a range of benefits on a sliding scale. $45,000 of sponsorship was sold within the first six weeks.

SHCCI achieved a breakthrough for the region, and one that impacted on the larger NSW Chamber community. Within weeks of winning the Local Chamber of Commerce Award, Kurt was invited to speak at the NSW Business Chamber Conference, various Chamber functions and address Chamber committees.

The NSW Chamber's interest was to understand how and why the Chamber grew so rapidly, the challenges encountered and what was done to overcome them. As a direct result, Duncan Burke, the Local Chamber of Commerce Relationship Manager NSW Business Chamber, initiated a keynote presentation for Kurt. Kurt was to address 11 town Chambers who were interested in pursuing a similar strategy to merge with the New South Wales north region.

In January 2016, three years after the first conversation about forming one large regional business Chamber, Kurt made the decision to hand over the responsibilities and resign. SHCCI had consumed a substantial amount of his time and he needed to concentrate on his own business, Sales Consultants.

SHCCI was in great shape for a successor to maintain the influence and continue member growth. The logical person was Vice Chair Sebastian Haret. He was in the ideal position to carry on the work having been there from the beginning. Kurt explained why he needed to resign but after multiple attempts to convince him to take over, it was plainly clear Sebastian did not want the chair role. This put Kurt in an awkward position. He needed to focus on his own business and at the same time he did not want to walk away and let hundreds of members down.

It was a testing year, trying to get Sales Consultants to where he wanted it to be and do the right thing by SHCCI. Being in caretaker mode was the best Kurt could do for the next 11 months—a position he was grossly uncomfortable with. The next annual general meeting was in the November. Fortunately, several months earlier Kurt managed to convince Sebastian to stand for the Chair role. Again, they discussed what needed to be done to ensure SHCCI's ongoing success. At the AGM, Sebastian was voted in. June decided not to renominate for her position and resigned.

224 Chapter 15 Southern Highlands Chamber of Commerce and Industry Ltd

Lessons learned

- When a high standard of professionalism is set as the norm, like-minded people are attracted. It creates a domino effect that impacts more people's lives than you may consciously be aware of.
- Join a not-for-profit organization you feel passionate about. Contribute your time and skills for the greater good, without expecting a return. You will be surprised at the friendships you develop, the new skills you learn and opportunities to get out of your comfort zone.
- Be innovative and try the untried. Obstacles and failure are an integral part of the journey. Learn from the mistakes and do not miss a beat. Keep moving forward.
- Do not listen to the critics or naysayers. They come out of nowhere when you are creating something no-one has done before. Be polite and acknowledge them, but do not buy into their pessimism. These are non-achievers who are quick to criticise.
- Ask questions to understand what the client really needs or wants, then ask why to discover their motive.
- Use a variety of communication tools to keep in regular contact with clients.
- Go beyond the client norms of expectation. You will be surprised how many will become advocates and refer you to others making your job easier—and more enjoyable.
- Work with the strengths of your support team because they will be on your side. Great outcomes can be achieved.
- Dreams do come true when you never give up.

The Most Unlikely Salesperson

Afterword

If you have reached this page, congratulations you have read the book. If not, you may have scanned through to this page before deciding what chapter to read first. Either way, I am glad you have the book and an opportunity to share my experiences.

Wherever you are in sales or considering a career in sales, I would encourage you to go for it. Or you may be highly experienced, with decades of sales under your belt, I am grateful to connect with a fellow salesperson.

Dreams do come true when you never give up

Let me ask you, were you able to relate to the sales journey, my failures and setbacks, how I felt, but continued to move forward? Has it inspired you to become a sales award winner? Have you had similar learning experiences as outlined in the Lessons Learned at the end of each chapter?

If you have questions about any of the content or would like to comment, then please send me an email, type in the subject line TMUSP, to kurt@salesconsultants.com.au. I will respond.

For more information about Sales Consultants go to www.salesconsultants.com.au

Wishing you great sales success!

With kind regards

Kurt

Other Publications

Another Book by Kurt Newman
21 Timeless Insights for Sales Success

The book is based on 25 years' experience in sales research, structured competence training and development and infield sales coaching across a number of industries.

This essential handbook could change your selling career, create greater insight into sales, boost sales, and develop the attitude you are aiming to achieve.

The book is filled with proven tips and practical how-to skills with questions at the end of each chapter. The latter is an option if you want to test yourself, or it can be used by sales managers to coach their salespeople and sales teams.

"If you picked up this book undoubtedly you want to be a highly successful professional salesperson or entrepreneur and deliver hard results for your clients and your life.

As you read this book, Kurt will take you on a personal journey describing critical sales skills and practical business development strategies that are simple, natural and easy to employ. You will witness first-hand Kurt in full flight, in a diverse range of selling and in-field sales training and coaching, business development and account management settings, across 15 industries.

You will observe Kurt emotionally and intelligently going the extra-mile, managing a broad range of business challenges, contexts and environments over several decades, overcoming difficulties and growing professionally to achieve outstanding results, accolades and a rich meaningful life while consistently delivering value for his clients.

You will learn how to apply Kurt's hard-won understanding and insights gained from marketing both tangible and intangible products and services, in just almost every sales environment imaginable—from kitchens and dining rooms, grimy industrial workshops, to shiny commercial and retail offices and showrooms, and all the way to the carpeted executive suites of corporate and community boardrooms.

This book is Kurt's Legacy, something that he knows will powerfully and meaningfully serve you and those you serve."

Peter Harrison
Master Coach and Trainer, EmergentQx Coaching Pty Ltd

Kurt sold the vision and the rest is history.
Duncan Burck

ISBN 978-0-645-83640-0

Printed in the USA
CPSIA information can be obtained
at www.ICGtesting.com
LVHW071140261023
762204LV00014B/428